access to his

Germany
Democracy to Dictatorship
c.1918–45 for WJEC

NICHOLAS FELLOWS

The Publishers would like to thank the following for permission to reproduce copyright material: WJEC for kind permission to use several questions in the Question practice sections. WJEC bears no responsibility for the example answers to questions taken from its past question papers which are contained in this publication.

Photo credits: p16 CPA Media Pte Ltd/Alamy Stock Photo; **pp44, 54** www.simplicissimus.info; **p77** Granger Historical Picture Archive/Alamy Stock Photo; **p97** INTERFOTO/Alamy Stock Photo; **p136** World History Archive/Alamy Stock Photo; **p150** Sueddeutsche Zeitung Photo/Alamy Stock Photo; **p183** World History Archive/Alamy Stock Photo.

Acknowledgements: Abrams Books, *Art of the Third Reich* by Peter Adam, 1992. Allen Lane, *The Weimar Republic* by Detlev J.K. Peukert, 1991. Berghahn Books, 'How likely were workers to vote for the NSDAP?' in Conan Fischer, editor, *The Rise of Nationalism and the Working Classes in Weimar Germany* by J. Falter, 1996. Blick + Bild Verlag, *The Man Who Wanted to Command* by Fritz Wiedemann, 1964. Bloomsbury Academic, *German History Since 1800*, Mary Fulbrook, editor, by R. Bessel, 1997. Bloomsbury Revelations, *The Nazi Dictatorship: Problems and Perspectives of Interpretation* by Ian Kershaw, 2015. D.C. Heath & Co., *Inside Hitler's Germany: Documentary History of Life in the Third Reich* by Benjamin Sax and Dieter Kuntz, 1992. Exeter University Press, *Nazism 1919–1945, Volume 2: State, Economy and Society 1933–39*, edited by Jeremy Noakes and Geoffrey Pridham, 1984. *GHIL Bulletin*, 'A Very German Revolution'? The Post-1918 Settlement Revaluated by Conan Fischer, Vol. XXVIII, No. 2, November 2006. Hamish Hamilton, *German History in Marxist Perspective: The East German Approach*, by Andreas Dorpalen, 1985. Hanseatische Verlagsanstalt, *Verfassungsrecht des Grossdeutschen Reiches* by E. Huber, 1939. *History Today*, 'The Rise of the Nazis' by Jeremy Noakes, January 1983. Hodder Arnold, *Nationalism and Society: Germany, 1800–1945* by Michael Hughes, 1988. Hodder Education, *Access to History: From Bismarck to Hitler: Germany 1890–1933* by G. Layton, 1995. Hodder & Stoughton, *Imperial and Weimar Germany* by John Laver, 1992. Houghton Mifflin, *Hitler and I* by Otto Strasser, 1940. Hurst & Blackett, *Mein Kampf*, translated by James Murphy by Adolf Hitler, 1939. Longman, *Hitler* by Ian Kershaw, 1991. Longmans, Green & Co., *Darkness Over Germany* by E. Amy Buller, 1943. Macmillan, *Modern Germany* by K.S. Pinson, 1966; *His Diaries, Letters, and Papers, Volume 3*, Eric Sutton, editor, by Gustav Stresemann, 1935; *Weimar and the Rise of Hitler* by A.J. Nicholls, 1968. Methuen, *The European Dictatorships, 1918–1945* by Stephen J. Lee, 1987. *Modern History Review*, 'Hitler' by Richard Overy, 1989. Oxford University Press, *Germany 1870–1945* by Peter G.J. Pulzer, 1997; *The Hitler Myth: Image and Reality in the Third Reich* by Ian Kershaw, 2001; 'Hitler and the Origins of the Second World War', *Proceedings of the British Academy, LIII* by Alan Bullock, 1968. Palgrave Macmillan, *From Weimar to Hitler: Germany 1918–33* by E.J. Feuchtwanger, 1993. Praeger, *The History of Germany Since 1789* by Golo Mann, 1968. Princeton University Press, *From Weimar to Auschwitz: Essays in German History* by Hans Mommsen, 1991. Sempringham, *Germany 1916–1941* by E.J. Feuchtwanger, 1997. Simon & Schuster, *The Rise and Fall of the Third Reich: A History of Nazi Germany*, Volume 2 by William L. Shirer, 1960. The New Press, *The Nazis: A Warning from History* by Laurence Rees, 1997. University of North Carolina Press, *The Nazi Voter: The Social Foundations of Fascism in Germany, 1919–1933* by Thomas Childers, 1983. *Western Mail*, 'How Germany Tackles Unemployment' by Gareth Jones, 1933. Yale University Press, *The Logic of Evil: The Social Origins of the Nazi Party, 1925–1933* by William Brustein, 1996.

Every effort has been made to trace all copyright holders, but if any have been inadvertently overlooked, the Publishers will be pleased to make the necessary arrangements at the first opportunity.

Although every effort has been made to ensure that website addresses are correct at time of going to press, Hodder Education cannot be held responsible for the content of any website mentioned in this book. It is sometimes possible to find a relocated web page by typing in the address of the home page for a website in the URL window of your browser.

Orders: please contact Bookpoint Ltd, 130 Park Drive, Milton Park, Abingdon, Oxon OX14 4SE. Telephone: +44 (0)1235 827827. Fax: +44 (0)1235 400401. Email education@bookpoint.co.uk Lines are open from 9 a.m. to 5 p.m., Monday to Saturday, with a 24-hour message answering service. You can also order through our website: www.hoddereducation.co.uk

ISBN: 978 1 5104 5917 5

© Nicholas Fellows 2020

First published in 2020 by
Hodder Education,
An Hachette UK Company
Carmelite House
50 Victoria Embankment
London EC4Y 0DZ

www.hoddereducation.co.uk

Impression number   10   9   8   7   6   5   4   3   2   1
Year   2024   2023   2022   2021   2020

All rights reserved. Apart from any use permitted under UK copyright law, no part of this publication may be reproduced or transmitted in any form or by any means, electronic or mechanical, including photocopying and recording, or held within any information storage and retrieval system, without permission in writing from the publisher or under licence from the Copyright Licensing Agency Limited. Further details of such licences (for reprographic reproduction) may be obtained from the Copyright Licensing Agency Limited, www.cla.co.uk

Cover photo © Everett Collection Historical/Alamy Stock Photo
Typeset by Gray Publishing
Printed in the UK by CPI Group Ltd

A catalogue record for this title is available from the British Library.

Contents

CHAPTER 1 Context: Germany in 1914 — 1

CHAPTER 2 The challenges facing the Weimar Republic 1918–23 — 4
1. The collapse of the imperial regime of Kaiser Wilhelm II — 4
2. The Treaty of Versailles and its impact on Germany — 7
3. The Weimar constitution — 11
4. Challenges to Weimar from the left and right — 15
5. The emergence of the National Socialist German Workers' Party — 21
6. The economic crisis — 25
7. The occupation of the Ruhr — 27
8. Key debate: What was the nature of the German Revolution? — 30

CHAPTER 3 Foreign and economic policy 1924–9 — 33
1. The appointment of Gustav Stresemann as chancellor — 34
2. Was there an economic recovery under Stresemann? — 35
3. Attempts to aid German economic recovery: the Dawes Plan and Young Plan — 38
4. Foreign policy under Gustav Stresemann — 42
5. Key debate: How far did Germany recover in the years 1924–9? — 49

CHAPTER 4 The changing fortunes of the Nazi Party 1924–33 — 52
1. The recovery of the Nazi Party in the 1920s — 53
2. The strength of the Nazi Party by 1929 — 57
3. The changing fortunes of the Nazis by 1932 — 58
4. The reasons for growing support for the Nazi Party — 60
5. Key debate: Who voted for the Nazis? — 65

CHAPTER 5 The crisis of the Weimar Republic 1929–33 — 69
1. The impact of the Great Depression — 70
2. The Brüning government and presidential rule — 73
3. The roles of Hindenburg, Papen and Schleicher — 76
4. The collapse of Weimar democracy — 80
5. Political intrigue and Hitler's appointment as chancellor — 82
6. Key debate: Was the creation of a Nazi dictatorship inevitable? — 84

Question practice: AS level — 87

CHAPTER 6 Developments in Nazi control of Germany after 1933 — 96
1. Hitler's consolidation of power 1933–4 — 96
2. Propaganda — 104
3. Indoctrination and terror — 108
4. The Nazi political system — 111
5. Was Hitler a totalitarian dictator? — 116

	6	Support for the regime	118
	7	Opposition and resistance	120

CHAPTER 7 Nazi racial, social and religious policies 1933–45 — 125

1. Nazi racial ideology — 126
2. Anti-Semitism — 127
3. Policies towards 'asocials' — 132
4. Social policies — 134
5. Workers — 141
6. The Churches — 142
7. The effectiveness of *Volksgemeinschaft* — 145

CHAPTER 8 Nazi economic policy 1933–45 — 149

1. The performance of the economy 1933–9 — 149
2. The wartime economy — 154
3. The role of individuals — 155
4. Trade unions — 159
5. Conclusion: Nazi economic policy — 161

CHAPTER 9 Nazi foreign policy and the Second World War 1933–45 — 163

1. The aims of Nazi foreign policy to 1939 — 164
2. The outbreak of war — 169
3. German success in western Europe — 173
4. The turning point of the Second World War — 175
5. The Wannsee Conference (1942) and the Final Solution — 176
6. The defeat of Germany — 180
7. The impact of war on society — 182

Question practice: A level — 190

Exam focus: WJEC AS and A level — 199

Timeline — 208

Glossary of terms — 210

Further reading — 215

Index — 217

Introduction: about this book

This book has been written to support the study of the following courses:

- Unit 2: Weimar and its challenges c.1918–1933 (AS level)
- Unit 4: Nazi Germany c.1933–1945 (A level).

The writer hopes that student readers will regard the book not simply as an aid to better exam results, but as a study which is enjoyable in itself as an analysis of a very important theme in history.

The following explains the different features of this book and how they will help your study of the course.

Beginning of the book

Context

Starting a new course can be daunting if you are not familiar with the period or topic. This section will give you an overview of the history and will set up some of the key themes. Reading this section will help you get up to speed on the content of the course.

Throughout the book

Key terms

You need to know these to gain an understanding of the period. The appropriate use of specific historical language in your essays will also help you improve the quality of your writing. Key terms are in boldface type the first time they appear in the book. They are defined in the margin and appear in the glossary.

Sources

Historical sources are important in understanding why specific decisions were taken or on what contemporary writers and politicians based their actions. The questions accompanying each source will help you to understand and analyse the source.

Key debates

The key debates between historians will help you think about historical interpretations and understand the different points of view for a given historiographical debate.

Chapter summaries

These written summaries are intended to help you revise and consolidate your knowledge and understanding of the content.

Summary diagrams

These visual summaries at the end of each section are useful for revision.

Refresher questions

The refresher questions are quick knowledge checks to make sure you have understood and remembered the material that is covered in the chapter.

Question practice

There are opportunities on pages 87 and 190 to practise AS level and A level exam-style questions, respectively. The exam hint below each question will help you if you get stuck.

End of the book

Timeline

Understanding chronology (the order in which events took place) is an essential part of history. Knowing the order of events is one thing, but it is also important to know how events relate to each other. This timeline will help you put events into context and will be helpful for quick reference or as a revision tool.

Exam focus

This section gives advice on how to answer questions in your exam, focusing on the different requirements of your exam paper. The guidance in this book has been based on detailed examiner reports since 2017. It models best practice in terms of answering exam questions and shows the most common pitfalls to help ensure you get the best grade possible.

Glossary

All key terms in the book are defined in the glossary.

Further reading

To achieve top marks in history, you will need to read beyond this textbook. This section contains a list of books and articles for you to explore. The list may also be helpful for an extended essay or piece of coursework.

Online extras

This new edition is accompanied by online material to support you in your study. Throughout the book you will find the online extras icon to prompt you to make use of the relevant online resources for your course. By going to www.hoddereducation.co.uk/accesstohistory/extras you will find the following:

Activity worksheets

These activities will help you develop the skills you need for the exam. The thinking that you do to complete the activities, and the notes you make from answering the questions, will prove valuable in your learning journey and helping you get the best grade possible. Your teacher may decide to print the entire series of worksheets to create an activity booklet to accompany the course. Alternatively they may be used as standalone activities for class work or homework. However, don't hesitate to go online and print off a worksheet yourself to get the most from this book.

Who's who

A level history covers a lot of key figures so it's perfectly understandable if you find yourself confused by all the different names. This document organises the individuals mentioned throughout the book by categories so you know your Goebbels from your Göring!

Further research

While further reading of books and articles is helpful to achieve your best, there's a wealth of material online, including useful websites, digital archives, and documentaries on YouTube. This page lists resources that may help further your understanding of the topic. It may also prove a valuable reference for research if you decide to choose this period for the coursework element of your course.

Dedication

Keith Randell (1943–2002)

The *Access to History* series was conceived and developed by Keith, who created a series to 'cater for students as they are, not as we might wish them to be'. He leaves a living legacy of a series that for over 20 years has provided a trusted, stimulating and well-loved accompaniment to post-16 study. Our aim with these new editions is to continue to offer students the best possible support for their studies.

CHAPTER 1

Context: Germany in 1914

The country 'Germany' as we know it today did not exist until 1871. Before then, there were many individual states spread across central Europe where German was the main language. However, during the 1860s, the largest and most powerful of these states, **Prussia**, brought about unification. This was achieved through a series of successful wars against Denmark in 1861, Austria in 1866 and France in 1870–1, and led to the declaration of the **German Empire** at Versailles, in defeated France.

The political system

The chief minister of Prussia, **Otto von Bismarck**, played a major role in the unification. He was chosen as the first chancellor (prime minister) of the united Germany and his influence meant that he had almost total authority. As a Prussian aristocrat, Bismarck ensured that Prussian power was preserved in the new Germany by the terms of the new **constitution**:

- The King of Prussia was proclaimed Kaiser, giving him power over the other 25 different states.
- The Kaiser appointed the chancellor and other imperial ministers who were directly responsible to him and therefore independent of the *Reichstag*.
- There was an element of democracy in the constitution as all men over the age of 25 were eligible to vote in elections to the *Reichstag*. However, the power of the *Reichstag* was limited as the Kaiser could ignore its decisions, and it could be dissolved at any time.
- The German army was accountable only to the Kaiser and took an oath of allegiance to him.
- Prussia's power was enhanced as Austria, although it was German speaking, was excluded from the new German state. This had resulted in the creation of a *Kleindeutschland* as opposed to a *Grossdeutschland*.

However, Germany was a **federal state** and power was divided between the states and the federal or imperial government.

KEY TERMS

Prussia The wealthiest, most powerful and largest German state in the 1800s, making up 62 per cent of the population of the German Empire.

German Empire This is also known as the Second Reich, 1871–1918, or Kaiserreich.

Constitution The rules and principles that govern a state.

Reichstag The German parliament. It had limited powers.

Grossdeutschland **and *Kleindeutschland*** A debate within the states of Germany in the nineteenth century as to whether a unified Germany should include Austria, *Grossdeutschland*, or exclude Austria, *Kleindeutschland*. It was the latter which prevailed.

Federal state A state in which powers are shared between central and regional governments.

KEY FIGURE

Otto von Bismarck (1815–98)

Minister president of Prussia and then chancellor of Germany from 1871 until 1890. He worked closely with the kaisers, dominating both domestic and foreign affairs, until replaced by Wilhelm II.

KEY FIGURE

Kaiser Wilhelm II (1859–1941)

Emperor of Germany from 1888 until his abdication in 1918. He aimed to create a German Empire abroad and build a large navy and army to rival other European powers. His policy of *Weltpolitik* brought him into conflict with other European powers and was a factor in the outbreak of the First World War. As Germany faced military defeat in 1918, he abdicated and fled to the Netherlands.

KEY TERMS

Autocrat Rule by one person, usually a monarch, who will have absolute power.

Socialism A political and economic theory that argues the means of production should be owned by the community for its collective benefit.

Junkers The landowning aristocracy, they were particularly dominant in Prussia and other parts of eastern Germany.

The first three kaisers kept Bismarck as their chancellor and the political system appeared to be quite successful as the kaisers and Bismarck had the same political outlook. However, in 1888, **Kaiser Wilhelm II** came to the throne. He wanted to rule Germany by himself and forced Bismarck to resign in 1890. From then until 1918 the Kaiser ruled Germany as an **autocrat**, with the chancellor having very little power.

The German economy

Germany had begun industrialising in the nineteenth century, but industrial growth really took off between 1890 and 1913. Industries, such as coal, iron, steel and textiles, were well established and, in the period up to the outbreak of the First World War, there was dramatic growth in the new industries of chemicals, electrics, petrochemicals and mechanical engineering. Companies such as Daimler and Benz developed cars, while AEG and Siemens became huge electrical enterprises. In particular, Krupps became a major armaments producer.

By the outbreak of the First World War in 1914, Germany was Europe's leading industrial power and able to compete with Britain's supremacy. Its industrial output was second only to that of the United States, making it a powerful and wealthy country.

German society

Industrialisation brought about much social change. This was seen most noticeably in population growth and in the rapid urbanisation that took place. It meant that by 1910 more people lived in towns and cities than in rural areas. Berlin was the largest city with a population of over 2 million, but other towns, such as Cologne and Munich, had populations of over half a million. This rapid population growth, however, created other problems such as overcrowding and poor living conditions. Although unemployment was not a major problem, the standard of living of many workers was low.

These developments led to a greater interest in politics by the working classes. What followed was a growth in **socialism** and trade unionism as well as support for a new political party, the Social Democratic Party (SPD), which represented the interests of the workers. By 1913, the SPD was the largest party in the *Reichstag*, but had little influence on government policy.

These rapid changes also created a divide in German society between the landowners, or *Junkers*, who sympathised with the army and other elite groups in society, and the working classes. The *Junkers* saw the new working class as a threat to stability, while the middle classes also felt threatened by the growth in socialism as they saw its ideas as a challenge to their economic position.

Industrialisation also attracted a large number of immigrants to Germany who contributed greatly to its economic growth but caused further social disruption.

Foreign affairs

After the fall of Bismarck, Germany had become very isolated in Europe, with Austria-Hungary its only reliable ally, which was very weak economically, militarily and politically. Under Kaiser Wilhelm II, Germany had attempted to become a world power, following a policy of **Weltpolitik**, and attempted to acquire an overseas empire as the Kaiser was envious of the British Empire. The Kaiser also built up the German navy in the years before the First World War and the British saw this as an attempt to challenge its dominance. Germany also had a very large army which made it a threat on mainland Europe.

The tensions caused by the Kaiser's policies and the need to defend its only reliable ally, Austria-Hungary, were major reasons for going to war in 1914. The declaration of war by the Kaiser resulted in a surge in patriotic fervour, with the main political parties agreeing a political truce. There was great expectation of a swift victory based on the **Schlieffen Plan**, but this failed, and Germany was drawn into a war of attrition. By 1916, the government had become a virtual military dictatorship. The civilian population also suffered as food shortages and inflation sapped morale. It was this collapse in morale, as well as military failure in 1918 with the **Ludendorff Offensive**, that led to the collapse of the regime, the abdication of the Kaiser and the signing of the armistice in November 1918.

Defeat in the First World War led to a dramatic period of German history, which is the focus of this book. The Weimar Republic that emerged from defeat faced many challenges and in 1933 was replaced by Adolf Hitler. He, and his Nazi Party, soon established a one-party state and took Germany into the Second World War. By 1945, Germany had been defeated again, was divided, and faced many social and economic problems.

> **KEY TERMS**
>
> **Weltpolitik** The policy of the German government in the 1890s and 1900s by which it sought to advance German interests throughout the world.
>
> **Schlieffen Plan** Drawn up by General Schlieffen to avoid Germany fighting a war on two fronts by defeating France on the Western Front before dealing with the threat from Russia. The plan was to defeat France in six weeks, but this failed because of Belgian, British and French resistance. Russia also mobilised more quickly than the Germans expected and so more men had to be sent to the Eastern Front, weakening the German attack in the west. Its failure led to trench warfare and a war of attrition.
>
> **Ludendorff Offensive** A German offensive launched in the spring of 1918 on the Western Front, designed to win the war before large numbers of US troops arrived to aid the French and British.

CHAPTER 2

The challenges facing the Weimar Republic 1918–23

The Weimar Republic replaced the Kaiserreich in 1919. It faced numerous challenges in its early years from both the left and right wing, yet was able to survive these.

This chapter examines the reasons why the republic was established and considers the political, economic and social challenges it faced by focusing on the following themes:

- The collapse of the imperial regime of Kaiser Wilhelm II
- The Treaty of Versailles and its impact on Germany
- The Weimar constitution
- Challenges to Weimar from the left and right
- The emergence of the National Socialist German Workers' Party
- The economic crisis
- The occupation of the Ruhr

The key debate on page 30 of this chapter considers the nature of the German Revolution of 1918.

KEY DATES					
1918	Sept.	Ludendorff accepted that Germany was unable to win the First World War	1919	Aug.	Weimar constitution adopted
			1920	March	Ruhr rising
	Nov.	Naval mutiny at Kiel			Kapp *Putsch*
		Wilhelm II abdicated	1923	Jan.	French and Belgian troops occupied the Ruhr
		Armistice signed			
1919	Jan.	Spartacist uprising in Berlin		Jan.–Nov.	Hyperinflation
	June	Treaty of Versailles signed		Nov.	Beer Hall *Putsch* in Munich

KEY FIGURE

General Ludendorff (1865–1937)

Ludendorff was a German general who, with Hindenburg, became virtual military dictators of Germany between 1916 and 1918. He attempted to control the constitutional reform in 1918 but failed and was dismissed. Later, he supported both the Kapp *Putsch* and the early activities of Hitler.

1 The collapse of the imperial regime of Kaiser Wilhelm II

■ *What was the impact of the First World War on Germany?*

In the spring of 1918, Germany had launched a massive attack against Allied forces in France. Germany's hope had been to defeat the Allies before large numbers of American troops arrived, following the US entry into the First World War in 1917. At first, the attack was very successful, but the strength of the Allies and German war-weariness brought the advance to a halt. This led to the chief of staff, **General Ludendorff**, informing his superior, Field Marshal Paul von Hindenburg, and the chancellor that the war was lost. Ludendorff offered two pieces of advice to the government:

- it should appeal to the USA for an armistice
- a more democratic regime should be created.

The news of impending defeat was a shock to the German people, who had become accustomed to hearing from the army commanders that they would win the war. This sense of shock was only added to as Germany had defeated Russia in the east and German troops were still in France and Belgium. However, many in Germany were also weary of the war because of food shortages caused by the naval blockade. During the final two years of the war, the British navy successfully blockaded German ports and prevented the German merchant fleet from functioning. This resulted in severe food shortages, with many Germans facing starvation. In the winter of 1916–17, the supply of potatoes ran out and people were left with just turnips. The food shortage meant that civilians were vulnerable to disease and it is possible that some 750,000 Germans died from a combination of hunger and disease.

The growth of revolutionary activity

The navy, which had been largely inactive during the war, was now ordered to sea. However, the sailors at the naval base at Kiel, seeing it as a last desperate but futile move, **mutinied**. This resulted in similar action in the ports of Bremen and Lübeck before unrest spread to other cities across Germany. **Soviets** or councils, similar to those established in Russia following the **Bolshevik Revolution of 1917**, were established to run affairs. Popular discontent was becoming increasingly revolutionary. It was very clear that the government was losing control and that attempts to change the government from an autocracy to a **constitutional monarchy** under a civilian government would fail as people demanded the abdication of Wilhelm and immediate peace.

As a result of this failure, the Kaiser **abdicated** on 9 November 1918. Power was passed to a Council of People's Representatives, a temporary government under **Friedrich Ebert**, the leader of the largest political party, the **Social Democratic Party (SPD)**. This temporary government would rule Germany until a national assembly could be elected.

The defeat of revolutionary activity

Ebert feared that Germany would follow Russia into revolution, which would lead to civil war and add further to the problems that the country faced. He was concerned that it would disrupt **demobilisation**, add to the problem of food supply and make peace negotiations even more difficult.

However, Ebert was able to defeat the revolutionary threat for the following reasons:

- He maintained the support of the army by not reforming it or replacing it with a new force.

> **KEY TERMS**
> **Mutiny** The refusal of the armed forces to obey orders.
> **Soviet** A Russian word for an elected council, often comprised of workers.
> **Bolshevik Revolution of 1917** The Bolsheviks were the majority within the Russian Social Democratic Party, which, under its leader Lenin, seized power in October 1917 and established the world's first communist state.
> **Constitutional monarchy** A system where the monarch's powers are limited by a constitution.
> **Abdication** The act of a monarch giving up his or her throne.
> **Social Democratic Party (SPD)** In Germany, a moderate socialist party, which should not be confused with Russia where the Social Democrats were more radical, with one part forming the Bolshevik or Communist Party.
> **Demobilisation** The removal of troops from active service at the end of a war.

> **KEY FIGURE**
> **Friedrich Ebert (1871–1925)**
> Ebert was co-chairman of the SPD and became leader of the German provisional government in 1918. He oversaw both the armistice and the transition to democracy. He then became president of the Weimar Republic in 1920.

- The working class was divided between the Communist Party of Germany (KPD), which wanted to establish a soviet-style of government and the SPD, which wanted a parliamentary form of government.

The impact of the First World War on Germany

The war had an enormous political impact on Germany, bringing to an end the rule of the Kaiser. However, it also had a large economic and social impact.

Economic impact

The war had a considerable economic impact on Germany:

- Industrial production had fallen so that it was only two-thirds that of 1913.
- National income was only a third of that of 1913.
- There were 600,000 widows and some 2 million children without fathers. As a result, the state was spending one-third of its budget on war pensions by 1925.
- Many Germans had invested in **war bonds**, but the face value of those bonds had been eroded by inflation, with the result that many lost most or all of their wealth.

Social impact

The war served only to deepen divisions within German society, with huge gaps in the living standards between the rich and the poor. This situation had been made worse by the restrictions placed on workers' earnings during the war, while factory owners had been able to make large profits.

Food shortages continued as the British naval blockade, introduced during the war, was tightened, intending to put further pressure on Germany to agree to the terms of the armistice. This created further tensions within society as those living in cities accused those in the countryside of hoarding food.

During the war, many women had worked in factories and although this helped to maintain levels of income while husbands were away fighting, others believed that this had damaged traditional family values.

Germany was, therefore, in a dangerous state when the Kaiser abdicated, and faced many serious problems. Ebert was able to sign an armistice after the Kaiser's abdication and announce that a new republic would be established which would guarantee:

- freedom of speech
- freedom of worship
- better working conditions.

Even though a new constitution was drawn up, there was considerable opposition to the concept of a democratic government, which would lead to further challenges to the new regime. These developments helped to create the **stab-in-the-back myth**, which claimed that Germany had lost the war because it had been betrayed by politicians such as Ebert.

> **KEY TERMS**
>
> **War bonds** In order to finance the First World War, the German government encouraged people to invest in government funds in the belief that their money was secure and they were helping the war effort.
>
> **Stab-in-the-back myth** The belief that the army had not lost the war but had been let down by groups at home, such as Jewish people and socialists. This made it much harder for the new Weimar government to gain popular support.

SUMMARY DIAGRAM

THE COLLAPSE OF THE IMPERIAL REGIME OF KAISER WILHELM II

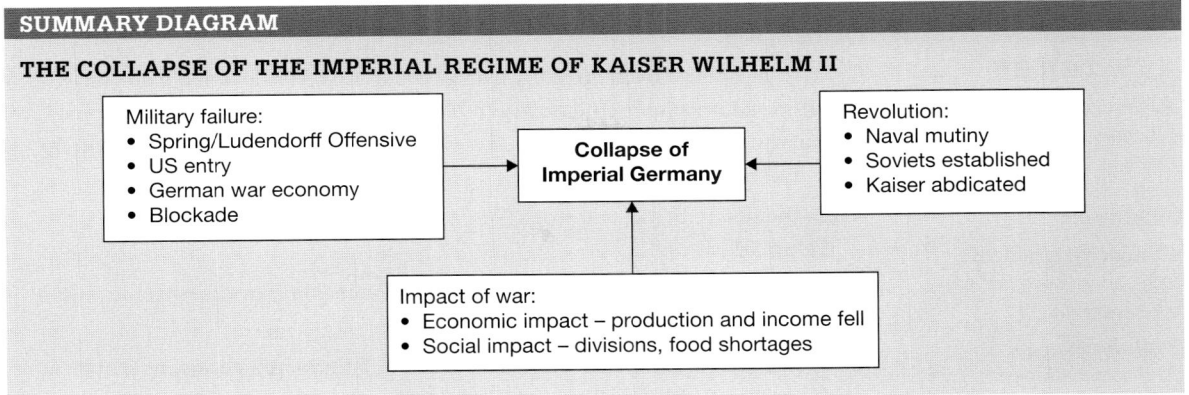

2 The Treaty of Versailles and its impact on Germany

■ *What was the impact of the Treaty of Versailles on Germany?*

The psychological shock of the defeat had a profound impact on the German people and would play a significant role in their reaction to the **Treaty of Versailles**. The military position of Germany when the armistice was signed on 11 November 1918 meant that the German government hoped it would be able to negotiate a moderate peace with the Allied powers. However, instead of being able to recover its strength and position as a great power, Germany was given little choice but to sign a treaty whose terms were viewed as harsh by a nation that was still finding it difficult to accept the reality of defeat.

Germany did not expect to be forced to pay **reparations** for anything other than the damage that it had caused in northern France and Belgium. It expected that it would be able to unite with other German-speaking areas, such as Austria, and be able to join the new **League of Nations**. Not only were these hopes dashed, but as a result of the treaty, Germany suffered far-reaching losses. It lost:

- 10 per cent of its land
- 12.5 per cent of its population
- 16 per cent of its coal
- 48 per cent of its iron industry.

These losses had a severe impact on Germany's economic position.

It also lost all of its overseas colonies, all of which Germany's new leaders claimed would have a considerable impact on its ability to pay reparations. These losses also destroyed its position as a major power. Even more humiliating for many was the war guilt clause (clause 231 in the Treaty of Versailles), which stated that Germany was guilty of starting the war and would therefore deserve the punishments of the Allied forces.

KEY TERMS

Treaty of Versailles The Allied powers met in Paris during 1919–20 and drew up five treaties with the defeated powers and created the League of Nations. The Treaty of Versailles was signed with Germany on 28 June 1919 and was much harsher than the Germans had expected, leading to national outrage.

Reparations Money and goods paid by a defeated power to cover the cost of damages caused by war.

League of Nations An organisation set up at the end of the war to help maintain peace, and to improve living and working conditions; it is often seen as the forerunner of the United Nations. The League was the brainchild of US President Woodrow Wilson. However, the US senate refused to approve it and the USA never joined the League. The defeated powers were initially not allowed to join.

7

Land lost

Germany lost land from virtually every border area. While it had expected to lose **Alsace-Lorraine** on the northern border with France, and possibly some land in the east to Poland, the scale of the losses was seen as a humiliation by many Germans.

> **KEY TERMS**
>
> **Alsace-Lorraine** Largely French-speaking provinces that had been taken by Germany in the Franco-Prussian War of 1870–1.
>
> **Plebiscite** A people's vote on an issue, similar to a referendum.
>
> **Mandates** The supervision of former German and Turkish colonies that were administered by the Allies after the First World War.

- In the north, Schleswig was given a **plebiscite** and voted to return to Denmark.
- In the east, Upper Silesia, which was rich in coal and contained steelworks, was given to the new state of Poland.
- West Prussia and Posen were also given to Poland, which meant that Germany was now split into two, with East Prussia separate from the rest of Germany.
- Hultschin was lost to the new state of Czechoslovakia.
- In the south, *Anschluss*, or union, with Austria was forbidden (see page 10).
- In the west, Alsace-Lorraine, which had been taken from France in the Franco-Prussian War of 1870–1, was given back.
- Eupen and Malmedy were granted to Belgium.
- Two other areas were also placed under control of the League or Allied forces. The Saarland, which was a rich industrial area, was placed under League of Nations control before a plebiscite would be held in fifteen years to decide its future. The Rhineland, which bordered France, was demilitarised and was occupied by Allied forces for fifteen years in order to improve the security of France.

There were considerable colonial losses, mostly in Africa and the Pacific Ocean:

- Togoland and the Cameroons were to be run by Britain and France as **mandates**.
- German South West Africa was mandated to South Africa.
- German East Africa was mandated to Britain.
- New Guinea to Australia.
- Samoa to New Zealand.
- The Marshall, Mariana and Caroline Islands to Japan.

Military losses

Germany's military strength had been a source of great pride for the nation. It was its military power in the 1860s that had allowed the German states to unite, but concerns about its recovery after the First World War led to its drastic decrease. Many Germans argued that the reduction would make Germany more vulnerable to attack.

- The army was reduced to no more than 100,000 men, all of whom would have to be volunteers.

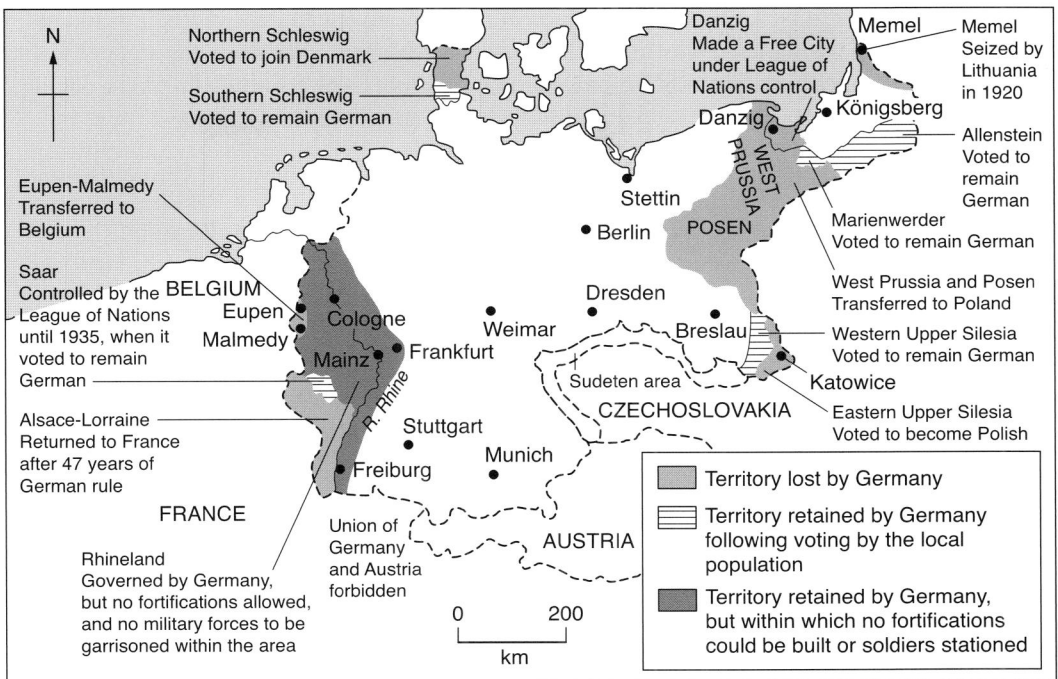

Figure 2.1 The terms of the Treaty of Versailles 1919.

- The general staff was disbanded.
- The navy was reduced to no more than 15,000 men.
- Germany was not allowed tanks, aircraft, submarines or poison gas.

These reductions angered Germany as, not only was the military a source of great pride, but also none of the other Allies were disarmed to the extent that Germany was in the 1920s, despite **Wilson's Fourteen Points** calling for disarmament.

Reparations

When the treaty was drawn up and signed in June 1919 it was not known how much damage had been caused and, therefore, reparations were not fixed in the treaty. Instead, the Allies established a Reparations Commission. Its job was to find out how much Germany could pay and fix a final sum. The Commission did not report until 1921, when it set a sum of £6600 million, which would be paid in instalments over many years. Most Germans considered this sum to be outrageous and argued that the country could not afford to pay it. However, such claims have caused considerable debate, with many historians arguing that it was well within Germany's capabilities and others arguing that the demands were much less than those imposed on Russia by Germany at the **Treaty of Brest-Litovsk**.

> **KEY TERMS**
>
> **Wilson's Fourteen Points** When the USA entered the First World War its president had drawn up the Fourteen Points to explain what the USA was fighting for. The aim was to create a more just world. One of the Fourteen Points called for disarmament as many believed the First World War had been the result of an 'arms race'.
>
> **Treaty of Brest-Litovsk** The treaty signed between Germany and Russia in March 1918 that ended the war in the east. It was much harsher than Versailles, with Russia losing 62 million people, 27 per cent of farmland, 26 per cent of railway lines and 74 per cent of iron and coal resources.

> **KEY TERMS**
>
> **Diktat** A dictated peace, where a treaty is imposed without negotiation.
>
> **Self-determination** The right of people of the same race to decide their own government.

> **ONLINE EXTRAS** WWW
>
> Get to grips with analysing the reliability of sources by completing Worksheet 1 at www.hoddereducation.co.uk/accesstohistory/extras

> **SOURCE QUESTION**
>
> How useful is Source A as evidence for the reaction of the German people to the Treaty of Versailles?

> **KEY TERMS**
>
> **Austro-Hungarian Empire** Austria-Hungary had been Germany's closest ally since 1879. The multinational empire ended when Austria was forced to accept defeat. The 8-million-strong state of Austria, despite being German in language and culture, was forbidden to join with Germany. The new states created from the empire had German-speaking minorities.
>
> **Successor states** Term used to describe the states created from the break-up of the Austro-Hungarian Empire, such as Poland and Czechoslovakia. These were often weak and this would make it easy for Germany to take them over in the 1930s.

It can be suggested that the actual sum was almost an irrelevance. It would not have mattered how much Germany was required to pay since any amount would have led to protests as many Germans did not think that they should be paying anything and could not accept that they had actually lost the war.

War guilt

The territorial, military and economic losses and reparations were sufficient to anger most Germans. This was reflected in the hostile reaction to the signing of the Treaty of Versailles, which saw demonstrations on the streets of Germany, and in newspapers, such as the *Deutsche Zeitung*, which called for revenge. However, the war guilt clause only added to the sense of injustice as Germany was forced to accept the blame for starting the war. Many in Germany thought that the war was a just conflict which had been brought on by Germany's enemies threatening the security of the nation.

> **SOURCE A**
>
> From the pan-German newspaper, *Deutsche Zeitung*, published 28 June 1918. Quoted in K.S. Pinson, *Modern Germany*, Macmillan, 1966, p. 398.
>
> *Vengeance! German nation! Today in the Hall of Mirrors of Versailles the disgraceful treaty is being signed. Do not forget it! In the place where, in the glorious year of 1871, the German empire in all its glory had its origin, today German honour is being carried to its grave. Do not forget it! The German people will, with unceasing labour, press forward to reconquer the place among the nations to which it is entitled. Then will come vengeance for the shame of 1918.*

German reaction to the Treaty of Versailles

The Allies gave Germany fourteen days to consider the terms of the treaty. However, in reality, the Germans had little choice but to sign it. The naval blockade was still in force and the Allies were in the Rhineland and poised to invade. As a result, many Germans viewed the treaty as a **diktat**, but they still disapproved of the government signing it and the government lost further public support. Most Germans believed that their treatment was not in keeping with the Fourteen Points, with **self-determination** given to states such as Latvia, Lithuania and Estonia, but denied to Germany. As a result of the treaty, many Germans now found themselves living under foreign rule, in Poland or Czechoslovakia, or in occupied areas.

Although, at first sight, the treaty appeared tough on Germany, many historians have argued that it was not as harsh as it seems. The overarching German view that they had not lost the war meant that, no matter what the terms of the treaty, there would have been opposition. But, even with the losses, Germany was still powerful. Its position had, in many ways, been strengthened in central Europe with the collapse of the **Austro-Hungarian Empire** and the defeat of Russia. This meant that Germany was still the strongest regional power, a position reinforced by the creation of a number of small **successor states**.

Despite Germany's remaining power and influence, the signing of the treaty played a major role in tipping the country into chaos, particularly as Ebert's government was very weak. It led to attacks on the government from the right-wing nationalists, who could not accept the terms of the treaty, to the French occupation of the Ruhr and **hyperinflation**, as Germany battled to pay reparations (see pages 27–9). However, how far these events were due to the treaty is a matter of debate.

> **KEY TERMS**
>
> **Hyperinflation** A very rapid rise in prices. In Germany, this was caused by the government printing large amounts of money so that the value of the currency fell dramatically.
>
> **Sovereignty** Where ultimate power to make decisions resides.

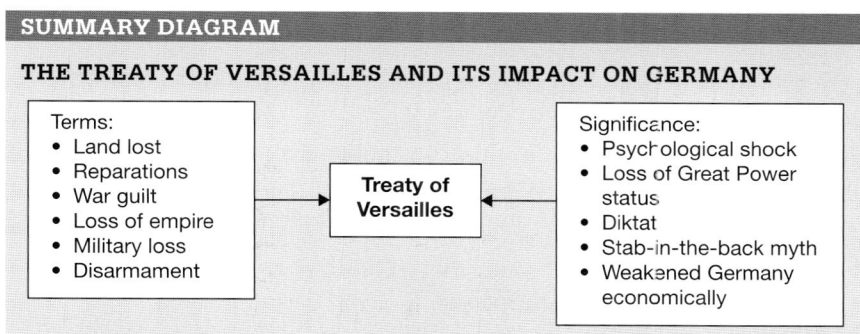

SUMMARY DIAGRAM
THE TREATY OF VERSAILLES AND ITS IMPACT ON GERMANY

3 The Weimar constitution

■ *How far reaching were the changes brought about by the Weimar constitution?*

The establishment of the Weimar Republic

As a result of the Kaiser's abdication in November 1918, Germany would change from an authoritarian state, where the ruler appointed the chancellor, to a democracy and republic, where **sovereignty** was based on the people. This was a major change for Germans. The support of the people for the new regime was further limited as the new democratic government signed the Treaty of Versailles, giving the impression that it was weak, unlike the strong rule of the kaisers.

During the autumn of 1918, the draft for a new constitution had been drawn up and elections for a National Assembly took place in January 1919. The turnout for the elections was high, with over 80 per cent of the electorate taking part. The results saw Ebert's SPD emerge as the largest party, winning 165 seats and 38 per cent of the vote (see Table 2.1, see page 12).

The National Assembly met at Weimar, hence the name for the new republic, because Berlin was considered unsafe owing to communist unrest (see pages 15–17). Ebert was elected president of the new republic and the Centre and German Democratic parties joined the Social Democrats in a coalition government. It appeared as if the new government was off to a strong start

Table 2.1 National Assembly seats, January 1919

Party	Number of seats
Social Democratic Party	165
Centre Party	91
German Democratic Party	75
German National People's Party	44
Independent Social Democratic Party	22
German People's Party	19

as 75 per cent of the electorate had voted for these three parties, all of which supported the new republic and democracy.

Despite this apparent success, the final constitution which was produced by the Assembly has often been seen as making the fall of the Weimar Republic virtually inevitable. The main features of the constitution were:

- Germany was a republic.
- Sovereignty was based on the people.
- It was a federal state, as the empire had been. This meant that individual states retained their power over matters such as education, police and churches.
- The central government was responsible for foreign policy, taxation and the armed forces.
- The head of the central government was the president, with two chambers, the *Reichstag* and the *Reichsrat*.

The *Reichstag* and *Reichsrat*

- Members of the *Reichstag* were elected every four years by **universal suffrage**, with everyone over the age of twenty eligible to vote.
- Members were elected by **proportional representation**.
- The chancellor and ministers had to have the support of the *Reichstag* and had to resign if they lost its support.
- The *Reichstag* initiated and approved legislation.
- The *Reichsrat* was made up of delegates from each state. It could **veto** legislation, although this could be overturned if the *Reichstag* voted two-thirds in favour.

The president

- Elected by popular vote every seven years.
- Head of the armed forces.
- Summoned and dissolved the *Reichstag*.
- Appointed the chancellor and the government.

> **KEY TERMS**
>
> **Universal suffrage** An electoral system in which every adult has the right to vote.
>
> **Proportional representation** An electoral system by which the number of seats given to a party depends on the number of votes it gains.
>
> **Veto** The right to block laws or decisions.

At the same time, a bill of rights was passed which guaranteed personal liberty, equality before the law, freedom of movement, expression, conscience and the right of association.

The constitution was approved in July 1919 by 262 votes to 75, with the Nationalists and the Independent Social Democratic Party (USPD) voting against it.

The challenges facing the Weimar constitution

It is perhaps not surprising, as the republic lasted for only fourteen years, many of which were troubled, that the constitution has been highly criticised. Some historians have even argued that the terms of the constitution did much to facilitate the rise to power of the Nazis. Such claims have focused on three main issues:

- The use of proportional representation.
- The relationship between the president and the *Reichstag*, in particular Article 48 which gave the president emergency powers.
- The continuation of some traditional institutions of Imperial Germany.

It is important to consider the validity of these claims. In particular, there has been much focus on the system of proportional representation.

Proportional representation

The system allocated the number of seats within the *Reichstag* in proportion to the total number of votes cast for each party. This meant that many small parties, such as the Nazis (see pages 21–4), gained representation, with the result that none had a majority and governments were made up of a coalition of a number of parties. These coalitions were often unstable and, therefore, short lived, with frequent changes in government. It is argued that frequent changes did much to damage confidence in the new democracy and left many desiring a return to a more conservative or authoritarian alternative.

It would be difficult to argue against this claim as there were twenty different cabinets between February 1919 and January 1933. However, it must be remembered that for much of the period governments were battling against serious economic problems which did little to encourage stability. People constantly changed support for political parties as they looked for one that could solve the problems.

The relationship between the president and the *Reichstag*

The relationship between the president and the *Reichstag* was meant to produce a system whereby there were checks and balances to ensure that neither would become too powerful. The aim was to produce a presidency that could limit the powers of the *Reichstag* and prevent it from becoming too powerful. However, in achieving this, it gave a large amount of power to the president. It also raised the question of where ultimate authority actually resided. Was it with the *Reichstag* or the president?

Article 48

The president was also given the powers to suspend civil rights in the event of an emergency and to issue presidential decrees. Although the aim was to ensure that government continued, it meant that in practice the president could override the powers of the *Reichstag*. This situation would arise in 1923–4 during the Ruhr and hyperinflation crises and again from 1930–3, following the Wall Street Crash and the collapse of the Müller government (see page 72). However, in 1923 presidential powers were used to good effect to deal with the impact of the French and Belgian invasion of the Ruhr (see pages 27–9).

The continuity of imperial institutions

There were a number of areas where traditional, conservative institutions remained in place and were able to exert a great deal of influence. This can be seen in:

- The civil service, which often upheld the conservative values of Imperial Germany.
- The judiciary, whose sympathies were not with the values of the republic.
- The army, which had held great status under the Kaiser and was not sympathetic to democracy.

The result of this was that conservative forces within Germany still exerted great influence and clashed with the desire of the republic to extend civil liberties and democracy.

How strong was the new constitution?

Despite the criticisms, there were a number of strengths in the new constitution. It was democratic, with universal suffrage and the system of proportional representation. Although this is often seen as weakness because governments were short lived, it is often forgotten that there was much continuity in terms of membership of the governments, with ministers often continuing to serve different chancellors. While proportional representation led to many small parties gaining representation and government through coalitions, this was not new for Germany as coalitions had been present under imperial rule. It might also be argued that proportional representation ensured that a wide range of interests were represented in the *Reichstag*. The preservation of traditional institutions, although seen as challenging the ideals of the new republic, meant that experience was available to the new regime. Perhaps the greatest criticism of the new constitution has been reserved for the emergency powers available to the president under Article 48 and used in the period 1930–3 to undermine democracy. However, this provision was to ensure that government would continue to function during a crisis and worked well dealing with the invasion of the Ruhr and hyperinflation in the years 1923–4, suggesting that when it was used properly it was a strength rather than a weakness. It might, therefore, be argued that it was the peculiar and challenging circumstances rather than the actual constitution that weakened the new republic.

Chapter 2 The challenges facing the Weimar Republic 1918–23

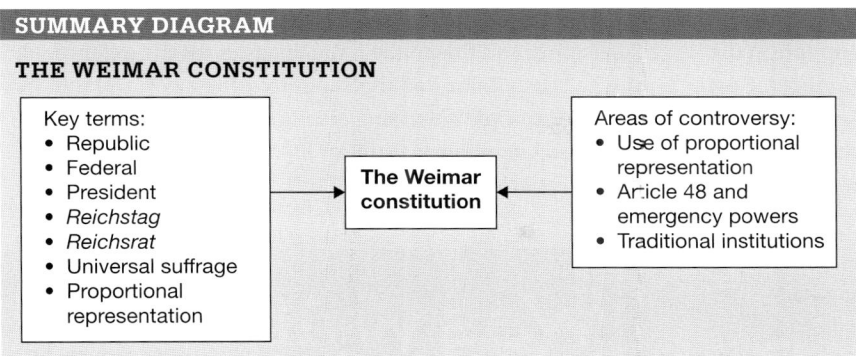

4 Challenges to Weimar from the left and right

▪ *How serious were the challenges to the Weimar Republic from the left and right?*

It is perhaps unsurprising that the Weimar government faced challenges from both the left and right of the political spectrum in the years 1919–23. There was limited support for the new republic, with many Germans wanting a return to the traditional, authoritarian government of the Kaiser. The regime was further weakened by signing the Treaty of Versailles in June 1919. However, even before this there had been political unrest, particularly from the left with the attempted establishment of workers' soviets in many towns and cities at the end of the war.

The Spartacist rising

With the ending of the war, many workers hoped that a soviet-style government would be established and that industries would be **nationalised**. However, the failure of the revolutions at the end of 1918 ensured that this did not happen. The decision to give power to parliament and a lack of genuine reform led to the resignation of the Independent Socialists from the Council of People's Representatives and the formation of the Spartacists, the forerunners of the KPD.

The Spartacists attempted to seize power in Berlin in January 1919 and it was their actions that led to the National Assembly meeting in Weimar rather than the capital. The revolt lasted from 5 to 12 January. Its aim was to overthrow the provisional government and establish a soviet-style government. On 5 January, the Spartacists occupied public buildings and called for a general strike to bring down the government, which they believed was betraying the revolution.

The rising was never a serious threat to the government, even though there were three days of brutal street fighting, which resulted in the deaths of over 100 people. The rising was poorly supported, with only a few workers,

KEY TERM

Nationalised When an industry is owned and run by the government.

KEY FIGURES

Gustav Noske (1868–1946)
A basket-maker who became a trade unionist and SPD member. He was the first defence minister in the early Weimar governments.

Rosa Luxemburg (1871–1919)
Known as 'Red Rosa'. She was a founder of the Spartacus League and imprisoned during the war. She helped to form the Communist Party but was murdered while in police custody during the Spartacist rising.

Karl Liebknecht (1871–1919)
A German socialist who, with Luxemburg, was co-founder of the Spartacus League and Communist Party. He was assassinated during the rising.

KEY TERM

Freikorps The Free Corps, a right-wing group of former soldiers. Nationalist in their outlook, they acted as a paramilitary group who were willing to take action against communist activity.

trade unionists and Social Democrats joining. The rising also failed to gain support in the rest of Germany and this made it much easier for the defence minister, **Gustav Noske**, to crush it. He had the support of the army and the *Freikorps*, with about 400,000 troops. The rising also saw the murder of two of the Communist leaders, **Rosa Luxemburg** and **Karl Liebknecht**, which further reduced the organisational capacity of the party.

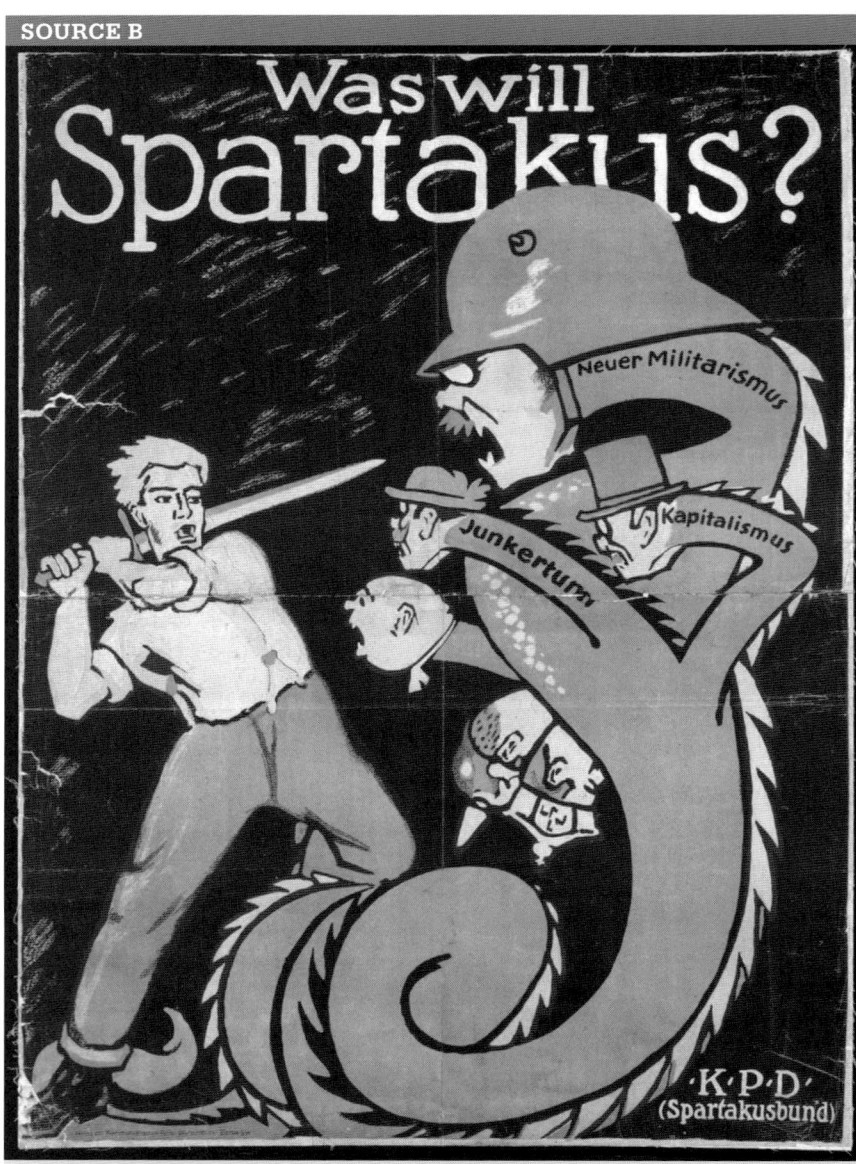

'What does Spartacus want? Fighting the new militarism, capitalism and landowners.' A KPD poster from 1919.

> **SOURCE QUESTION**
> What is the battle portrayed in the poster in Source B?

> **SOURCE C**
>
> From an article from a SPD newspaper, *Vorwärts*, published in early January 1919.
>
> *The despicable actions of Liebknecht and Rosa Luxemburg soil the revolution and endanger all its achievements. The masses must not sit quietly for one minute longer while these brutal beasts and their followers paralyse the activities of the republican government and incite the people more and more to a civil war.*

SOURCE QUESTION

What is the view of Source C about the Spartacist rising?

However, although the Spartacist revolt had been crushed, this did not mean that the threat from the left had ended. There were a series of strikes throughout the country over the next four months and soviets were set up in cities such as Bremen and Munich. The collapse of the **Bavarian monarchy** allowed the leader of the USPD, **Kurt Eisner**, to take the political lead there, but he was assassinated in February 1919. In the confusion that followed, a Bavarian soviet republic was set up, but this was crushed after a month by the *Freikorps* and the army in what became known as the **White Terror**.

Despite the crushing of the left-wing unrest, which removed the immediate threat to the republic, it increased polarisation within society and led many on the right to believe that the country faced a soviet-style revolution. This fear appeared to come to fruition in the Ruhr in March 1920 when the KPD was able to take control of much of the region. Once again, this was crushed by the army and *Freikorps*, but it led to the feeling on the left that the army was undemocratic.

How serious was the threat from the left?

The almost continuous unrest among the left in the early years of the republic gave the impression to many in Germany that the country was facing a soviet-inspired threat, which was added to by propaganda from the right. This fear appeared to be confirmed by the success the left enjoyed in elections throughout the period, securing some ten to fifteen per cent of the vote. However, although strikes were a regular feature of life, it did not mean that large numbers were willing or about to undertake revolutionary activity. There were a wide range of reasons why left-wing activity failed to threaten the government:

- The government was able to suppress left-wing activities. Leaders such as Luxemburg were killed, reducing the effectiveness of groups, while the threat of brutal action deterred others.
- Leadership was often poor, particularly after the deaths of Luxemburg and Liebknecht. There were also divisions between leaders over the tactics to be adopted.
- There were divisions between different groups.
- The government was able to make concessions, which further split its opponents.

KEY TERMS

Bavarian monarchy Bavaria was one of the oldest states in Europe, but was part of Imperial Germany, and kept its monarchy until November 1918.

White Terror First used to describe the suppression of the soviet or 'Red' republic in Bavaria in 1919, it became used to describe the murders and violence that took place in 1919–22.

KEY FIGURE

Kurt Eisner (1867–1919)

A journalist and a socialist. He organised the socialist revolution that overthrew the Bavarian monarchy in November 1918. He proclaimed the People's State of Bavaria but was assassinated by a nationalist in 1919.

The threat from the right

There was much dislike of the new government from the right of the political spectrum, particularly from army officers, civil servants and the judiciary, who all longed for a return to the authoritarian rule of the Kaiser. There were some who were willing to take action to remove the republic, while others focused on rebuilding their own position.

There were also a number of extreme right-wing political parties. They were able to play effectively on the supposed insult to the nation that the new government had committed by signing the armistice and the Treaty of Versailles. These patriotic and often anti-Semitic groups had developed during the First World War, but were able to gain more support in the chaos that followed defeat, often arguing that members of the new government had Jewish links. One of the most notable of these was the German Workers' Party under Anton Drexler, whose meetings were attended by Adolf Hitler, which put forward the view that Germany had been betrayed by Jewish people. There were also more mainstream right-wing parties, such as **German National People's Party (DNVP)**, whose aim was to combat the left and establish a more conservative, nationalist government.

> **KEY TERM**
>
> **German National People's Party (DNVP)**
> A coalition of nationalists that included the Fatherland Party and the Pan-German League. Many of its members were racists and extremists. Its support came from landowners and industrialists, but it also had backing among the middle classes and was the largest of the more radical right-wing parties.

Table 2.2 Weimar-era political parties

Party	Main views and support
ZP (Centre Party)	Created in the nineteenth century to protect Catholic interests, attracted wide range of supporters
DDP (German Democratic Party)	Formed from the old National Liberal Party, it gained support from the professional middle class
DNVP (German National People's Party)	A right-wing party, monarchist and anti-republic
DVP (German People's Party)	Founded by Gustav Stresemann, it initially disliked the republic but it became a supporter of parliamentary democracy and attracted support from the Protestant middle and upper classes
KPD (German Communist Party)	Opposed the republic and wanted revolution
NSDAP (National Socialist German Workers' Party – Nazis)	As the name suggests it was a mixture of nationalism and socialism, but the socialism was largely abandoned as the party followed a more right-wing agenda
SPD (German Social Democratic Party)	Moderate socialists and were the party of the working class and trade unions. They supported parliamentary democracy
BVP (Bavarian People's Party)	A regional party formed from elements of the Centre Party in 1919. Its aim was to uphold the interests of Bavaria
USPD (Independent German Social Democratic Party)	Broke away from the SPD and contained more radical socialists, with some later joining the KPD, but others returned to the SPD

The Kapp *Putsch*

The opportunity for right-wing groups came when the government began to disband the *Freikorps* and reduce the size of the German army in accordance with the terms of the Versailles treaty. A rising began when it was proposed to disband two brigades of the army stationed close to Berlin. **Wolfgang Kapp** and General Lüttwitz led 12,000 troops into Berlin, proclaimed Kapp, the founder of the wartime patriotic Fatherland Party, as chancellor and seized the main buildings in the capital.

> **SOURCE D**
>
> From a proclamation by Wolfgang Kapp, 13 March 1920. Quoted in John Laver, *Imperial and Weimar Germany*, Hodder & Stoughton, 1992, p. 43.
>
> The Reich and nation are in grave danger. With terrible speed we are approaching the complete collapse of the State and of law and order. The people are only dimly aware of the approaching disaster. Prices are rising unchecked. Hardship is growing. Starvation threatens. Corruption, usury, nepotism and crime are cheekily raising their heads. The Government, lacking authority, impotent, and in league with corruption, is incapable of overcoming the danger …
>
> From the east we are threatened by destruction and violation by war-like Bolshevism. Is this Government capable of resisting it? How are we to escape internal and external collapse?
>
> Only by re-erecting a strong State … there is no other way but a government of action.

The army refused to put the rising down despite government requests and, as a result, the government was forced to flee. It appeared as if the threat was serious. However, the government was saved by the trade unions responding to a government request to call a general strike, which not only brought the capital to a standstill but also the rest of the country. This action paralysed public services, including water, electricity and gas, and after four days Kapp and his 'government' fled the city.

> **SOURCE E**
>
> From an appeal by the Social Democrats, March 1920.
>
> We refuse to buckle under this military pressure. We did not bring about the revolution to make this bloody *Freikorps* regiment legal. Workers! Comrades! Go on strike, put down your work and stop the military dictatorship. There is only one way to prevent the return of a Kaiser: shut down the economy!'

KEY FIGURE

Wolfgang Kapp (1858–1922)

A Prussian civil servant who helped to found the Fatherland Party. He wanted to see the Kaiser restored.

SOURCE QUESTION

How accurate are Kapp's comments in Source D about the situation in Germany in 1920?

ONLINE EXTRAS

Test your understanding of the value of a source by completing Worksheet 2 at **www.hoddereducation. co.uk/accesstohistory/extras**

SOURCE QUESTION

According to Source E, why was there opposition to the Kapp *Putsch*?

How serious a threat was the rising?

The crushing of the rising would suggest that the government had been successful. It had been able to defeat the rising and during the crisis it had been able to retain the support of the people of Berlin. However, the fact that the rising had taken place and the army's unwillingness to come to the aid of the republic is a clear indication of its weak position. It also suggests that the army had the right to behave as it saw fit, a position that had already been accepted by the **Ebert–Groener Pact**. The supreme army command had agreed to support the government and use troops to maintain it in return for Ebert opposing revolutionary socialism and the authority of army officers. In reality, the army had become a **'state within a state'**. This was made even clearer by developments in Bavaria where the army was able to install a right-wing government, leading to the state becoming a hotbed for radicalism, culminating in the Munich *Putsch* of 1923 (see pages 23–4).

The aftermath of the Kapp *Putsch*

The elections of June 1920 resulted in further loss of support for democratic parties, such as the SPD, and saw gains for the right wing, which was determined to abandon the programme of social and economic reforms. This served only to encourage further hostility from many workers, reflected in the left-wing risings of 1921 and 1923. At the same time, the extreme right wing also continued to grow as disputes with the Allies over the peace terms and reparations (see pages 25–6) created further resentment.

> **KEY TERMS**
>
> **Ebert–Groener Pact** Agreed in November 1918; by this, Groener, the supreme army commander, agreed to support the new government under Ebert and use troops to maintain the stability of the republic.
>
> **State within a state** Where another power can threaten the authority of the government.

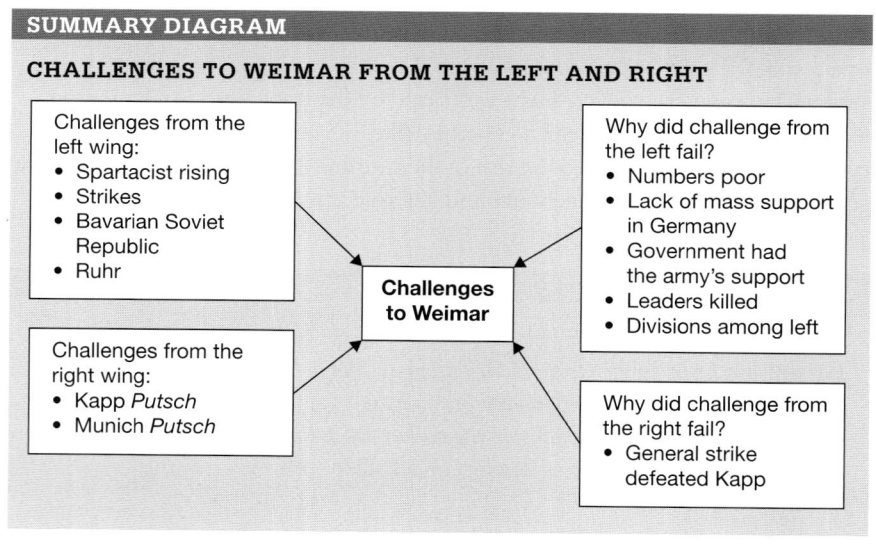

SUMMARY DIAGRAM

CHALLENGES TO WEIMAR FROM THE LEFT AND RIGHT

Challenges from the left wing:
- Spartacist rising
- Strikes
- Bavarian Soviet Republic
- Ruhr

Challenges from the right wing:
- Kapp *Putsch*
- Munich *Putsch*

Why did challenge from the left fail?
- Numbers poor
- Lack of mass support in Germany
- Government had the army's support
- Leaders killed
- Divisions among left

Why did challenge from the right fail?
- General strike defeated Kapp

5 The emergence of the National Socialist German Workers' Party

■ *Why did the Nazi Party emerge and how strong was it by 1923?*

The National Socialist German Workers' Party (NSDAP or Nazis) had begun as the German Workers' Party (DAP) under the leadership of Anton Drexler. Although there was little to suggest that Adolf Hitler would become a powerful political figure, his right-wing attitude resulted in his being employed as a spy by the Bavarian section of the German army. His investigations led to his attending meetings of the DAP, which he believed, because of its name, was a left-wing revolutionary group. However, he soon discovered that it was committed to extreme nationalism, anti-Semitism and **anti-capitalism**. Hitler joined the group and soon became a committee member. It did not take long before he was working with Drexler in drawing up the party's 25-point programme in February 1920. The party's name was also changed to the NSDAP.

> **KEY TERM**
>
> **Anti-capitalism**
> Opposition to a system which operates on the principle of private ownership and profit.

Nazi ideology

The 25-point programme was designed to appeal to the fears and prejudices of many Germans with its focus on nationalism, the reversal of the Versailles treaty and socialism:

> **SOURCE F**
>
> Selected points from the (25-point) Programme of the German Workers' Party read by Hitler at a meeting in a Munich beer cellar, 24 February 1920.
>
> 1 *We demand the union of all Germans in a Greater Germany on the basis of the right of national self-determination.*
>
> 2 *We demand equality of rights for the German People in its dealings with other nations, and the revocation of the peace treaties of Versailles and Saint-Germain.*
>
> 3 *We demand land and territory (colonies) to feed our people and to settle our surplus population.*
>
> 4 *Only members of the nation may be citizens of the State. Only those of German blood, whatever their creed, may be members of the nation. Accordingly, no Jew may be a member of the nation.*
>
> 7 *We demand that the State shall make it its primary duty to provide a livelihood for its citizens. If it should prove impossible to feed the entire population, foreign nationals (non-citizens) must be deported from the Reich.*
>
> 14 *We demand profit sharing in large industrial enterprises.*
>
> 15 *We demand the extensive development of insurance for old age.*
>
> 25 *We demand the creation of a strong central power of the Reich.*

> **SOURCE QUESTION**
>
> In what ways did the programme in Source F appeal to the concerns of the German people at the time?

Nationalism

The opening points of the party programme made it clear that aggressive nationalism was an important aspect of Nazi beliefs. Germany had lost a great deal of land and economic resources as a result of the Treaty of Versailles and it was, therefore, crucial that this was overturned. However, the 25 points went beyond this as they demanded the creation of a *Reich* which included all German people who lived beyond the boundaries of Imperial Germany and would therefore include Germans who lived in the Baltic or Sudetenland. But the demands went even further than this as Hitler wanted **Lebensraum**, which required territorial expansion in the east and the conquest of land in Poland, Russia and Ukraine. Germany could obtain food supplies and raw materials from this territory, which would allow Germany to become a great power.

Racism

Hitler's ideas were built on his concept of race, believing as he did in **Social Darwinism** and the survival of the fittest. This would inevitably lead to a struggle between races, with the strongest defeating the weakest. In Hitler's view, the **Aryans**, as represented by the Germans, were the master race, and would dominate inferior races. As a result, expansion east where there were, according to Hitler, inferior races, such as Slavs and Jewish people, was easily justifiable.

Anti-Semitism

Hitler had an irrational belief that Jewish people were responsible for all of Germany's problems, and therefore used them a scapegoat. As a result, he thought that they had to be removed. This belief was not new and had been present in medieval Europe, when attacks on Jewish communities were not unusual. The belief had grown and in the nineteenth century developed further, based on nationalism and racism, so that by 1900 anti-Semitic political parties were able to win seats in the *Reichstag*.

Anti-democracy

Hitler believed in strong, authoritarian government and saw democracy as weak and ineffective. There was much support for this view in Germany, where there was a tradition of militarism and a strong state. Hitler also believed that democracy was responsible for the betrayal of Germany in 1918, when democratic politicians had surrendered, referring to them as the **November criminals**. Democracy, Hitler also believed, led to the growth of an even greater enemy, communism.

Socialism

The 25-point programme also contained a number of points that had a distinctively socialist aspect, with demands for some social reforms. Hitler accepted these ideas because they had popular appeal and at the start the party

> **KEY TERMS**
>
> **Lebensraum** 'Living space', Hitler's aim for land in the east to settle the surplus German population.
>
> **Social Darwinism** A belief that the world comprised a struggle between the different races.
>
> **Aryans** The non-Jewish peoples of northern Europe who, Hitler believed, were supreme or the 'master race'.
>
> **November criminals** Those who agreed to the armistice; was later used as a term of abuse for those who supported the republic.

needed to appeal to as many as possible. However, Hitler was never really committed to these ideas and this would lead to disagreements within the party. Instead, Hitler promoted the idea of **Volksgemeinschaft**, or people's community. This concept remained very vague, although what does emerge was that it was an attempt to overcome class differences and create a new national identity. People were supposed to work together for the benefit of the nation and promote national values. However, it could only appeal to those who were members of the state and were willing to sacrifice their individual freedom.

The growth of the Nazi Party to 1923

Initially, it was Hitler's own popularity, and the speeches that he gave, which attracted the public's attention and led to a growth in party membership. He established armed squads to protect party meetings and intimidate the opposition, particularly the Communists. Hitler gave the party a clear identity, with the Nazi salute, the swastika and a uniform. Concerned by his increasing influence, Drexler and others attempted to limit Hitler, but failed, and the subsequent power struggle resulted in Drexler resigning and Hitler becoming chairman and leader (Führer) of the party.

The party was further strengthened in the period from 1921 to 1923 by a number of actions:

- Armed squads, the **Sturmabteilung (SA)**, were set up in 1921 as a paramilitary group under the leadership of **Ernst Röhm**. These squads were used to intimidate other parties and carry out acts of violence.
- The party set up its own newspaper in 1921, the *Völkischer Beobachter* (*People's Observer*).
- Hitler won the support of **Julius Streicher** and **Hermann Göring**, the latter providing him with valuable contacts in Munich society, which helped to make the party respectable.

As a result of these developments, the party had a membership of about 20,000 by 1923, with its strongest support in Bavaria. However, it was still a fringe party.

The Munich *Putsch*

By 1923, Bavaria was ruled by a conservative Catholic regime under the control of **Gustav von Kahr** that wanted to unite all right-wing elements and restore the values of pre-war Germany. The state had become home to a variety of ultra-nationalist groups, including the Nazi Party. The Nazis had joined an association of right-wing groups in the region, and in September 1923 they began to plan a *putsch* in Munich before marching on Berlin to establish a **military dictatorship** with the support of Ludendorff, the renowned army commander from the First World War.

KEY TERMS

Volksgemeinschaft
A people's community that was socially unified and racially pure.

Sturmabteilung (SA)
Members were known as the Stormtroopers or Brownshirts, after the colour of their uniform. Many were supporters of the more radical or socialist aspects of Nazism.

KEY FIGURES

Ernst Röhm (1887–1934)
Röhm had been an early member of the Nazi Party. He had been involved in the formation of the SA and had become its leader. He turned the SA into a powerful force and wanted a genuine national socialist revolution, including further social and economic reform, and a greater political role for the SA, amalgamating it with the army, and with him as its commander. However, he was a homosexual and this, and his supposed plotting against Hitler, led to his arrest and death in the Night of the Long Knives (pages 101–3).

Julius Streicher (1885–1946)
Streicher was a prominent Nazi, and founder and publisher of the anti-Semitic newspaper *Der Stürmer* (*The Striker*). He was also involved in publishing anti-Semitic children's books. After the war he was convicted of crimes against humanity at the Nuremberg trials and was executed.

KEY FIGURES

Hermann Göring (1893–1946)

Göring came from a well-to-do family, which helped to give Nazism greater respectability. He was popular because he was witty and played a crucial role in the rise of Nazism. Göring was willing to use violence and murder to consolidate Nazi power and was involved in the *Reichstag* fire (pages 97–8) and the Night of the Long Knives (pages 101–3). He gained a range of titles and after 1936 was 'economic dictator' and then in 1939 was officially named as Hitler's successor. However, with the failure to win the Battle of Britain during the Second World War he became more isolated and his influence declined. He killed himself in 1946 before his scheduled execution.

Gustav von Kahr (1862–1934)

An ultra-conservative Bavarian politician who helped to turn the state into a centre of radical nationalism after the First World War. He blamed Germany's problems on the government in Berlin. Initially he plotted with Hitler in 1923, but fearing failure he abandoned his support for the *putsch*.

KEY TERMS

Military dictatorship Rule by the armed forces.

Putsch An uprising, usually by a small group in an attempt to overthrow the government.

By October 1923, the army commander in Bavaria, General von Lossow, was disobeying orders from Berlin and plotting with Kahr and Hitler. However, by November, with the failure of the coup appearing likely, Lossow and Kahr abandoned the plan, but Hitler decided to continue. On 8 November, while Kahr was addressing a meeting in a Munich beer hall, Hitler and the Nazis stormed in, took control and declared a national revolution. Kahr and Lossow, under pressure, agreed to cooperate, but the chief of the army command, General von Seeckt, ordered the armed forces to resist the ***putsch***. The following day, 3000 Nazis attempted to take Munich, but lacking sufficient support the *putsch* was easily crushed. Sixteen Nazis were killed and Hitler was arrested on charges of treason.

Impact of the Munich *Putsch*

The defeat of the *putsch* appeared to show the strength of the new republic. It had been able to withstand a serious challenge during a difficult year (see pages 27–9). The army had not supported the overthrow of the regime as Hitler had hoped. However, the response of the judiciary raised serious concerns for the future of Weimar and democracy:

- Despite Hitler being arrested for treason he was given the minimum sentence of five years and also told that he would be released early on probation.
- The conditions in which Hitler was kept at Landsberg prison were comfortable.
- Hitler was released after less than ten months.
- Ludendorff was acquitted on the grounds that he was only present at the *putsch* by 'accident'.

Hitler was able to use his trial to generate publicity for the Nazi Party as his words were well reported in newspapers. He used his time in prison to develop his ideas and write his book, *Mein Kampf* (*My Struggle*), in which he outlined his ideas for the future of Germany. Hitler also used the time to think about Nazi tactics and concluded that he would not be able to seize power by force, but would have to work within the democratic system, which the Nazis could then destroy once they were in power.

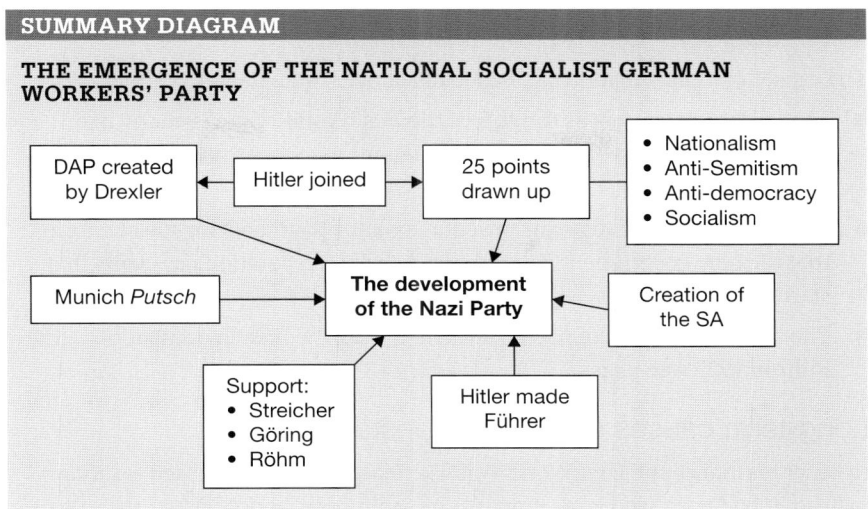

6 The economic crisis

■ *Why did Germany suffer an economic crisis?*

The German economy had grown dramatically in the years before the First World War and had become the strongest in Europe, overtaking Britain in many areas, particularly in the new industries, such as petrochemicals. The country had many advantages:

- Considerable natural resources of coal and iron ore.
- Advanced engineering and petrochemical industries.
- An advanced banking system.
- A well-educated workforce.

However, the First World War did considerable damage to the economy:

- Land containing valuable natural resources was lost (see page 7).
- Inflation had hit the economy, with prices rising four-fold during the war.
- National debt had grown from 5000 million marks in 1914 to 144,000 million by 1919.
- The cost of reparations.

The cost of the war and reparations had already caused inflation, with the value of the mark declining dramatically from 8.9 marks to the US dollar in January 1919 to 493.2 in January 1922. However, economic problems came to a head in 1923 with hyperinflation. Many Germans believed this was the result of the Treaty of Versailles and the cost of reparations, while others blamed the supposed greed of Jewish people. Some historians now argue that the fundamental cause of hyperinflation was the decision of the government to print increasing amounts of paper money to pay off interest on its debts.

The causes of hyperinflation

The causes of hyperinflation can be looked at over three phases of time:

- The long-term cause was the cost of the First World War. Germany had borrowed large sums of money to fund the war and was now faced with huge debts.
- The medium-term cause was brought about by payments for social reforms that the new government had promised and the reparation payments that started from 1921.
- The short-term cause of paying strikers during the French occupation of the Ruhr in 1923 (see pages 27–9).

Long-term causes of economic instability

In order to finance the First World War, Germany had not increased taxation; instead, it had borrowed large amounts by selling war bonds. When the sale of these bonds proved insufficient, the government simply allowed the national debt to grow. As a result, by the end of the war, only sixteen per cent of the cost had been raised from taxation. Victory would have allowed the government to claim reparations from the defeated nations, but defeat meant the opposite.

Medium-term causes of economic instability

The government needed to reduce the gap between its expenditure and income, but this could be done only by cutting spending or increasing taxation. However, both options were unpopular and would cause both political and social problems for an already unpopular regime. It decided to follow a policy of **deficit financing**, but this allowed inflation to continue. The reparations that Germany now had to pay only added to the difficulties as the payments had to be in **hard currency**, such as gold or US dollars. However, in order to pay reparations the government printed more marks and sold them to obtain the stronger currencies of other countries, which sent the value of the mark into further decline (see Table 2.3, page 27).

Table 2.3 clearly shows that although inflation had been climbing sharply, it was in 1923 that it soared. Even before then, Germany had struggled to pay some of its reparations and it had been allowed to postpone some of its instalments. In order to try and solve the problem there had been an international conference at Genoa, Italy, in 1922. However, in July 1922 Germany again requested another postponement and this set in motion the final phase of the inflationary crisis.

Short-term causes of economic instability

The French government had become increasingly convinced that Germany was deliberately attempting to avoid paying reparations and the French premier, Raymond Poincaré, was determined to secure what he believed was rightfully French. Therefore, when the German government defaulted on payments in

> **KEY TERMS**
>
> **Deficit financing**
> The policy whereby the government spends more than its income in order to stimulate economic growth.
>
> **Hard currency**
> A currency that financial markets consider to be reliable because its value does not fluctuate.

December 1922 he ordered French and Belgian troops to occupy the Ruhr in order to make Germany pay in goods what it was not paying in money. The invasion of the Ruhr set in motion a string of events that would send the mark into freefall and create an economy that relied on the **black market** and **barter**.

Table 2.3 Hyperinflation: exchange rate and wholesale prices

Date	Exchange rate of German marks against the US dollar	Wholesale price index. The index is created from a scale of prices starting with 1 for 1914
July 1914	4.2	1
January 1919	8.9	2
January 1920	14.0	4
January 1921	64.9	14
January 1922	191.8	37
January 1923	17,792	2,785
July 1923	353,412	74,787
September 1923	98,860,000	23,949,000
November 1923	200,000,000,000	750,000,000,000

> **KEY TERMS**
> **Black market** The underground economy where goods are sold at unregulated prices.
> **Barter** An exchange where goods are swapped rather than sold for money.
> **Passive resistance** The refusal to work or cooperate with occupying forces.

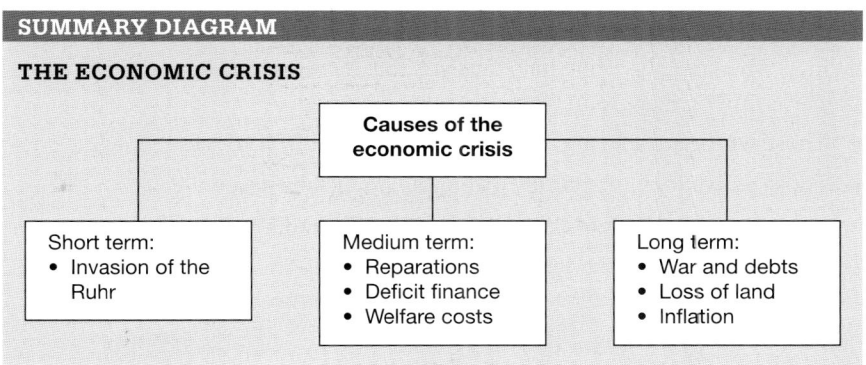

SUMMARY DIAGRAM
THE ECONOMIC CRISIS

Causes of the economic crisis
- Short term:
  - Invasion of the Ruhr
- Medium term:
  - Reparations
  - Deficit finance
  - Welfare costs
- Long term:
  - War and debts
  - Loss of land
  - Inflation

7 The occupation of the Ruhr

■ *What was the impact of the invasion of the Ruhr?*

The occupation of the Ruhr by French and Belgian troops did much to unite Germany. The government, under Chancellor **Wilhelm Cuno**, played on nationalist sentiment and supported the workers in the Ruhr who went on strike and adopted a policy of **passive resistance**. The government promised to carry on paying the wages of the workers. However, the government was unable to collect taxes from the region; the French also stopped coal being taken from the region to other parts of Germany, forcing fuel to be imported.

> **KEY FIGURE**
> **Wilhelm Cuno (1876–1933)**
> Cuno was a businessman and economic expert involved in the armistice, reparation negotiations and post-war international conferences. He was chancellor 1922–3 during the French occupation of the Ruhr and hyperinflation. He resigned as a result of a no-confidence vote.

In order to pay the striking workers, the government was forced to print even more money and, as a result, by August 1923 money was virtually worthless, with it costing more to print the currency than it was actually worth. As a consequence, German people had to barter in order to obtain goods; there was starvation in many towns and cities as food became virtually unobtainable. Unrest broke out all over Germany and food was seized from farms.

With the economy on the verge of complete collapse, a new coalition government under **Gustav Stresemann** was formed. He ended passive resistance. In reality he had little choice, but it caused great anger among nationalists who saw it as another example of surrender to the Allies, which may have encouraged Hitler's actions in Munich in November (see pages 23–4). Stresemann also faced other challenges:

- Some of the DNVP were planning a coup to bring in a dictatorship.
- The KPD were planning uprisings in Saxony, Hamburg and Thuringia.
- There were plans for a nationalist coup in Bavaria.

The impact of the 1923 crises

The dramatic decline in the value of the mark ruined many people. Historians have often argued that it was those, such as pensioners, civil servants or members of the middle class, who were either on **fixed incomes** or reliant on savings, who were the worst hit. However, that picture could be viewed as too simple as among that group there were some winners:

- Those who were able to pay off loans or debts with worthless money.
- Those who bought up property from the financially desperate.
- Businessmen who were able to borrow cheaply and invest in new enterprises.

Yet, those who were dependent on their savings did suffer. Investments in banks went down in value and those who had bought government bonds found they were now worthless.

More recent research by historians has suggested that generalisations are difficult and individual circumstances would determine how people were affected. However, for the following groups, it does appear that their outcome remained similar:

- Peasants and farmers: they were able to survive as not only was food in demand but they were often self-sufficient so were less affected by the price rises.
- Industrial workers: they had seen real wages and their standard of living improve in the period to 1922, but, after that, wage rises did not keep pace with price rises and they suffered a considerable decline.
- Lower middle class (*Mittelstand*): many were able to exploit market conditions and made gains.
- Civil servants: they had been doing well in the period before hyperinflation, but as they were on fixed incomes, they suffered considerable losses. Many

---

KEY FIGURE

Gustav Stresemann (1878–1929)

Stresemann founded the DVP in 1919. Initially opposed to Weimar, he changed his view, became chancellor in 1923 for 100 days, and was foreign minister from 1923 until his death in 1929. He wanted to see the Versailles treaty revised, but saw the best way was to work with the Allied powers, which brought a number of foreign policy successes.

KEY TERM

Fixed income Where people rely on a guaranteed set income, be it from a salary or bonds. It does not change in response to economic changes.

had bought war bonds and lost out on those as well. However, if they were buying a property with a mortgage they might have been able to make gains.
- Retired: it is often argued that they suffered the most as they were dependent on a fixed income.
- Business owners: they often did well as they bought up property and paid off mortgages. They also gained if they sold goods overseas as the exchange rate was in their favour and meant that German goods were cheap to import.

However, the focus on the economic results ignores the human consequences, which were possibly even more far-reaching. Mortality rates increased as people's diets deteriorated, leading to an increase in diseases such as scurvy. The crises also had an impact on behaviour. Studies have suggested that there was an increase in crime, a decrease in morality reflected in the growth in prostitution, a growth in the number of suicides and a greater willingness to find scapegoats for problems, such as Jewish people.

In particular, some historians have argued that the crises led to a loss of faith in the government and was seen as further evidence of the failings of democracy.

Conclusion: how did Weimar survive the crises of 1919–23?

The Weimar Republic faced a significant number of challenges in the years 1919–23, but the fact that it survived may suggest that the Weimar was stronger than it appeared. The challenge from the far left was not as serious as that from the extreme right, as the left was not powerful enough to lead a revolution against the republic. However, the government failed to appreciate the extent of the opposition to the republic from the extreme right and instead focused on the threat from the left. Ultimately, it was the persistence of old, traditional values and attitudes among many of the national institutions that was the most serious problem the government faced.

The movements led by Kapp and Hitler in the early 1920s were, like the challenges from the left, too weak and disorganised, but the more serious danger from the right was just below the surface, as seen in the election results, which saw a move away from the democratic parties. This was made more serious because the supporters of democracy found it increasingly difficult to create and maintain working coalition governments. In the period from 1919 to 1923, the longest government lasted just eighteen months.

The political problems, in addition to hyperinflation and the Ruhr crisis, resulted in problems for the government, even if it did survive. However, in 1923 there was little alternative to the republic and hostility had not reached unbearable levels. The government was also fortunate that hostility could be directed against the occupying French and Belgian forces, rather than the government. Moreover, the workers were not suffering as badly as when there was mass unemployment in the early 1930s. As a result, although the problems were serious, they were nothing like those that the republic would come to encounter.

SUMMARY DIAGRAM

THE OCCUPATION OF THE RUHR

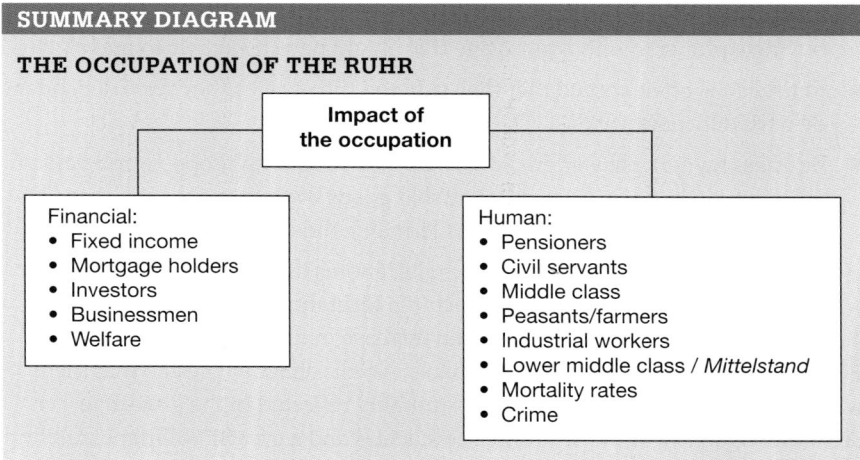

8 Key debate

■ *What was the nature of the German Revolution?*

Until recently, the period 1918–19 attracted little attention from historians; instead, research on Weimar focused on its collapse and the rise of the Nazi Party. However, with the division of Germany after the Second World War, the revolution of 1918–19 attracted more academic debate. East German writers saw Ebert as saving capitalism by crushing the revolution of the masses and betraying the left wing, but this view was dismissed by those in the West as communist propaganda.

INTERPRETATION 1

From Andreas Dorpalen, *German History in Marxist Perspective: The East German Approach*, Hamish Hamilton, 1985, pp. 314–15.

To anyone viewing revolutions as engines of social progress, Ebert's concern with restoring order carried little conviction. It seemed a manoeuvre to salvage the old power apparatus in open betrayal of the revolution and the government's own supporters. In its blind struggle against revolution ... the new regime did not purge the bureaucracy of its non-democratic elements, but retained the old imperial officials right up to the minister level. In the same vein, Ebert entered an alliance with the old militarist forces – those mortal enemies of the nation – thus shielding the officer corps from all revolutionary aspirations inside and outside the Army. Similarly the government sanctioned a pact between labour unions and private capitalist employers.

ONLINE EXTRAS **WWW**

Get to grips with finding out how and why different historical interpretations have been formed by historians by completing Worksheet 3 at www.hoddereducation.co.uk/accesstohistory/extras

In the West, historians such as Erich Eyck (1970) and K.D. Erdmann (1950) argue that there were only two options for Ebert, the first was to allow a communist dictatorship to develop while the second was to establish a parliamentary democracy.

However, these traditional views have been subject to more academic scrutiny since the relaxation and ending of the Cold War. Thus, historians have closely studied the Councils that were established in November 1918 and this has led to a reassessment of the situation in Germany.

- Most have argued that the chances of a Soviet-style regime were limited and that Ebert overestimated the threat from the left, while underestimating the challenge from the right. This view has been reinforced by writers such as Eberhard Kolb (2004) and Reinhard Rürup (2000), who argued that few workers fell under the control of the revolutionary left.
- There was a desire for a more radical transformation of society, which, if it had been pursued, might have led to a more secure democratic regime being established.

As a result, the revolution brought about little more than political and constitutional change and failed to alter the social and economic structure of the country.

> **INTERPRETATION 2**
>
> From Michael Hughes, *Nationalism and Society: Germany, 1800–1945*, Hodder Arnold, 1988, p. 184.
>
> *There is still dispute among historians as to whether there was a genuine revolution in November 1918. In view of the fact that there was so little real change – the removal of the Kaiser and the other German monarchs was of symbolic rather than real significance – it is more accurate to talk of a potential revolution which ran away into the sand rather than the genuine article. The republic that eventually emerged contained at once too much and too little of the old Germany: powerful institutions centres of the old ruling class remained intact and were not subject to democratic control while many Germans saw the republic as originating in a revolution and therefore illegitimate.*

ONLINE EXTRAS

Test your understanding of how you might use your knowledge to support or challenge an interpretation by completing Worksheet 4 at www.hoddereducation.co.uk/accesstohistory/extras

Ebert's belief that the threat from the extreme left was severe led to his relying on the old elite and this was a major factor in the eventual failure of the republic. His policies created bitterness on the left and the Communists never forgave the SPD. The USPD split, with some joining the Communists and others the SPD, with the result that the left remained severely divided, making it much harder for them to resist the advances of Nazism.

However, more recent work by Conan Fischer (2006) has challenged the view that the revolution failed to bring about fundamental social change. He maintains that it is too simplistic to see the revolution as a weak compromise. Instead, he argues that, given the circumstances of Germany's defeat, the revolution was a remarkable achievement.

> **INTERPRETATION 3**
>
> From Conan Fischer, 'A Very German Revolution'? *The Post-1918 Settlement Revaluated*, GHIL Bulletin, Vol. XXVIII, No. 2, November 2006, pp. 31–2.
>
> *1918 was, indeed, a very German revolution, but then, on the whole, countries do tend to get the revolutions they have earned. On those terms Germany's revolutionary settlement was sufficiently practical yet visionary to offer the country a viable future, for it represented a readiness on each side to accommodate the other, and thus was a triumph of moderation over utopian extremism in all its forms.*

ONLINE EXTRAS WWW

Develop your understanding of linking interpretations to the wider historical debate by completing Worksheet 5 at **www.hoddereducation.co.uk/accesstohistory/extras**

CHAPTER SUMMARY

Although it was clear by the late summer of 1918 that Germany had lost the First World War, the people were still shocked by the defeat and many blamed the new Weimar government rather than the army. Although Ludendorff tried to introduce reforms to preserve the old regime, it did not satisfy people and popular disquiet led to the abdication of the Kaiser and his replacement by the democratic Weimar Republic.

The republic faced challenges from both the left wing, with the Spartacist rising, and the right wing, with both the Kapp *Putsch* and the Munich *Putsch*, in its early years, which threatened its very survival. It also had to sign the very unpopular Treaty of Versailles, which resulted in further criticism of the new government.

There were also economic and social challenges, the most serious of which was the French and Belgian invasion of the Ruhr, which led to the government printing more money to pay the striking workers who followed a policy of passive resistance. This was a major factor in the hyperinflation which hit the country in 1923 and ruined the savings of many, further adding to the regime's unpopularity.

Refresher questions

Use these questions to remind yourself of the key material covered in this chapter

1. What was the impact of defeat in the war on the German people?
2. What was the 'stab in the back' myth? Why was it believed?
3. Did the revolution of 1918–19 achieve its aims?
4. What were the problems facing Ebert's government?
5. Why was the Treaty of Versailles so unpopular with the German people?
6. What were the strengths and weaknesses of the Weimar constitution?
7. Why did the Spartacist revolt fail?
8. What did the right wing want? Why did it fail to achieve its aims?
9. Which was a greater threat to Weimar, the Kapp *Putsch* (1920) or the Munich *Putsch* (1923)?
10. What did the Nazi Party represent in the period 1919–23?
11. What were the causes of hyperinflation?
12. Who gained and who lost from hyperinflation?
13. Why was Weimar able to survive the years 1919–23?

CHAPTER 3

Foreign and economic policy 1924–9

In comparison with the period 1918–23, the years 1924–9 are usually seen as the golden years of the Weimar Republic. There were signs of economic stability and an improvement in Germany's foreign position, as well as a decline in political extremism and a cultural flowering. This chapter will consider the accuracy of this view by examining the extent of the economic recovery and the achievements of Stresemann's foreign policy by focusing on the following themes:

- The appointment of Gustav Stresemann as chancellor
- Was there an economic recovery under Stresemann?
- Attempts to aid German economic recovery: the Dawes Plan and Young Plan
- Foreign policy under Gustav Stresemann

The key debate on page 49 of this chapter considers the extent of the recovery in the period 1924–9.

KEY DATES

1923	Aug.	Stresemann became chancellor
	Nov.	Stresemann government fell but he remained foreign minister
1924	April	Dawes Plan
	May	Elections to *Reichstag* saw gains by extremist parties
1925	Feb.	Ebert died
	April	Hindenburg elected president
	Oct.	Locarno Conference
1926	April	Treaty of Berlin with USSR
	Sept.	Germany joined the League of Nations
1927		Fall in agricultural prices
1929	June	Young Plan
	Oct.	Stresemann died
		Wall Street Crash
	Dec.	Anti-Young Plan referendum

In the summer of 1923, the Weimar Republic had seemed close to collapse. Hyperinflation had set in and the currency was worthless. There were foreign troops occupying the Ruhr and the government appeared to lack a clear policy to deal with the problems. There were also challenges from both the left and right wings of the political spectrum; on the left there was an attempted communist rising in Saxony, while in Bavaria, an ultra-right state government refused to obey the national government and this would eventually lead to the abortive Munich *Putsch* in November. However, within a few months, some sense of stability had been restored. How far was this due to the appointment of Gustav Stresemann as chancellor in August 1923?

1 The appointment of Gustav Stresemann as chancellor

■ *How important was Stresemann's appointment as chancellor?*

Some historians have argued that the appointment of Gustav Stresemann as chancellor, even though he served in that role for just 103 days, and the establishment of the Great Coalition in August 1923 signalled the start of a period of recovery and stability for the republic. In support of this, there was economic recovery, a new currency, foreign loans and declining support for extreme parties both on the left and right wings of the political spectrum. In addition, Germany had become well known as a cultural centre and more a part of European affairs, encouraged by Stresemann as foreign minister. However, there were still those who were bitter, having been ruined by inflation or resentful of the humiliation of Versailles.

Unlike the previous chancellor, Cuno, Stresemann was willing to take hard political decisions. This was seen very clearly in the actions he took within the first 100 days of his appointment:

- He ended passive resistance in the Ruhr and began again to pay reparations. Although this was unpopular with many nationalists, who saw it as a surrender, he was aware that it was the only way to get the French out of the Ruhr and get the economy going again.
- Guided by the finance minister, Hans Luther, he cut government spending to help reduce the deficit. This resulted in over 700,000 public employees losing their jobs.
- In December 1923, a new currency, the Rentenmark, under the supervision of **Hjalmar Schacht**, was introduced. The old worthless currency was withdrawn and the new currency, which provided stability, was brought in.
- Stresemann's policies won him some international sympathy and he was able to persuade the Allies to hold an international conference to discuss Germany's situation. This led to the establishment of the Dawes Committee and the publication, in April 1924, of the Dawes Plan (see pages 38–40).

Politically, it also appeared as if the extreme left and right had been defeated. However, there were still problems and under the surface there still lurked unease, discontent and extremism.

KEY FIGURE

Hjalmar Schacht (1877–1970)

Schacht was a highly respected financier and economist. He stabilised the economy in the 1920s and was president of the Reichsbank under the Weimar Republic until his resignation over the Young Plan. He returned as president in 1933 and became minister of economics in 1934, drawing up and overseeing the New Plan and deficit financing. However, he gradually lost influence and disagreed with the emphasis on rearmament. He resigned as minister in 1937 and president of the Reichsbank in 1939. He made links with the resistance, was put in a concentration camp, but survived both that and the following war trials.

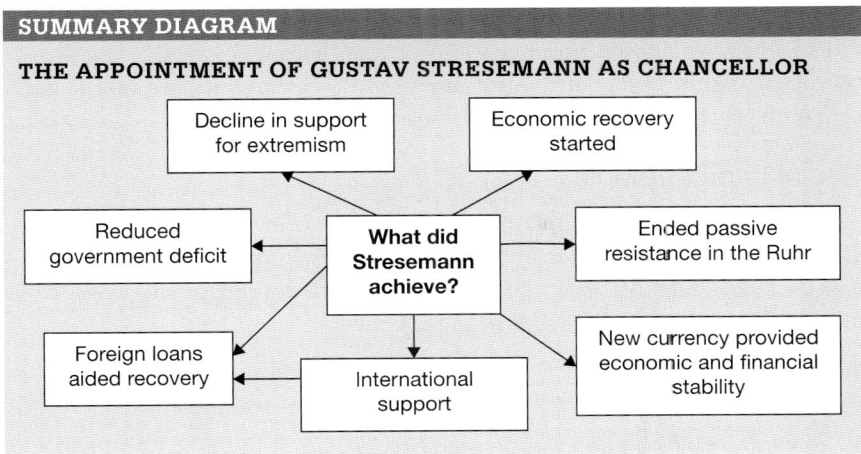

2 Was there an economic recovery under Stresemann?

■ *How strong was the economic recovery under Stresemann?*

Most accounts suggest that the changes brought in by Stresemann brought about a period of growth and prosperity for the German economy in the years 1924–9, before the **Great Depression** undermined all the achievements. However, whether Stresemann's policies led to an economic recovery is a matter of debate.

Arguments for an economic recovery

In November 1923, the introduction of the new currency, the Rentenmark, began the process of achieving financial stability. This process was completed the following year when the Reichsmark was introduced. This helped to restore confidence in the currency as the old, worthless mark was destroyed. There was also some compensation for those who had their savings destroyed by inflation, but the level was so low that many still remained resentful. Industrial production also recovered so that, under Stresemann, it was better than in the periods 1919–23 and 1930–3, returning to the 1913 levels by 1927 and surpassing it in both 1928 and 1929.

However, how far the industrial recovery was due to government policies is debatable. Production levels rose, often because of the use of more efficient methods of production, particularly in coal mining and steel production, and because of overseas investment which totalled some 25.5 billion marks. Foreign banks saw the advantages of high interest rates, while foreign business, such as Ford, invested in factories because their mass production methods were more

> **KEY TERM**
>
> **Great Depression** The severe economic depression from 1929 to 1993. It started in the USA with the Wall Street Crash and resulted in mass unemployment.

efficient. Costs were also reduced because of the power of large **cartels**, such as IG Farben, which were able to lower their costs because of their purchasing power. All of this resulted in a significant rise in exports, which grew by 40 per cent in the period, bringing with it increases in wages.

> **KEY TERM**
> **Cartel** A group of companies which control the market and prices through a joint monopoly.

Social improvements

Not only did wages rise but there were improvements in social conditions. The Weimar constitution aimed to improve social provision through the creation of a welfare state, and this was to be achieved by a series of progressive taxes. This allowed a number of measures to be implemented:

- The maximum working week was limited to 48 hours.
- A state scheme for arbitration in the event of strikes was established.
- There were benefits and war pensions for the widows and the wounded.
- Provision was made for youth clubs and sports facilities.
- A new national insurance code extended welfare provision.
- The unemployment insurance law created a system that covered some 17 million people and offered benefits for three-quarters of the year and at 75 per cent of pay.

The state also provided subsidies for many public works, such as parks and sports facilities. However, it was in the field of housing that the greatest advances were made. Between 1924 and 1931 over 2 million houses were built and a further 200,000 renovated, which played a significant role in reducing the number of homeless. These improvements, alongside a growth in consumer spending reflected in the number of cars being bought, appeared to suggest that the economy was recovering, but government spending exceeded income and problems were being stored up for the future.

Arguments that the German economy was weak

Although the changes to the currency appeared to have created stability, they also created economic problems. The currency change led to an increase in the cost of exports and this forced employers to look for ways to cut their costs, which often resulted in workers being made redundant. The situation was made worse by the fact that this happened at the same time as there was an increase in the numbers entering the workforce because of a baby boom in the years before the First World War. As a result, some 5 million more people were looking for work and this created unemployment that was not resolved despite economic growth in the years 1927–9, with unemployment reaching 2 million by January 1928. Unemployment never fell below 1.3 million in this period and by 1929 it was averaging 1.9 million.

Economic growth was not consistent. Although production levels did rise, there was a decline in 1926. Meanwhile, in overseas trade, imports were always higher than exports.

Perhaps, most significantly, the agricultural sector did not benefit from any of these gains, particularly in the period after 1927 and this was important as farmers made up one-third of Germany's population. Farmers from across the world were overproducing goods and this resulted in a considerable fall in prices. By 1929, nearly one-half of all German farms were failing to make a profit, with income per head some 44 per cent below the national average. There was also growing anger in the countryside that the government was favouring towns at the expense of the countryside, importing cheap food in return for access to foreign markets for industrial goods. As a result, there were large-scale peasant protests in areas such as Schleswig-Holstein, where peasants began to give their support to the Nazis (see pages 57 and 66). Agriculture had still not recovered from the First World War and grain production was only three-quarters of its 1913 figure. This had a knock-on effect on the rest of the economy as the spending power of a significant section of the population was reduced and this led to a fall in demand in other sectors of the economy.

The social policies pursued by the government meant that the country was continually running deficits. The government continued to increase its spending and by 1928, public expenditure had reached 26 per cent of **gross national product (GNP)**, which was twice the pre-war figure. Perhaps more importantly, it relied on foreign loans, particularly from the USA and the Dawes Plan (see pages 38–40), to be able to balance the books and this meant that it was susceptible to any future dislocation in the world economic system. Hyperinflation had seen many savers lose considerable amounts of money and, therefore, there was a greater reluctance to invest, which increased Germany's reliance on international investors, making the country even more dependent on overseas finance.

> **KEY TERM**
>
> **Gross national product (GNP)** The total value of products and services produced by a country.

Germany had always been heavily reliant on exports to stimulate economic growth, but it was hit by the reduction in world trade, which did not return to pre-1914 levels. Other countries were also willing to introduce **tariffs** to protect their own industries from foreign competition and this limited export opportunities even further. This difficulty was compounded by a loss of raw materials, such as coal and iron ore, due to the territorial losses of the Treaty of Versailles.

These problems have led some to argue that the German economy was already in a poor state before the Great Depression and that its problems had been disguised because of foreign loans. Even Stresemann commented in 1928 that 'Germany is dancing on a volcano. If the short-term credits are called in, a large section of our economy would collapse.'

Germany: Democracy to Dictatorship c.1918–1945 for WJEC

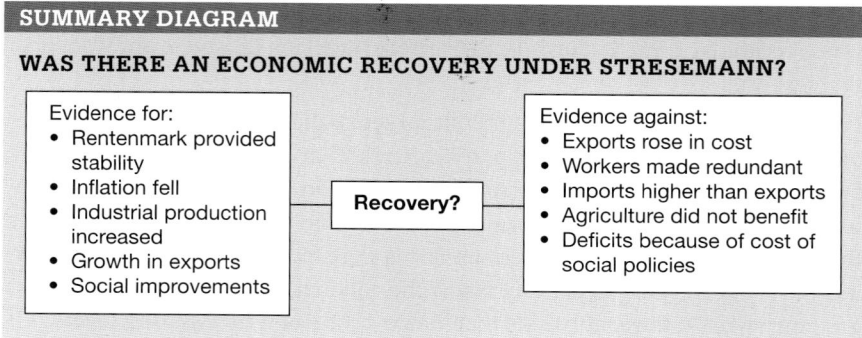

SUMMARY DIAGRAM

WAS THERE AN ECONOMIC RECOVERY UNDER STRESEMANN?

Evidence for:
- Rentenmark provided stability
- Inflation fell
- Industrial production increased
- Growth in exports
- Social improvements

Recovery?

Evidence against:
- Exports rose in cost
- Workers made redundant
- Imports higher than exports
- Agriculture did not benefit
- Deficits because of cost of social policies

3 Attempts to aid German economic recovery: the Dawes Plan and Young Plan

▪ *How successful were the Dawes Plan and Young Plan in bringing about economic recovery?*

Although both the Dawes Plan and Young Plan were part of Stresemann's scheme to deal with the question of reparations, they were also central to his foreign policy aims of reconciliation and gaining international recognition. Stresemann also recognised that Germany needed help if the economy was to recover from the post-war problems.

The Dawes Plan 1924

One of Stresemann's first actions had been to end passive resistance in the Ruhr and restart reparation payments. This led to the establishment of the Dawes Committee, under the chairmanship of the US banker Charles Dawes, which considered the problems facing the German economy.

? SOURCE QUESTION

In Source A, what hope does the report provide that Germany will be able to recover its economic stability?

SOURCE A

From the Dawes Report, 1924.

We have approached our task as businessmen anxious to obtain effective results. We have been concerned with the technical, not the political aspects of the problem presented to us.

The committee has had to consider to what extent the balancing of the budget and the stabilization of the currency could be re-established permanently in Germany as she actually is at the present moment, with limitations as to her fiscal and economic rights over part of her area.

> We should say at the outset we have been unable to find any practical means for insuring permanent stability in the budget of currency under these conditions, and we think it unlikely that such means exist.
>
> The task would be hopeless if the present situation in Germany accurately reflected her potential capacity. Proceeds from Germany's national production could not in that case enable her both to meet her national needs and insure payment of her foreign debts.
>
> But Germany's growing and industrious population, her great technical skill, the wealth of her material resources, the development of her agriculture on progressive lines, her eminence in industrial science, all these factors enable us to be hopeful with regard to her future production.

ONLINE EXTRAS WWW

Get to grips with source evaluation by completing Worksheet 6 at **www.hoddereducation.co.uk/accesstohistory/extras**

Although the plan did not reduce the actual reparations sum to be paid, the instalments over the first five years were now to be calculated according to Germany's ability to pay. The plan also provided some 800 million marks in loans to help finance an expansion in government spending at both a national and a local level, and loans were also made available to industry and German banks.

This plan had many advantages for Germany:

- France promised to evacuate the Ruhr during 1925.
- Germany gained money for its cash-starved economy through both loans and future investments.
- The international community recognised that Germany needed international help.

In the short term, the plan was certainly a success. The country received twice as much money from abroad as it paid in reparations. The payment of reparations to France also helped to improve relations between the two countries. However, it also tied Germany closely to the fortunes of the US economy, which would have severe consequences in 1929. In order to guarantee the loans, some assets of the German railway system were given to the USA and a measure of foreign control over the national bank was put in place. Within Germany there was also opposition. Extreme nationalists and those on the far right saw the plan as a national humiliation. They argued that Germany should not be paying reparations and they should be cancelled. They considered it demeaning that a once great power should be dependent on other countries for financial aid, even though it was a temporary measure until Germany had recovered.

The American financier and the agent for reparation payments also thought that the plan had been beneficial to Germany in the longer term.

SOURCE QUESTION

What evidence does the writer of Source B provide to suggest that the German economy was recovering?

ONLINE EXTRAS WWW

Get to grips with using contextual knowledge to support or challenge the view of a source by completing Worksheet 7 at www.hoddereducation.co.uk/accesstohistory/extras

SOURCE B

From Gilbert Parker, the American financier and the agent for reparation payments, reporting to the Reparations Commission in December 1928.

German business conditions generally appear to have righted themselves on a relatively high level of activity. A year ago, it will be recalled, German business was in the midst of a process of expansion which threatened to result in over-production in certain of the principal industries ... As the year 1928 comes to a close, it appears that this over-expansion has been checked before it reached dangerous proportions, and that a condition of relative stability has now been attained ... Since 1924, when stabilization was achieved and the execution of the Experts' Plan began, Germany's reconstruction has at least kept pace with the reconstruction of Europe as a whole, and it has played an essential part in the process of European reconstruction.

The Young Plan 1929

The question of reparations remained an issue throughout the period, even though there appeared to be evidence of economic recovery. The Dawes Plan had only ever been a temporary measure and in 1929 the Inter-Allied Reparations Commission set up a committee of financiers under the chairmanship of Owen Young, a US banker. His committee's report suggested a new scheme of payments:

- Germany's reparation bill was to be reduced from 132 billion marks demanded in 1921 to 37 billion.
- Payments were to be spread over 58 years, with the last payment scheduled for 1988.
- The foreign controls over the German economy that were in the Dawes Plan were ended.
- This would help government spending and, after some negotiation, was accepted by the German government.

Opposition to the Young Plan

Although the period from 1924 to 1929 is often considered to be politically stable, the country was still governed by unstable coalitions. The two major political parties, the Social Democratic Party (SPD) and the German People's Party (DVP), disagreed over social and economic policies and this made it difficult for them to cooperate. In foreign affairs (see pages 42–8), the German National People's Party (DNVP) disliked Stresemann's policy of **rapprochement** with France and Britain. The election of Paul von Hindenburg as president in 1925 was a further sign of the weakness of the fledgling democracy. Although he was a much-respected military figure, his support for the republic was lukewarm. His election suggested that there was still much support for an old-style authoritarian regime and that the army and the old elites still had a lot of influence.

KEY TERM

Rapprochement The re-establishment of good relations.

The Young Plan provided a rallying point for Germany's right wing who were already angered by Stresemann's foreign policy (see pages 42–8), which they believed was a betrayal of national interest to the Allies. The right wing disagreed with the payment of reparations as it implied an acceptance of war guilt, which they opposed. As a result, the Young Plan had to be resisted.

A national committee, created by **Alfred Hugenberg**, the leader of the DNVP, was established to fight the plan. He was able to use his media empire, as he owned over 150 newspapers, a publishing house and the UFA film organisation, to promote his views, and gained support from other right-wing nationalist groups and individuals.

Hugenberg was joined in his opposition by the **Pan-German League**, the ex-servicemen's organisation, the *Stahlhelm*, and Hitler and the Nazi Party. The **National Opposition**, as opposition to the plan became known, drafted a 'Law against the Enslavement of the German People'. This attacked reparation payments and demanded the punishments of those who had agreed. The Opposition was able to gain sufficient signatures for its proposal for the issue to become a national referendum in December 1929. The plan was defended vehemently by ministers:

SOURCE C

From Gustav Stresemann: *His Diaries, Letters, and Papers*, Volume 3, edited by Eric Sutton, Macmillan, 1935.

Guilt lie. Every German Government, as also President von Hindenburg and the Foreign Minister, Dr. Stresemann, have indignantly repudiated the assertion that Germany was responsible for the World War. The campaign against this guilt lie will be carried on by the whole nation and by the appropriate Departments of State with all available resources. In provoking a campaign against the War Guilt lie, the Hugenberg Plebiscite is pushing at an open door. But in doing so it attempts to give the impression that a law passed in Germany can invalidate international treaties, it is suggesting to the German people a possibility which, as the originator of the proposal knows, unfortunately does not exist.

Do not the advocates of the plebiscite also see the significance of the Young Plan is not exhausted by the material provisions, but that its outstanding achievement is the final liberation from foreign occupation and the abolition of the control system which was so repugnant to every German feeling?

Although the Opposition won only 5.8 million votes, which fell well short of the required 21 million needed by the constitution for success, it was a clear indication of the opposition to the plan. It showed that there were still very strong nationalist sentiments within the country and it also brought Hitler further publicity and links with influential people, such as Hugenberg.

The plan itself did not last long as, with economic depression and the financial crisis, the Allies allowed Germany to suspend repayments in 1931. In 1932, they agreed to their ending.

KEY FIGURE

Alfred Hugenberg (1865–1951)

Hugenberg was a civil servant, banker, industrialist and media owner in the 1920s. He was appointed leader of the DNVP in 1928, but helped to fund Hitler's political campaigns.

KEY TERMS

Pan-German League A nationalist organisation, founded in 1891, it gradually became more racist in its views.

Stahlhelm A German First World War ex-servicemen's organisation. It was the paramilitary wing of the DNVP.

National Opposition Used to describe the political groups that came together in 1929 in opposition to the Young Plan and which opposed all reparation payments.

SOURCE QUESTION

On what grounds, according to Source C, did the government oppose the referendum?

ONLINE EXTRAS WWW

Test your understanding of the value of a source by completing Worksheet 8 at **www.hoddereducation.co.uk/accesstohistory/extras**

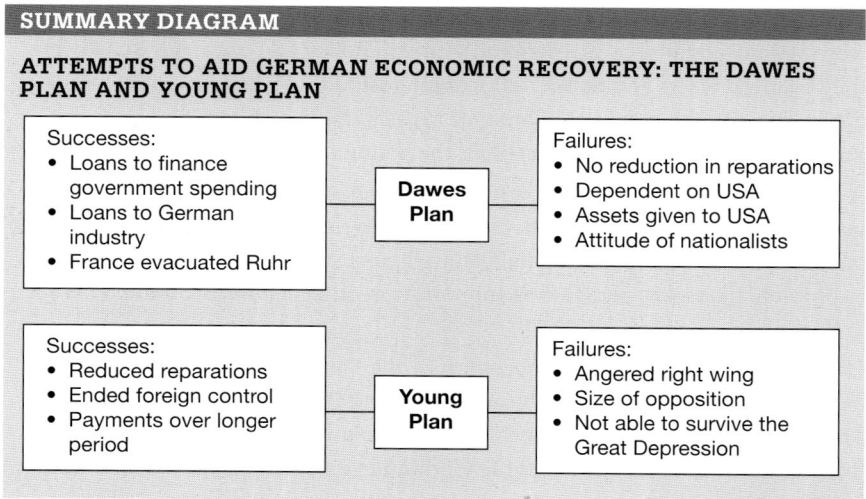

4 Foreign policy under Gustav Stresemann

How successful was Stresemann in achieving his foreign policy aims?

Although Stresemann was chancellor for only 103 days, he continued as foreign minister until 1929. His foreign policy was built around the concept of *Erfüllungspolitik* or 'fulfilment'. This was not a new policy and had been initiated by the chancellor, Joseph Wirth, and his foreign minister, Walther Rathenau, in the years 1921–2. In practice, the policy meant improving relations with Britain and France by accepting and complying with the terms of the Versailles treaty. It was based on the belief that once it became clear that Germany was willing to accept the terms and their good intentions, then the Allies would be willing to modify or revise the treaty. Many historians would argue that he practised his policy to good effect, rejecting the views of many nationalists that Germany had not lost the war and had been 'stabbed in the back'. Although he appeared to favour peace, he never lost sight of regaining lost territory and renegotiating Versailles. He was able to draw support from many of the middle class and it is arguable that had he not died in 1929 he might have successfully opposed the rise of extremism.

The foreign policy aims of Stresemann

The main aim of Stresemann was to free Germany from the limitations imposed by Versailles. He set out his aims in 1925:

> **SOURCE D**
>
> From a letter from Foreign Minister Gustav Stresemann to the ex-Crown Prince, 7 September 1925.
>
> *In my opinion there are three great tasks that confront German foreign policy in the more immediate future. In the first place the solution of the Reparations question in a sense tolerable for Germany ...*
>
> *Secondly, the protection of Germans abroad, those 10 to 12 million of our kindred who now live under a foreign yoke in foreign lands.*
>
> *The third great task is the readjustment of our eastern frontiers; the recovery of Danzig, the Polish Corridor, and a correction of the frontier in Upper Silesia.*
>
> *In the background stands the union with German Austria, although I am quite clear that this not merely brings no advantage to Germany, but seriously complicates the problem of the German Reich.*
>
> *... The question of a choice between east and west does not arise as a result of us joining the League. Such a choice can only be made when backed by military force. That, alas, we do not possess.*

SOURCE QUESTION

How useful is Source D in explaining Stresemann's foreign policy aims?

Not only does the letter show his desire to alter Versailles, it also rules out the possibility of offensive action, at least in part because of the lack of force, so his only choice was diplomacy.

The events of 1923 had made it clear to Stresemann that the French rightly had security concerns and that the only way to solve the problem was to build a friendship with them. However, he did recognise that in the German economy he had a powerful weapon. He realised that it was vitally important to world trade, and therefore, could be used to win the goodwill of both the USA, as was seen in the Dawes Plan, and Britain. Stresemann saw that cooperation with Britain and France was the best way for Germany to regain its position in Europe, even if this meant annoying hardliners within Germany who wanted the **Rapallo** friendship with Russia to become a formal alliance.

KEY TERM

Rapallo A pact signed with Soviet Russia in 1922. It included trade and secret military links.

How successful was Stresemann's foreign policy?

The best way to judge the success of Stresemann's foreign policy is to consider how far he achieved his aims in each of the events that took place in the period from 1924 to 1929. In summary, his aims were to:

- free Germany from the limitations of Versailles
- restore Germany as a great power and equal to Britain and France
- establish Franco-German friendship
- win the cooperation of Britain and the USA.

Germany: Democracy to Dictatorship c.1918–1945 for WJEC

SOURCE QUESTION

According to the cartoonist in Source E, how is Stresemann portrayed?

SOURCE E

'He looks to the right, he looks to the left – he will save me'. (It is worth noting that the little boy is the 'German Michael' – a stereotype for the naïve German.) A cartoon published by the *Simplicissimus* magazine in May 1923 about Stresemann.

Restoring foreign trust

The Dawes Plan did help to start the process of restoring relations and trust between France and Germany, with guarantees made through giving creditor nations some control over the rail and banking systems. It was also a success in so far as the Allies agreed not to occupy German cities in the event of non-payment. French troops were to be withdrawn from the Ruhr in 1925, restoring German control over its territory. Stresemann had also been able to win international support for the republic with foreign loans from the USA. Although right-wing Germans were opposed to the plan because of the principle of reparation payments, the *Reichstag* voted in favour of it in August 1924, providing Stresemann with a successful start.

The Locarno Pact

The Locarno Pact was agreed in 1925. Under the terms of the agreement, Germany, France and Belgium pledged that they would not use force to change the borders between them as laid down in the Treaty of Versailles. The terms were guaranteed by Britain and Italy, with all five signatories renouncing the use of force except in self-defence. As a result, Germany had formally abandoned the hope of regaining Alsace-Lorraine. France also agreed not to repeat its occupation of the Ruhr. The agreement was another step on the road to reconciliation and improving relations with the French as it appeared to give them the security they desired.

The success of the Locarno Pact showed that Stresemann had achieved many of his aims. He had improved relations with France by confirming the existing borders between the two nations. However, in reality, Germany was in no position to change the situation, so in practice it actually gave very little away. It could be argued that Germany was the big winner in this scenario as France's freedom of action was severely constrained as there could be no repeat of an invasion of the Ruhr and no annexation of the Rhineland, which would have given France greater security. Germany was also freed from its previous isolation and was treated as an equal by the other major powers. It might also be argued that because French relations with Germany were improving it made it less necessary for France to seek allies in the east against potential German aggression, which would improve Germany's position relative to other powers in central Europe.

Germany's position in central Europe was further strengthened by the terms of the Locarno Pact. Germany, Poland and Czechoslovakia signed arbitration treaties, which agreed to settle future disputes peacefully. However, unlike the western borders of Germany, the eastern borders were not accepted as final. This meant that the potential for German expansion in the east and the revision of Versailles had not been resolved. It is hardly surprising that the Polish people viewed the treaties as a major setback, only signing the treaties because they expected France to ensure they were upheld.

The Locarno Pact led to many believing that the arguments between France and Germany had finally ended. Stresemann and his counterpart in France, Aristide Briand, were jointly awarded the Nobel Peace Prize in 1926. People began to talk about the 'Locarno spirit' and this would be seen further in the signing of the Kellogg–Briand Pact in 1928.

The removal of Allied occupation forces

In 1925, the Allies agreed to remove their occupation forces from the Cologne area. Then, in 1926, they agreed to withdraw the Inter-Allied Monetary Control Commission, which monitored Germany's compliance with the military terms of Versailles, from Germany and reduce the number of occupying forces to 60,000. This was taken further in 1929 when they agreed to remove all remaining occupying forces from the Rhineland in 1930, which was five years ahead of the scheduled date, in return for a final settlement of the reparations issue. It was this that ultimately led to the Young Plan (see pages 40–1).

These were further successes for Stresemann. The removal of Allied forces from German soil suggested that greater trust towards Germany was developing. Reconciliation with France continued and some of the terms of the treaty were being revised in Germany's favour.

Germany joins the League of Nations

In 1926, as part of the Locarno Pact, Germany was admitted to the League of Nations. It was Aristide Briand who welcomed Germany as an equal and it was given a permanent seat on the Council of the League of Nations. There, it joined Britain, France, Italy and Japan. This was perhaps the clearest sign that old enmities were dying and that Germany was being treated as an equal. It appeared that Stresemann's policy of cooperation was paying off, even if some extreme nationalists in Germany still saw the League as a victors' club and did not want anything to do with it. Although it can be argued that Germany's entry to the League was purely symbolic, it did signify that Germany was no longer an outcast.

The Berlin Treaty

In the years from 1921 to 1924, relations with the western powers had been poor, culminating in the French invasion of the Ruhr in 1923 when Germany defaulted on reparation payments. The immediate post-war years had seen Germany viewed as an outcast, along with the new communist state of Russia. As a result, the two outsiders had come together to sign the Treaty of Rapallo in 1922, whereby the two nations re-established diplomatic relations.

Although Stresemann's primary concern was to establish good relations with the west, it did not mean that he wanted to abandon friendship with the USSR. His determination to remain on good terms with the USSR was reflected in the signing of the Treaty of Berlin in 1926. Arguably, this was double-dealing on the part of Germany but it must be remembered that its geographical position in the centre of Europe meant that it needed to reach understandings with both the east and west. The treaty itself reduced strategic fears regarding Germany's eastern front. However, by reaching an agreement with the Soviet Union it increased the pressure on Poland, which faced potentially hostile nations on either side of its borders. Germany's treaty with the USSR therefore coerced Poland to revise its frontiers with Germany in order to try and maintain its friendship. Through the treaty, Stresemann was also able to open the possibility of a large trade area and military cooperation.

Chapter 3 Foreign and economic policy 1924–9

SOURCE F

From the Treaty of Berlin Between the Soviet Union and Germany, 24 April 1926.

The German Government and the Government of the Union of Soviet Socialist Republics, being desirous of doing all in their power to promote the maintenance of general peace, and being convinced that that the interests of the German people and the peoples of the Government of the Union of Socialist Soviet Republics demand constant and trustful co-operation, having agreed to strengthen the friendly relations existing between them by means of a special Treaty have agreed upon the following provisions.

Article 1
The relations between Germany and the Government of the Union of Socialist Soviet Republics shall continue to be based on the Treaty of Rapallo. The German Government and the Government of the Union of Socialist Soviet Republics will maintain friendly contact in order to promote an understanding with regard to all political and economic questions jointly affecting their two countries.

Article 2
Should one of the Contracting Parties, despite its peaceful attitude, be attacked by one or more third Powers, the other Contracting Party shall observe neutrality for the whole duration of the conflict.

SOURCE QUESTION

According to Source F, what advantages were there for Germany in signing the friendship Treaty with the Soviet Union?

The Kellogg–Briand Pact

Germany's apparent policy of peaceful cooperation was further seen in 1928 when it signed the Kellogg–Briand Pact, an agreement which outlawed war 'as an instrument of national policy'. This had little practical effect as it proved impossible to implement, but it was used by Germany to show once again that it was cooperating with other nations and fully supportive of the 'Locarno spirit'.

Conclusion: how should Stresemann's foreign policy be viewed?

Historians have been greatly divided by Stresemann's foreign policy. Some have seen him as a 'great European' who worked hard for international reconciliation, whereas others have seen him as a hard-headed champion of his country's national interests. There is little doubt that he was a nationalist. Through the policy of fulfilment he hoped to remove the burden of reparations, regain territory lost to Poland, re-establish German military strength and even bring about *Anschluss* with Austria – he wanted to restore German power.

Despite this, his policy was vilified by the extreme right. His abandonment of passive resistance was seen as treasonous and his acceptance of the Dawes Plan was viewed as accepting the lie of 'war guilt' and enslaving the German economy. All of this culminated in a referendum on the Young Plan. Although opponents of the plan did not win the referendum, the level of support they gained showed just how much animosity there was towards Stresemann's approach.

How should Stresemann be viewed?

It would be hard to argue against the view that Stresemann did a great deal to change Germany's position both domestically and internationally. Given the position he inherited in 1923 it was remarkable, as internal and external forces appeared to be against him. However, international circumstances did favour him. There was little enthusiasm for further conflict, as seen in Britain's unwillingness to get involved in the Ruhr, and this made peaceful coexistence and the restoration of Germany's international position much easier. It might even be argued that, given the situation, he could have done more, particularly in terms of revising Germany's borders in the east with Poland.

Stresemann failed to win over the right, but that was never likely. But, more importantly, he failed to win over many moderates to his policy of reconciliation, perhaps because he did not have time before his sudden death in 1929, or because policies of compromise are never popular. Some historians have gone on to argue that, given more time, he could have won over the majority and prevented the more radical policies pursued by the Nazis in the period after 1933. Domestically, his policies brought short-term improvements, but they left the economy vulnerable to world fluctuations, as would be seen in the period 1929–33. However, many of the developments in this period were beyond his control.

Although the republic had not gained loyalty and still faced criticism from both the left and right wings, it appeared that attempts to overthrow it had ceased by 1929. Traditionalists were shocked by the cultural developments of the 1920s. The economy, while growing, was heavily dependent on foreign loans and the cost of the welfare state was a concern. Decisive actions from a strong government were needed if the problems were to be resolved. Despite this, there was no reason in 1929 to suggest that the collapse of the republic was inevitable.

Historians disagree as to the success of Stresemann, with Matthew Stibbe (2010) arguing that Stresemann had built up a fair degree of consensus in favour of a realistic foreign policy, Eberhard Kolb (2004) arguing that he was 'astonishingly successful' and Jonathan Wright (2002) describing him as 'Weimar's greatest statesman'. However, Martin Walsdorff (1972) challenged this view and argued that Stresemann failed to achieve his main aim of revising either Versailles or the Polish border and that any change he did achieve was slow, and that this led to the right wing becoming more critical and vociferous in its condemnation. Even though the silent majority had not been won over, Stresemann's death in October 1929, just before the Wall Street Crash, robbed the republic of one of its leading politicians and reduced its chances of survival.

5 Key debate

▇ How far did Germany recover in the years 1924–9?

Although the period 1924–9 is often seen as the high-water mark of the Weimar Republic, many historians have questioned the stability because it was quite limited in scope.

The German economic historian Knut Borchhardt (1991) argued that Germany was living beyond its means, with subsidies and the redistribution of wealth harming economic growth. He put forward the view that wages increased regardless of economic performance because of the power of trade unions and, therefore, profits and investments were squeezed so that growth was lower than might be expected. He argued that a recession had started before the crash of October 1929. However, such a view was challenged by many on the left, with Carl Ludwig Holtfrerich (1986) suggesting that the economy faltered because of a lack of entrepreneurialism and investment from industrialists. More recent research undertaken after the collapse of the East German state in 1990 and with the availability of new archive records suggests that it was both the workers and industrialists who contributed to the economic weakness. Such research has shown that the two groups were unwilling to cooperate and that although wages rose this was due more to local shortages of skilled labour than to any greed from the workers. This view also suggests that the lack of investment was the result of a lack of confidence among savers to lend and the government's concern to balance the budget.

Historians have also considered the impact of the welfare state on the republic. Although considerable advances were made in many areas, the republic had created a set of demands that could not be met even before the crash and encouraged unrealistic expectations among many Germans. This was particularly the case with unemployment insurance. The reforms also affected the attitude of the elite towards the republic. The welfare measures led to high taxation and historians have suggested that this and the redistribution of resources angered many of the elites, as did the arbitration system set up to resolve strikes, which owners believed favoured the workers. All of this, it has been claimed, led to tensions between owners and workers that would become more severe when the Depression hit. It has led historians, such as Werner Abelshauser (1997) to argue that 'the Weimar Republic was an over-strained welfare state' as the economic growth could not meet the expectations and aspirations.

The limited nature of such a recovery can be seen in Interpretation 1 and, Bessel argues, was reflected in the politics of the period.

> **INTERPRETATION 1**
>
> From R. Bessel, *German History Since 1800*, edited by Mary Fulbrook, Bloomsbury Academic, 1997, pp. 252–3.
>
> *Even during the years of 'relative stabilisation' all was not well with the Weimar Republic. The profound social, economic, political and psychological destabilisation which had set in with the First World War had not really been overcome; underlying economic problems remained, and the relative political stability of Weimar's 'golden years' rested on shaky foundations … While the two liberal parties saw their popular support dwindle and the (moderate) conservatives lost roughly two thirds of their supporters, many voters turned to special-interest parties – betraying a lack of faith in a democratic politics which focused on the common good.*

ONLINE EXTRAS
Get to grips with identifying the main view of an interpretation by completing Worksheet 9 at **www.hoddereducation.co.uk/accesstohistory/extras**

However, as Interpretation 2 shows, some historians have argued that the period was a 'golden age'.

> **INTERPRETATION 2**
>
> From Peter G.J. Pulzer, *Germany 1870–1945*, Oxford University Press, 1997, p. 3.
>
> *The era of Stresemann was the high noon of the Weimar Republic. Tempers dropped, political extremism subsided. In large part this was due to the return of prosperity. Between 1924 … and 1928 money wages doubled and the value of the currency was maintained. The standard of living was higher in 1928 than in 1913. Unemployment was generally below one million. In 1927 the expansion of the German state culminated in the introduction of a comprehensive unemployment insurance scheme. German industry regained its technical and organisational lead. The Dawes loan … encouraged modernisation.*

ONLINE EXTRAS
Get to grips with finding evidence to support or challenge the view of a historian by completing Worksheet 10 at **www.hoddereducation.co.uk/accesstohistory/extras**

CHAPTER SUMMARY

The period from 1924 to 1929 was, when compared with both the period before and after, a 'golden age' for the republic. It witnessed the establishment of a trustworthy currency, with the Rentenmark, which helped to create a more stable economy. However, although the economy grew, the recovery was relative, and the prosperity seen in these years was built on very shaky foundations because of the dependence on US loans. Although the governments of the period were more effective than previous, there was still opposition to some of Stresemann's foreign policy initiatives. Many nationalists thought that Stresemann was giving in to the Allies and his successes were not always celebrated. It is, therefore, possible to question whether by the end of the period the economic and social changes can be considered a success for the republic.

Refresher questions

Use these questions to remind yourself of the key material covered in this chapter.

1. What were the strengths and weaknesses of Stresemann's policies as chancellor?
2. What were the strengths of the economy in the period 1924–9?
3. What were the weaknesses of the economy in the period 1924–9?
4. Was there an economic recovery in the period 1924–9?
5. Did social conditions improve in the years 1924–9?
6. What were the aims of Stresemann's foreign policy?
7. What were the strengths and weaknesses of the Dawes Plan?
8. What did the Locarno Pact achieve?
9. How far did Stresemann improve relations with France?
10. Why did Germany sign the Treaty of Berlin with Russia?
11. Should Stresemann's foreign policy be viewed as a success?

CHAPTER 4

The changing fortunes of the Nazi Party 1924–33

The period following Hitler's release from jail was a time of reorganisation and consolidation for the Nazi Party. During the 'golden years' of the Weimar Republic, 1924–9, the party's success was limited despite a growth in membership. It was the onset of the Great Depression that transformed its position.

This chapter will examine why the party was able to take advantage of the situation and consider the role of Hitler, propaganda, the use of violence and the appeal of several of its policies by focusing on the following themes:

- The recovery of the Nazi Party in the 1920s
- The strength of the Nazi Party by 1929
- The changing fortunes of the Nazi Party by 1932
- The reasons for growing support for the Nazi Party

The key debate on page 65 of this chapter considers who voted for the Nazis.

KEY DATES

1924	Dec.	Hitler released from jail	1931	Feb.	SA in Berlin purged
		Nazis lost votes as economic growth continued			Goebbels put in charge of propaganda
1925		Hitler refounded the party		Oct.	Harzburg Front
1926		Bamberg meeting	1932	Jan.	Hitler received enthusiastic reception at Dusseldorf Industry Club
1927		Agricultural depression			
1928		Losses at the elections, but gains in the rural areas			
1929		Local election gains; majority in Coburg		March	Hitler won 37 per cent of vote in presidential elections
		Hitler involved in the Anti-Young Plan referendum		July	Nazis won 37 per cent of vote in *Reichstag* election
1930		Otto Strasser forced out of the party		Nov.	Nazis lost 2 million votes in *Reichstag* election
	Sept.	Nazis made major gains in elections		Dec.	Internal crisis in Nazi Party with radicalism and financial pressures
		Röhm appointed leader of the *Sturmabteilung* (SA)			

In the period from 1924 to 1932, following Hitler's release from jail after the failure of the Munich *Putsch*, support for the Nazi Party increased. However, it was only in the period from 1930 onwards that the party grew dramatically. The years before that were a period of struggle for the party to gain national recognition, despite the publicity that Hitler's trial had given the party. This is reflected in the election results to the *Reichstag* in this period (see Table 4.1, page 53).

However, despite not providing party growth, the trial did have enormous consequences as Hitler changed his tactics to gain power. Instead of trying to take power by force, as had been the case with the Munich *Putsch*, Hitler decided to win power through the ballot box, even though, as the election results show, this would be a slow process. It is even reported that while in prison he commented, in an account given by Kurt Ludecke of his visit to Hitler in May 1924: 'We shall have to hold our noses and enter the *Reichstag* against the Catholics and Marxist deputies. If out-voting them takes longer than our shooting them, at least the result will be guaranteed by their own constitution. Any lawful process is slow.'

Table 4.1 Support for the Nazis in the *Reichstag* elections 1924–33

Year	Number of seats in the *Reichstag*
May 1924	32
December 1924	14
1928	12
1930	107
July 1932	230
November 1932	196
1933	288

1 The recovery of the Nazi Party in the 1920s

How was the Nazi Party revitalised in the 1920s?

While the election results in this period were disappointing for the Nazis, in part because of the relative success of the Weimar Republic in this period, Hitler did use the time productively, enabling future party growth. During his time in prison he had written *Mein Kampf* (see page 24), which set out the party's position on a number of issues. Hitler was released from prison in December 1924 and the party, which had almost disintegrated while he was in jail, was refounded in February 1925. Hitler stated in the *Völkischer Beobachter* that it was 'a new beginning'.

Despite Hitler's focus on the Nazi Party while in prison, when he was released, the party was divided over a number of issues:

- There were disagreements about the tactics of gaining power, with some opposed to the policy of legality.
- There were disagreements between different regions, most notably between the party base in Bavaria and north Germany.
- There were significant differences between nationalist and anti-capitalist elements within the party.

Germany: Democracy to Dictatorship c.1918–1945 for WJEC

KEY FIGURES

Gregor Strasser (1892–1934)

He joined the Nazis in 1920 and took part in the Munich *Putsch*. He then led the party after Hitler was jailed in 1924. He built up a large following in north Germany and became the second most powerful member in the party after Hitler. He opposed Hitler's anti-Semitic beliefs and his support of big business. Gregor resigned in 1932 and was murdered during the Night of the Long Knives.

Otto Strasser (1897–1974)

Originally a member of the Social Democratic Party (SPD), he joined the Nazis in 1925. Like his brother Gregor, he was on the left wing of the party. He became disillusioned with the Nazis as they were not socialist and did little for the workers. He left the party in 1930 and, having survived the Night of the Long Knives, went into exile.

KEY TERM

Führerprinzip
The 'leadership principle', whereby a one-party state is led by an all-powerful leader.

SOURCE QUESTION

In Source A, how are Hitler and Ebert portrayed?

Divisions within the Nazi Party

The divisions within the party were seen most clearly in the influence of **Gregor Strasser** and his brother **Otto Strasser**. Gregor had joined the party in 1920 and supported Hitler during the Munich *Putsch* (see pages 23–4), but he was in favour of the more socialist element of the Nazi policies and was essentially the leader of the party in north Germany. This struggle for the direction of the party between Hitler, with his more nationalist aims, and Strasser, with his socialist views, came to a head in February 1926 at a special party conference in Bamberg.

The conference was, in some ways, a triumph for Hitler. The *Führerprinzip* principle of the party was upheld. This ensured that Hitler re-established his

SOURCE A

'Hitler's entry into Berlin.' A cartoon published by the *Simplicissimus* magazine in April 1924, just after Hitler's trial.

supremacy after his period in prison. It also meant that there was to be no place for disagreements. However, the party also upheld the 25 points of the original party programme (see pages 21–3) with its socialist elements. Therefore, although Hitler had regained his supremacy, the divisions between the nationalist and socialist elements within the party had not been healed.

Reorganisation of the party

A number of measures were taken to reorganise and improve the party structure during this period. Therefore, even though the Nazi Party's performance in elections did not indicate large growth, the foundations were still being laid for future progress.

One of the most important creations was the establishment of the *Gauleiters*. They controlled each region and were given the responsibility of creating district and branch groups. The *Gauleiters* were based in the regions, or *Gaue*, into which Germany was divided according to the system of proportional representation. This meant that a vertical system of control was created and reinforced Hitler's position at the apex. It was through this system that Joseph Goebbels emerged. He was *Gauleiter* in Berlin and, although he had originally been a supporter of Gregor Strasser, he switched his allegiance to Hitler. Berlin was traditionally a stronghold of the Social Democratic Party (SPD) and Goebbels showed determination and drive in trying to win support for the Nazis. He created a Nazi newspaper, *Der Angriff* (*The Attack*), and took considerable interest in propaganda, which led to his appointment as chief of party propaganda in 1930.

Once out of jail, Hitler also established a network of party-affiliated organisations, each designed to appeal to a particular group within the population. These included:

- the Hitler Youth
- the Students' League
- the Nazi Teachers' Association
- Union of Nazi Lawyers
- the Order of German Women
- the Nazi Welfare Organisation.

This last group was particularly important during the Depression as it ran soup kitchens and organised food collections and donations for people who were suffering.

The reorganisation led to a growth in party membership, as Table 4.2 (see right) shows.

This growth in membership allowed the party to expand its publicity operation, using door-to-door campaigns and leafleting. It also used direct mailing and distributed 600,000 copies of the 'Immediate Economic Programme' at the time of the July 1932 *Reichstag* election.

> **KEY TERM**
>
> **Gauleiters** Leaders of a regional area. The Nazi Party was organised into 35 regions.

Table 4.2 The growth in Nazi Party membership

Year	Members
1925	27,000
1926	49,000
1927	72,000
1928	108,000
1929	150,000

There was also a training programme for speakers, the aim of which was to further Nazi recruitment and spread propaganda, with over 6000 passing through the training school by 1933. Speakers were given licences, which ensured that quality was maintained, and provided with books and pamphlets on policies and propaganda techniques.

> **SOURCE QUESTION**
>
> What value is Source B to a historian?

SOURCE B

From a report of the Prussian state police in June 1930, on the NSDAP's speakers' school.

The training of speakers is accomplished by a correspondence course in the form of monthly instruction packages ... A participant at the Speakers' School is only finally recognised as an official party speaker after participating in the correspondence course for 12 months and speaking publicly thirty times within 8 months.

This year it is planned to hold a further, oral course at Herrsching. The precondition for attendance is a minimum of six months' satisfactory participation on the correspondence course ... Speakers in possession of a 'certificate of aptitude' are permitted to hold local training evenings at which they can train speakers according to the methods of the speakers' school.

KEY TERMS

Mittelstand Literal translation means middle class, but in Germany it refers specifically to the lower middle classes, which includes shopkeepers, craft workers and clerks. They were self-reliant but had come under increasing pressure from big business and industrial labour.

Schutzstaffel (SS) Commonly referred to as Blackshirts, so-called because of the colour of the uniforms. Set up in 1925 as an elite bodyguard for Hitler and then grew further to become a major paramilitary organisation under the control of Himmler. It developed a reputation for obedience and loyalty.

The party had initially attempted to win support among the workers, but these tactics were ineffective due to the workers' traditional support of the SPD, and therefore the party's core support was among the **Mittelstand**, those who had lost out from the war and inflation. Therefore, in the winter of 1927–8, the party changed its tactics and, with the onset of the agricultural depression, Hitler gave up his urban plan of appealing to the workers and played down his emphasis on the confiscation of land, which had worried many small farmers. This change led to the Nazis' making gains in rural areas in 1928.

One other important development was the creation of the **Schutzstaffel (SS)**, usually known as the Blackshirts. The organisation was created in 1925 and members swore absolute obedience to Hitler. However, numbers were small, with just 200 members in 1929. Although initially it was Hitler's personal bodyguard, the SS did develop its own identity when it was placed under Himmler's control later in 1929.

SUMMARY DIAGRAM

THE RECOVERY OF THE NAZI PARTY IN THE 1920S

How was the Nazi Party revitalised in the 1920s?

Strategy:
- Resolve divisions
- *Führerprinzip*
- Influence of Strasser
- Legality of achieving power

Structure:
- Regional *Gauleiters*
- Affiliated organisations
- Propaganda
- Membership

2 The strength of the Nazi Party by 1929

■ *How strong was the Nazi Party by 1929?*

By 1928, the party had recovered and was much better organised than it had been when Hitler came out of jail. The membership had quadrupled and Hitler's position was secure even if there were still disputes with Strasser and his supporters. The party had also succeeded in absorbing many other right-wing nationalist and racist groups within its ranks.

The 1928 *Reichstag* election

The improvements in organisation were not reflected in the election results of 1928, where the Nazis won just 2.6 per cent of the vote and twelve seats, meaning their worst performance in their election history. Therefore, even though the party had reorganised, it appeared that it would be virtually impossible for it to make an electoral breakthrough, particularly while the economy was recovering.

Despite this national failure, there were some signs of a breakthrough. The party did make gains in north Germany among the rural middle and lower-middle classes in areas such as Schleswig-Holstein where the agricultural depression had started to be felt. In this area it was able to win over ten per cent of the vote, prompting the following comment in the Nazi newspaper:

SOURCE C

From the Nazi newspaper, *Völkischer Beobachter*, published on 31 May 1928.

The election results from the rural areas, in particular, proved that with a smaller expenditure of energy, money and time, better results can be achieved there than in the big cities. In small towns and villages, mass meetings with good speakers are events and are often talked about for weeks, while in the big cities the effects of meetings with even three or four thousand people soon disappear. Local successes in which the National Socialists are running first or second are, surprisingly, almost invariably the result of the activity of the branch leader or of a few energetic members.

SOURCE QUESTION

What does Source C tell us about the electoral success of the Nazi Party?

Developments in 1929

During the late 1920s, Nazi Party membership continued to grow and by September 1929 had reached 150,000 (see Table 4.2, page 55). This increasing support was also reflected in the regional state elections of 1929. Similarly to the 1928 election, it appeared that the agricultural depression played a crucial role. Falling agricultural prices had started to cause disquiet, and demonstrations and protests were replaced by increasing violence as some farmers went bankrupt.

It was in Thuringia, a province in central Germany, where this had the greatest impact on Nazi votes as they trebled their previous performance, breaking the ten per cent barrier and winning 11.3 per cent of the vote, suggesting that in times of economic hardship the party did well. This trend would soon be put to the test with the Wall Street Crash in October 1929 and the onset of the Great Depression (see pages 70–2) which would provide a serious challenge for the republic.

The 1929 anti-Young Plan campaign provided the Nazis with a boost and led to an alliance with Hugenberg's Nationalist Party. This was particularly important as it gave the Nazis access to Hugenberg's media empire, which meant that their ideas could be spread more widely through mass circulation papers rather than just through their own newspaper. The alliance also helped to bring in funds; even Hugenberg himself provided money for Hitler's presidential campaign.

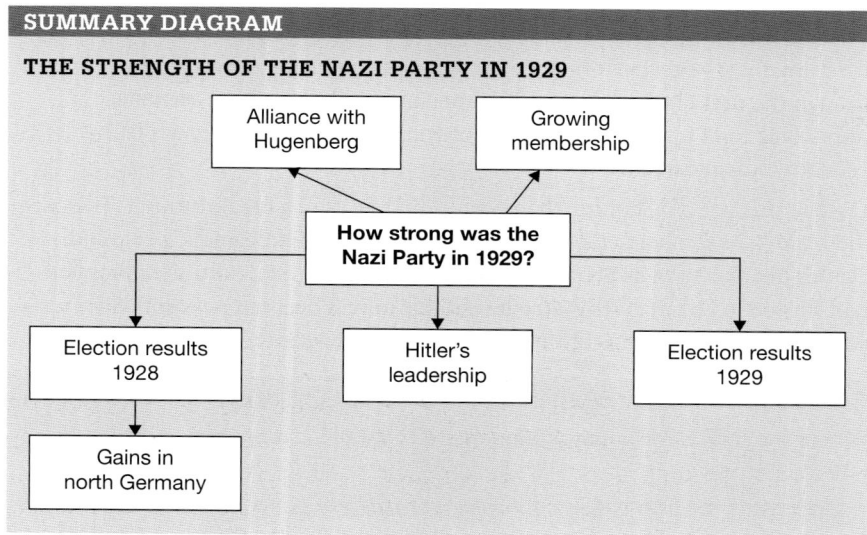

SUMMARY DIAGRAM

THE STRENGTH OF THE NAZI PARTY IN 1929

3 The changing fortunes of the Nazis by 1932

■ *Why was the Nazi Party able to make an electoral breakthrough in the early 1930s?*

The Great Depression provided the Nazi Party with its electoral breakthrough, as was seen in the 1930 election where it went from twelve seats in the *Reichstag* to 107. This breakthrough was due to a number of reasons:

- The Weimar government appeared weak and unable to deal with the crisis.

- Unemployment rose and the Nazis offered **public works schemes** to combat it.
- Many people were fearful of communism, particularly after events in the Soviet Union where the Russian Revolution provided clear evidence of the brutality of communism, and with support for it growing in Germany, others, particularly the middle class, turned to the Nazis.

> **KEY TERM**
>
> **Public works schemes** Employment schemes that are financed by the state in order to create jobs and reduce unemployment.

Table 4.3 *Reichstag* election results 1928–32

Date	NSDAP	DNVP	DVP	ZP	DDP	SPD	KPD	Others
May 1928								
Seats	12	73	45	78	25	153	54	51
Percentage	2.6	14.2	8.7	15.2	4.9	29.8	10.8	14.0
September 1930								
Seats	107	41	30	87	20	143	77	72
Percentage	18.3	7.0	4.5	14.8	3.8	24.5	13.1	13.8
July 1932								
Seats	230	37	7	97	4	133	89	11
Percentage	37.3	5.9	1.2	15.7	1.0	21.6	14.3	2.9

NSDAP, National Socialist German Workers' Party (Nazi Party); DNVP, German National People's Party; DVP, German People's Party; ZP, Centre Party; DDP, German Democratic Party; SPD, Social Democratic Party; KPD, German Communist Party.

In 1931, the Nazi Party was involved in the Harzburg Front, a short-lived coalition of radical right-wing parties designed to oppose the government of Chancellor **Heinrich Brüning**. It had been the intention of Hugenberg to agree on a right-wing candidate to oppose Hindenburg at the presidential election in 1932, but ideological differences prevented this from happening. However, by this time, Hitler saw himself as the champion of the radical right and refused to make any agreement with other groups that would restrict the Nazis' freedom of movement. In the presidential election of March to April 1932, Hindenburg was supported by the moderate left and centre, but despite this Hitler was able to poll some 37 per cent of the popular vote, which led to many believing that the Nazi Party had to be included in any government.

This electoral success continued and in the elections to the *Reichstag* in July 1932, the Nazi Party became the largest political party in Germany. This was certainly helped by the decline in support for other right-wing parties such as the DNVP and the collapse in support for both the DVP and DDP.

> **KEY FIGURE**
>
> **Heinrich Brüning (1885–1970)**
>
> Brüning began his career as a teacher before serving as an infantry officer. He was elected to the *Reichstag* in 1924 and became leader of the Centre Party in 1929. He was appointed chancellor in 1930. His failure to reduce the impact of the Depression led to him becoming known as the 'hunger chancellor'. He resigned in May 1932 following his plans to divide up bankrupt estates in eastern Germany, which lost him the confidence of Hindenburg.

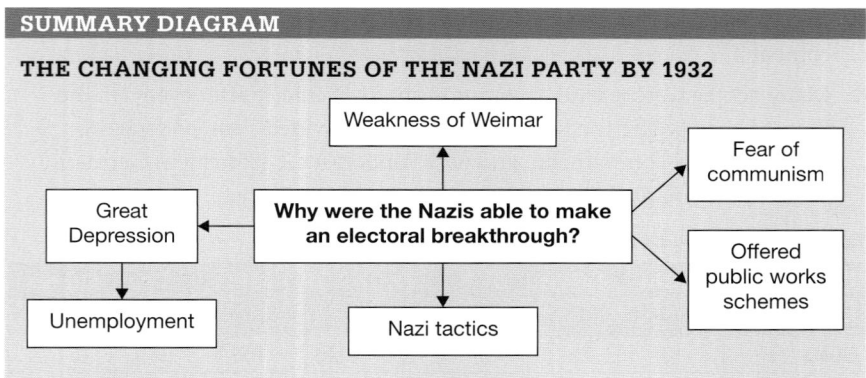

4 The reasons for growing support for the Nazi Party

■ Why did the Nazi Party become a mass movement?

The Great Depression transformed the Nazi Party and brought it mass appeal as it was able to exploit the social and economic discontent. Many historians have argued that without the Depression the Nazis would never have attracted mass support. However, other parties on both the left and right of the political spectrum offered radical solutions but did not enjoy similar electoral success, suggesting that there were other factors that brought about their appeal. The Nazis certainly used modern propaganda techniques as their improved party organisation was able to exploit a range of opportunities. There was also Hitler's reported charisma and appeal which attracted many, and Nazi policies appeared to offer simple solutions to problems that other parties seemed either unwilling or unable to tackle. The following section will consider the role of these issues in the increasing support for the party.

The role of Hitler

> **KEY TERM**
>
> **Messianic** Having the character of a messiah or saviour.

The decline in support of the party while Hitler was in jail had shown how indispensable he was to the movement. He provided the charismatic leadership that was essential to its success, offering an almost **messianic** vision, which inspired others. He was also a powerful speaker who had the ability to convince many in his audience that what he said would come true. Hitler's speeches were perfectly timed, building up tension before starting to speak and convincing many in his audience that he was speaking just to them. Although the message was often lacking in specific details, he convinced many that he could return Germany to its former greatness, which was particularly valuable at a time of despair and economic crisis, when other political parties appeared to offer no solutions to the economic ills of the country.

> **INTERPRETATION 1**
>
> From Otto Strasser, *Hitler and I*, Houghton Mifflin, 1940.
>
> *Adolf Hitler enters a hall. He sniffs the air. For a minute he gropes, feels his way, senses the atmosphere. Suddenly he bursts forth ... His words go like an arrow to their target, he touches each private wound in the raw, liberating the mass unconscious, expressing its innermost aspirations, telling it what it most wants to hear ... If he tries to bolster up his argument with theories or quotations from books he has only imperfectly understood, he scarcely rises above a very poor mediocrity. But let him throw away his crutches and step out boldly, speaking as the spirit moves him, and he is promptly transformed into one of the greatest speakers of the century.*

Hitler's speeches seemed to strike a chord with people, appearing to show an understanding of their plight, with even an opponent commenting:

> **INTERPRETATION 2**
>
> From E. Amy Buller, *Darkness Over Germany*, Longmans, Green & Co., 1943.
>
> *At one of the early congresses I was sitting around surrounded by thousands of SA men and as Hitler spoke I was most interested at the shouts and more often the muttered exclamations of the men around me, who were mainly workmen or lower-middle-class types. 'He speaks for me, he speaks for me.' 'Ach Gott [Oh God], he knows how I feel.' Many of them seemed lost to the world around them and were probably unaware of what they were saying. One man in particular struck me as he lent forward with his head in his hands, and with a sort of convulsive sob said, 'Gott sei Dank [God be thanked], he understands.'*

Hitler was able to vary his message to appeal to his audience, whether it was to those who were suffering from the Depression and were unemployed, or to the elite classes. Hitler became the unifying factor for all classes of society during the movement. However, some have argued that the Nazis did just as well in 1930 in areas where Hitler had not visited, as was seen in Neidenburg, east Prussia, where Nazi support rose from 2.3 per cent in 1928 to over 25 per cent in 1931 even though there was no local Nazi Party and there had been no organised mass rallies or visits from Hitler.

The role of the SA and violence

The SA was formed in 1920 and was designed to protect Nazi speakers. By 1933, it numbered some half a million members. Members were provided with a uniform; a brown shirt, with a swastika on the arm, which led to the nickname of the Brownshirts. For much of the period they were led by Ernst Röhm (see page 23), who wanted the Nazis to seize power and establish a new, radical state.

The organisation attracted many young men, often because they were searching for adventure and something to do, particularly once unemployment began to rise. For others, it was the uniform, meals and accommodation that attracted them, giving many a sense of belonging and comradeship. Their work involved distributing propaganda leaflets, protecting Nazi meetings and fighting the communists on the street. Although they were not allowed to carry arms, this did not stop the violence, with July 1932 witnessing the death of nearly 100 SA men, often in street fights with political opponents. These became martyrs for the Nazi cause and, while the SA was banned for a short period by Brüning in 1932, this was lifted by the next chancellor, Papen in an attempt to appease the Nazis.

The SA played an important role in the success of the Nazis. Although it was associated with violence and disorder, its rallies gave the impression of organisation and discipline, something many Germans believed was lacking in society. SA attacks on communists were also popular with the middle class, who feared a Russian-style revolution. Therefore, despite its behaviour, it helped to give the impression that the Nazis would provide a firm and strong government.

> **SOURCE QUESTION**
>
> How useful is Source D in explaining the appeal of the SA?

SOURCE D

From an SA decree by Franz Pfeffer von Salomon, the leader of the SA, published 3 November 1926.

The only form in which the SA appears to the public is that of the military formation. This is one of the most powerful forms of propaganda. The sight of a large number of calm, disciplined men whose total will to fight may be seen or sensed makes the most profound impression on every German, and speaks to his heart in a more convincing language than writing and speech and logic can ever do. Where whole hosts march purposefully, stake life and existence for a cause, all must be great and true.

KEY TERM

Mass suggestion
A psychological term suggesting that people can be unified by the atmosphere of an occasion.

The role of propaganda

Many historians have stressed the importance of propaganda in the appeal of Nazism. Hitler himself had commented on its value in *Mein Kampf*:

> **SOURCE QUESTION**
>
> What does Source E tell us about Nazi propaganda?

SOURCE E

From Adolf Hitler, *Mein Kampf*, translated by James Murphy, Hurst & Blackett, 1939.

The receptive powers of the masses are very restricted, and their understanding is feeble. On the other hand, they quickly forget. Such being the case, all effective propaganda must be confined to a few bare essentials and those must be expressed as a far as possible in stereotyped formulas.

ONLINE EXTRAS

Test your understanding of the limitations of sources by completing Worksheet 11 at **www.hoddereducation.co.uk/accesstohistory/extras**

Nazi propaganda was designed to appeal to public emotions, particularly through the use of mass meetings and rallies. The atmosphere created by large-scale rallies led to many being drawn in by the 'collective will' or '**mass suggestion**', whereby people were simply united by the atmosphere. This was achieved through a whole range of techniques, including uniforms, torches, music and flags, with many saying how these occasions led to their becoming Nazi supporters.

In 1934, Goebbels commented that 'Propaganda was our sharpest weapon in conquering the state, and remains our sharpest weapon in maintaining and building up the state.' Goebbels was placed in charge of propaganda in April 1930. Propaganda was sent out from party headquarters to local areas, where it was adapted to fit local circumstances. Different pamphlets and posters were produced for different groups so that the message was specifically tailored to their social and economic interests:

- Farmers were told that high taxes were crippling them and the Nazis offered them benefits to offset the agricultural depression.
- The unemployed were offered bread and work.
- The *Mittelstand* were told that Marxism and the control of large department stores were to blame for their situation.
- Industrialists were reassured that the Nazis would not embark on a mass nationalisation programme.

The party was also quick to seize on modern technology to get its message across. Perhaps the most dramatic was Hitler's use of planes during the 1932 presidential campaign, which allowed him to get to as many places as possible. His 'Flight over Germany' campaign allowed him to make four or five major speeches per day. The party also made use of radio and film to portray Hitler's messages, and loudspeakers ensured that the message was heard by as many as possible.

The Nazi movement was also able to play on a number of existing elements that helped to unite the people and these also played a crucial role in Nazi propaganda. The Nazis exploited German nationalism and the discontent that had been created by the First World War and the Treaty of Versailles and promised to restore German pride. They also played on the cult of the Führer, who, it was argued, had a vision to make Germany great again, while also creating a national community or *Volksgemeinschaft* which would unite the people. At the same time, propaganda also blamed a number of groups for the problems Germany faced and created scapegoats. These included:

- The Jewish community, who had long been used in Europe as scapegoats and were now accused of making fortunes while ordinary Germans suffered.
- The communists, who particularly worried the middle class, property and factory owners given events in the Soviet Union and the threat that they posed.
- The 'November criminals', who were the politicians who had signed the armistice and helped to create the weak Weimar Republic.

However, the importance of propaganda in explaining Nazi success has been challenged by the work of historians such as Jeremy Noakes (1983). He has argued that its importance has been overemphasised and the Nazis did well electorally in areas where there was little propaganda and vice versa. He has suggested that propaganda simply reinforced existing views, rather than creating them.

Economic motives

The work of historians such as William Brustein (1996) has argued that people voted for the Nazis for primarily economic reasons rather than the xenophobia which was often stressed in party propaganda. This interpretation puts forward the view that between 1930 and 1933, the Nazis offered a third way between state-planning Marxism and free-market capitalism. The Nazis proposed a system whereby the economy would serve the needs of the state and there would be public investment in industry in order to boost the economy. Germany would become self-sufficient through a policy of **autarky**, which would mean that the interests of Germany would be put first and an economic zone dominated by Germany would be created. Those who were in debt would be protected, and, in particular, farmers would be supported with controls on prices and imports, while unused land in the east would be seized and resettled.

> **KEY TERM**
>
> **Autarky** Self-sufficiency in both food and raw materials.

Brustein argued that these policies helped to attract support from blue-collar or working-class voters, particularly those who worked in depressed industries who were attracted by policies that offered support. This led him to conclude:

> **INTERPRETATION 3**
>
> From William Brustein, *The Logic of Evil: The Social Origins of the Nazi Party, 1925–1933*, Yale University Press, 1996, p. 184.
>
> *The Nazi party did not gain its phenomenal mass constituency because of its emphasis on xenophobia but rather because the party designed a series of innovative programs that appealed to material interests of a broad constituency overwhelmed by the Depression. Xenophobia alone could not have brought the Nazis to power.*

Anti-Semitism

Most historians no longer argue that Hitler's virulent anti-Semitism helped to win mass support. It may have played a role in attracting some of the original supporters to the party, but there is little evidence to support the argument that it helped to win the Nazis votes. Hitler himself also played down anti-Semitism in some of his election campaigns, particularly as support for the Nazis grew among some of the elite classes, where his anti-communist stance was much more popular. It is also worth stressing that even Jewish historian Daniel Goldhagen (1996), who argued that Germany developed a desire to eliminate Jewish people, stressed that anti-Semitism did not play an important role in Nazi electoral success.

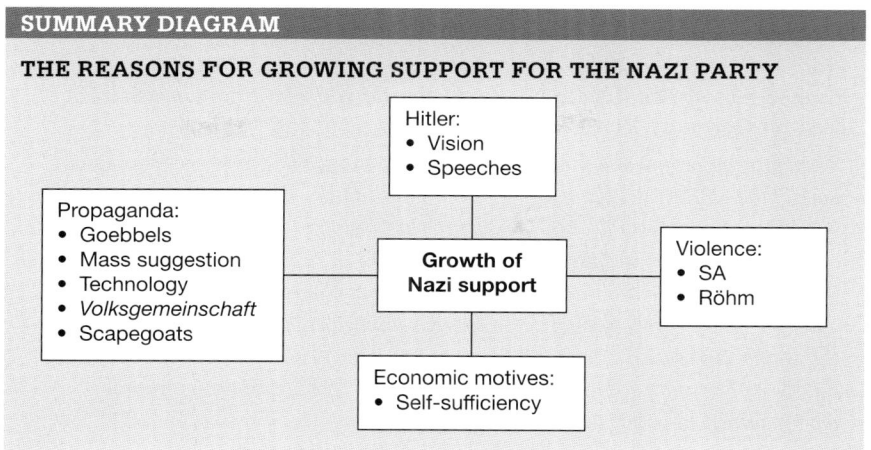

5 Key debate

■ *Who voted for the Nazis?*

Support for the Nazi Party grew dramatically in the years 1929–32. This has resulted in much debate among historians as to why people supported extremist parties. The Nazis never gained an absolute majority, although this was never likely, given the large number of political parties in Germany and the system of proportional representation. Despite this, Nazism did become a mass movement in this period and it has led to considerable argument as to why so many were attracted to the party.

Until the 1980s, many historians believed that the key group in the Nazi movement was the *Mittelstand*, which gave the Nazis the majority of their support. It was, according to most accounts, this group, along with the elite groups that conspired in January 1933, which helped bring Hitler to power. This interpretation enabled left-wing historians to argue that the working class could not be blamed for the developments within Germany. However, in the 1990s, this view was challenged as the working class in Britain and the USA began voting for right-wing governments, and this has led to more sophisticated approaches being taken in analysing voting patterns in Nazi Germany. Historians started to consider local issues and religious factors. Local studies have shown more complex patterns than previously thought, while the collapse of East Germany has also opened up archive material which has allowed historians, such as Conan Fischer, to show that workers were attracted to Nazism in greater numbers than had originally been thought.

> **INTERPRETATION 1**
>
> From J. Falter, 'How likely were workers to vote for the NSDAP?' in Conan Fischer, editor, *The Rise of Nationalism and the Working Classes in Weimar Germany*, Berghahn Books, 1996, pp. 34 and 40.
>
> *Therefore, according to our estimates, probably one in three workers of voting age backed the NSDAP ... From July 1932 onwards more workers would have voted NSDAP than voted KPD or SPD respectively ... on a regular basis more than a quarter of National Socialist voters were workers ... In terms of its electoral support the NSDAP was clearly Protestant dominated, but otherwise in social terms it was a distinctly heterogeneous party ... There is unmistakable over-representation from the middle classes, a fact certainly disputed by nobody as of yet. On the other hand it no longer appears admissible, given so high a proportion of voters from the working class, to speak of a middle-class party.*

This research does not mean that the importance of the *Mittelstand* should be dismissed, but it suggests their dominance was less than once thought. It now appears that religion and community influences played a greater role in determining voting behaviour, but it should not be forgotten that the Nazis did make considerable electoral gains from parties who had middle-class support and/or a Protestant identity. On the other hand, Catholic parties, the Communists and SPD were largely able to withstand the Nazi advance, as Dick Geary has shown in his book *Hitler and Nazism* (1993). Geary has shown that the Nazis were unable to make large inroads where:

- Catholicism and socialism were well established, with the structure of the Catholic Church and trade unions being strongly founded.
- Catholicism and Socialism were both well organised and had effective propaganda to oppose Nazism.
- Both groups had built up their resilience and loyalty due to attacks and persecution under the Kaiser and were more able to resist Nazi advances.

A study of the geographical voting patterns has shown that Nazi support was higher in the north and east than the south and west. The Nazis gained their highest levels of support in the area from the North German Plain to Schleswig-Holstein, which was both largely rural and Protestant, whereas attempts at breakthrough in Catholic areas and in large industrial areas were less successful. However, even these generalisations have to be taken carefully as Silesia, which was Catholic and industrial, did record a high Nazi vote.

There are two other issues that should be considered in any analysis of voting patterns. First, the Nazis often attracted those who had lost faith in the prevailing system and believed that their position in society was under threat. This is often described as the 'politics of anxiety'. These people included many of the middle class who wanted to escape from the crisis following the First World War and return to what they viewed as 'the good old days'. This view was most clearly developed in the work of Thomas Childers in his book *The Nazi Voter* (1983), where he argued:

> **INTERPRETATION 2**
>
> From Thomas Childers, *The Nazi Voter: The Social Foundations of Fascism in Germany, 1919–1933*, University of North Carolina Press, 1983, p. 268.
>
> [By 1930] the NSDAP had become a unique phenomenon in German electoral politics, a catch-all party of protest, whose constituents, while drawn primarily from the middle-class electorate were united above all by a profound contempt for the existing political and economic system.

Secondly, the Nazis attracted considerable support from the young in Germany:

- Nearly half the Nazi membership in the period before 1933 had been born in the years between 1904 and 1913.
- Some 60 per cent of those aged between 20 and 30 who joined political parties, joined the Nazis.
- Many of these joined the SA, particularly as unemployment rose and there seemed little hope for their future, whereas Nazism appeared to offer them some hope and, with the SA, something to do.

Although this recent work has shown that the Nazis had become a broad party and that to do this they had had to make some inroads into working-class areas, they still gained most of their support from Protestant, rural and middle-class voters, as is shown in Interpretation 3.

> **INTERPRETATION 3**
>
> From Jeremy Noakes, 'The Rise of the Nazis', *History Today*, January 1983.
>
> The Nazis did best in the rural areas and small towns of the Protestant parts of Germany, particularly in the north and east. They won much of their support from the most rooted and traditional section of the German population – peasant farmers, self-employed artisans, craftsmen and small retailers … In urban areas the party did best in those towns and cities which were administrative or commercial centres with large civil servant and white collar populations, rather than in industrial centres; and they tended to win most support in upper-middle-class districts. Nazi support also tended to be strongest among the younger generation. This was particularly true of the membership, which was also overwhelmingly male.

CHAPTER SUMMARY

Following the failure of the Munich *Putsch*, Hitler abandoned the policy of seizing power through force. With his release from jail in 1924, he rebuilt the party and branched out, creating many Nazi-founded organisations. This helped to lay the foundations for future electoral success, yet the Nazis' performances in elections until 1930 were disappointing. It was only really with the onset of the Great Depression that they were able to make significant progress. In this, they were helped by the appeal of Hitler himself, the propaganda skills of Goebbels, the violence of the SA and the attraction of some of their economic policies. As a result, by mid-1932 they were the largest party in the *Reichstag*. The reasons for this dramatic growth in support have been the topic of historical debate.

Refresher questions

Use these questions to remind yourself of the key material covered in this chapter.

1 In what way did the tactics of the Nazi Party change in the period after 1923?

2 In what ways was the Nazi Party reorganised in the period 1924–9?

3 What issues divided the Nazi Party in the period 1924–30?

4 Why did the Nazis perform badly in the 1928 election?

5 In what ways did the Nazi position improve in 1929?

6 How important a role did Hitler play in the appeal of Nazism?

7 Why did the violence of the SA help to win support for the Nazi Party?

8 In what ways did Goebbels develop Nazi propaganda?

9 Explain the role of each of these elements in gaining the Nazi Party support: a) economic policies of the Nazis and b) anti-Semitism.

10 Which social groups tended to vote for the Nazis? Why?

11 In which regions of Germany did the Nazis win most support? Why?

CHAPTER 5

The crisis of the Weimar Republic 1929–33

The collapse of share prices in the USA during the Wall Street Crash of 1929 led to the Great Depression, which is the context for the collapse of the Weimar Republic. The Weimar governments were unable to deal with the political, social and economic consequences of the Depression, leading many in Germany to look to alternatives to solve their problems. It has been argued that without the Depression, the Nazi Party would never have gained support and come to power.

This chapter examines the extent to which this view is true and looks at the reasons for the collapse of the republic by focusing on the following themes:

- The impact of the Great Depression
- The Brüning government and presidential rule
- The roles of Hindenburg, Papen and Schleicher
- The collapse of Weimar democracy
- Political intrigue and Hitler's appointment as chancellor

The key debate on page 84 of this chapter considers whether the creation of a Nazi dictatorship was inevitable.

KEY DATES

1928	May	Müller's Grand Coalition
1929	Oct.	Wall Street Crash
1930	March	Brüning replaced Müller as chancellor
	Sept.	Nazis made large gains in *Reichstag* elections
	Dec.	Economic measures imposed by presidential decree
1931	July	Five major German banks failed
1932	Jan.	Unemployment reached 6.1 million
	April	Presidential election, Hindenburg re-elected
1932	June	Papen replaced Brüning as chancellor
	July	Nazis largest party in elections to the *Reichstag*
	Sept.	No-confidence vote in Papen's government
	Nov.	Nazi support in elections to *Reichstag* declined
	Dec.	Schleicher replaced Papen as chancellor
1933	Jan.	Schleicher dismissed as chancellor, replaced by Hitler

1 The impact of the Great Depression

■ *How serious was the impact of the Great Depression on Germany?*

Most historians see the collapse of the US stock market in October 1929 and the subsequent Great Depression as the most important cause of the failure of the Weimar Republic. Although the **Wall Street Crash** occurred in the USA and primarily affected the west, it had a profound impact on Germany because of its reliance on US loans. The crash played a significant role in the rise in popularity of the Nazi Party, even if it was not ultimately responsible for their accession to power.

The economic impact of the Depression

The collapse of the US economy following the Wall Street Crash in October 1929 resulted in US businesses and banks curtailing loans to Germany and recalling the loans they had already made. Even before the crash, unemployment in Germany had been rising and by the spring of 1929 it had already reached 2.5 million. The crash only made matters worse (see Table 5.1, left).

It is important to remember that the German economy already had a number of weaknesses before 1929:

- The **balance of trade** was in deficit; Germany was importing more than it was exporting.
- The number of unemployed averaged 1.9 million by 1929.
- A significant number of farmers were already in debt and had experienced falling incomes.
- Government finances were in deficit.

It might, therefore, be suggested that even without the Wall Street Crash the German economy faced the serious possibility of a depression. It could be argued that the crash was simply the setting rather than the cause of the collapse of the Weimar Republic.

As unemployment continued to rise, people had less money to spend and demand for goods plummeted. This resulted in more people losing their jobs as the economy entered a vicious downward spiral as production was cut back even further. The result was that by 1932, nearly 33 per cent of the workforce was unemployed and on top of this figure there were others who were either working shorter hours, had taken pay cuts to keep their jobs or were simply not registered. The impact of this was huge, with poverty rising and many workers unable to pay rent or feed their families. Industrial production fell to 42 per cent of its 1929 level.

> **KEY TERMS**
>
> **Wall Street Crash**
> The collapse of share prices on the New York Stock Exchange, based on Wall Street, in October 1929.
>
> **Balance of trade**
> The difference between the value of goods exported and imported. Where a country imports more than it exports then it has a deficit and is considered to be in the 'red'.

Table 5.1 Unemployment in Germany (thousands), 1928–33

Year	January	July
1928	1862	1012
1929	2850	1251
1930	3218	2765
1931	4887	3990
1932	6042	5392
1933	6014	4464

Farmers had already been hit by an agricultural depression caused by overproduction due to improved farming techniques and a reduced demand in food products from Europe. The result was that they faced high interest rates and falling prices. The Depression worsened their situation and, by 1932, 18,000 farmers had gone bankrupt, with some **tenant farmers** evicted from holdings that had been in their families for generations.

Industry also suffered, with 50,000 businesses collapsing between 1930 and 1932, while five major banks failed in 1931. The collapse of banks only added to the crisis. Most banks had only small amounts of money reserves, and, therefore, when **Kredit Anstalt** folded, customers of other banks feared that this was just the beginning of the end of the whole banking system. As a result, they began to withdraw their money. This forced banks to close as they ran out of cash and the government was forced to support them, further increasing the economic crisis.

France blocked an emergency loan to Germany, which might have helped to ease the crisis and stimulate the economy. It was increasingly clear that Germany was in a very weak situation and, although help for it was limited as the loan was blocked, it was agreed that there should be a one-year suspension of reparation payments. Then, in 1932, with no sign of improvement, a committee of financial experts from the League of Nations agreed that reparations and inter-Allied debts should be cancelled. However, this did not solve the crisis in Germany, and economic problems continued to fuel political instability.

> **KEY TERMS**
>
> **Tenant farmer** A farmer who rents land from a landlord.
>
> **Kredit Anstalt** An Austrian bank that went bankrupt in July 1931. The collapse encouraged other investors to withdraw money from other banks and helped to initiate the Great Depression.

The social impact of the Depression

Rural areas were already suffering from low prices and unemployment, but now the hardships spread through urban areas. Savings had been wiped out by the inflation of 1923–4 and millions could not feed themselves. Malnutrition was common and was accompanied by diseases that arose from poverty, poor diet and poor housing. As well as physical hardship, there was mental stress resulting from feelings of shame, hopelessness and inadequacy in a society that valued hard work.

With the prospect of long-term unemployment for many, people faced the challenge of feeding their families and keeping the house warm on the limited income provided by social benefits. However, the impact was not just confined to the working class. The middle class also struggled to survive as there was little demand for their services and, in some ways, this had an even greater impact, as their pride and respectability was lost.

These developments appeared to signal the collapse of traditional German society and values and so it is not surprising that many lost faith in the government. It seemed to have no answers to problems, and therefore many people turned to political extremism which appeared to offer simple solutions.

The political impact of the Depression

Although the scale of the economic downturn in the USA was comparable with that in Germany, the political impact was far less. The economic crisis in Germany became a political one as there was already a lack of confidence in the system and these events simply further weakened the republic's position. It led to a feeling of gloom and despondency, reinforcing people's hostility to the republic and the failings of a democratic system. It contributed to the collapse of **Müller's coalition government**, which had a majority in the *Reichstag* at the time, and to the increase in the number of anti-democratic deputies. Following this, it meant that it was nearly impossible for any government to gain a majority and simply furthered the decline in parliamentary government. Unlike other democracies, such as the USA, France or Britain, Germany did not have the tradition of parliamentary democracy to fall back on in times of crisis.

The economic collapse also had an impact on government revenue. This fell dramatically as less revenue was raised from taxes. Yet, at the same time, government expenditure rose as a result of the increase in benefit payments that had to be made to the unemployed. When the benefit system had been introduced it had been assumed that it would not have to cope with more than 800,000 unemployed, and that periods of unemployment would be short; but the number was nearly four times greater by 1930 and rising, and the periods of unemployment were long lasting. As a result, the government struggled to meet the demands, creating further difficulties for the already weak republic.

KEY TERM

Müller's coalition government This was one of the longer-lasting governments during the Weimar period, surviving from May 1928 until March 1930. It was the last Weimar government that had a majority in the *Reichstag* and its collapse led to the start of rule by emergency decree and presidential government. It was often called the Grand Coalition and was made up of the German Social Democratic Party (SPD), Centre Party (ZP), German Democratic Party (DDP) and German People's Party (DVP), with the SPD returning to government for the first time since the start of the period.

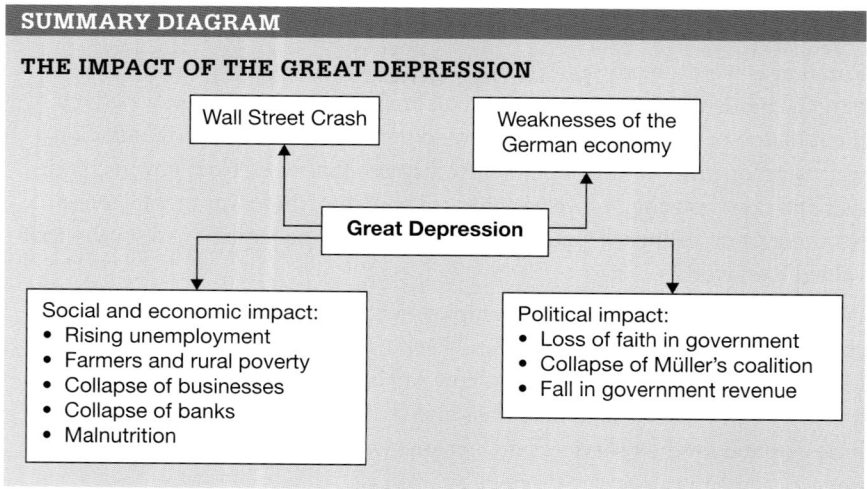

SUMMARY DIAGRAM

THE IMPACT OF THE GREAT DEPRESSION

- Wall Street Crash
- Weaknesses of the German economy

→ Great Depression →

- Social and economic impact:
  - Rising unemployment
  - Farmers and rural poverty
  - Collapse of businesses
  - Collapse of banks
  - Malnutrition

- Political impact:
  - Loss of faith in government
  - Collapse of Müller's coalition
  - Fall in government revenue

2 The Brüning government and presidential rule

■ *How did parliamentary democracy turn into presidential government?*

The Grand Coalition government created in 1928 was a broad coalition of left-wing and moderate parties under the socialist Chancellor **Hermann Müller**. Although the election results saw parties sympathetic to the republic stabilise and the SPD make gains, it was not typical of the period and did not hide the weaknesses of the parliamentary system. There were still problems created as a result of proportional representation and the difficulty of maintaining a coalition between different parties, which often put their own interests first.

In this instance it was the issue of unemployment insurance which created difficulties within the coalition as the different parties wanted different approaches to the problem. The SPD, which gained most of its support from the working classes, did not want to contemplate cutting benefits, whereas the DVP wanted cuts, and many industrialists argued that the whole system was simply too expensive and should be abolished. Attempts at compromise between the different parties and interest groups over the issue of spending cuts failed. This led to the resignation of the cabinet when President Hindenburg refused to grant Müller emergency powers to approve his budget, which might have created stability. More importantly, Müller's resignation also led to the end of democracy.

> **KEY FIGURE**
>
> **Hermann Müller (1876–1931)**
>
> Müller had been foreign minister at the start of the Weimar period and had signed the Treaty of Versailles. He had briefly been chancellor in 1920 and became leader of the SPD in the same year. He became chancellor again in 1928, but resigned in 1930 when Hindenburg refused to support him.

Table 5.2 Germany's governments 1928–32

Chancellor	Dates in office	Type of government
Hermann Müller (SPD)	May 1928 to March 1930	Parliamentary government. Coalition cabinet of SPD, ZP, DDP and DVP
Heinrich Brüning (ZP)	March 1930 to May 1932	Presidential government dependent on emergency decrees. Coalition cabinet from the centre and right
Franz Papen (ZP)	May to December 1932	Presidential government dependent on emergency decrees. Many non-party cabinet members
General Kurt Schleicher (non-party)	December 1932 to January 1933	Presidential government dependent on emergency decrees. Many non-party members

The Brüning government 1930–2

The fall of the Müller coalition gave Hindenburg the opportunity to appoint the right-wing conservative Heinrich Brüning (see page 59) as chancellor in March 1930. Brüning's Centre Party (ZP) did not have a majority in the *Reichstag* as he faced opposition from both the extreme left and right. Therefore, he stated that if he was defeated in his bid to win support for increasing taxes and welfare spending, he would ask for the *Reichstag* to be dissolved and rule by emergency decree through Hindenburg, using Article 48 of the constitution.

As a result, parliamentary democracy was replaced by 'presidential government'. Brüning became ever more reliant on Article 48, with the number of emergency decrees rising from five in 1930 to 44 in 1931 and 66 in 1932. His policy of reducing expenditure worsened the economic situation, leading to his being known as 'the hunger chancellor', and may have unintentionally played a significant role in Nazi success by calling unscheduled elections in 1930. Some historians have argued that he was concerned that if he continued a policy of spending rather than reducing expenditure, then it would have led to hyperinflation. Others have suggested that he wanted to provoke a crisis so that reparations would be cancelled. The government was also criticised by contemporaries for its failure to bring in public works schemes in the summer of 1931. This failure gave the impression that the government was in a state of paralysis and unable to deal with the crisis, further fuelling support for the extremist parties. However, other historians have suggested that with the economy weak even before the Depression there was actually very little that he could have done to improve the situation.

The fall of Brüning's government

Although Brüning helped to secure the re-election of Hindenburg in the spring 1932 presidential election, he was dismissed as chancellor in May. This was the result of a number of issues, including:

- the banking crisis
- attempts at land reform
- political intrigue.

The closure of banks created a fear of a financial crisis and also fuelled unemployment, which reached some 5 million by the end of the year and resulted in demonstrations. This led to the creation of the **Harzburg Front**, which tried to bring down the government and force new elections, but at this time Brüning still had the backing of the president.

The issuing of a decree to create allotments for the unemployed from some landed estates in Prussia angered landowners, who saw it as an attack on property and associated it with communism. It led to the right wing, led by Schleicher, pushing for the resignation of Brüning. Hindenburg was a Prussian landowner; he was concerned by Brüning's proposals and, under pressure from the right, withdrew his support and dismissed him. Dependent on Hindenburg's support, as he lacked a majority in the *Reichstag*, Brüning's land reform policy took away the backing of the man who had kept him in power.

Historians have debated how far Brüning's period as chancellor was responsible for the collapse of democracy. Although he refused to work with the Nazis and upheld the rule of law, his presidential rule meant that Germany had become accustomed to rule by decree, which undermined democracy. The different views of his chancellorship are reflected in the following interpretations:

> **KEY TERM**
>
> **Harzburg Front** A right-wing nationalist alliance, formed in 1931, against Brüning's government.

INTERPRETATION 1

From E.J. Feuchtwanger, *From Weimar to Hitler: Germany 1918–33*, Palgrave Macmillan, 1993, p. 277.

Brüning was the last chancellor to govern with any kind of constitutional legitimacy. His personal integrity, intelligence and devotion to duty have never been doubted by men of goodwill. He was also secretive and sometimes paranoid. The debate about his place in history is focused on two main issues. The first question is whether his method of government by decree can be regarded as a last attempt to preserve a non-dictatorial political system or should be seen as a stepping stone to dictatorship. The second question is whether there were any realistic alternatives to Brüning's policies.

INTERPRETATION 2

From Hans Mommsen, *From Weimar to Auschwitz: Essays in German History*, Princeton University Press, 1991, pp. 125 and 140.

He deliberately intended his policies to deepen the economic crisis as he hoped this would enable Germany to get over the worst of the crisis before other comparable states ... Breaking the spirit of the constitution, and replacing it with formal legalisms was his doing. This contributed to the final destruction of the Weimar Republic just as surely as the systematic escalation of the economic crisis, which deliberately engineered, produced the atmosphere of utter hopelessness ... which Hitler could exploit more effectively than any other.

There is one thing that is clear: Brüning's dismissal led to a period of further instability and a rapid turnover in chancellors.

SUMMARY DIAGRAM

THE BRÜNING GOVERNMENT AND PRESIDENTIAL RULE

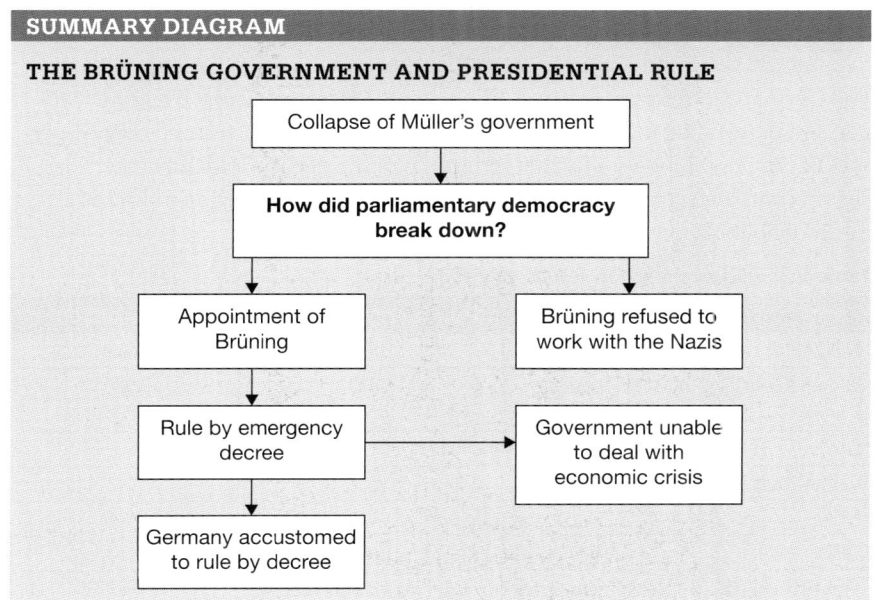

3 The roles of Hindenburg, Papen and Schleicher

■ *Why the results of the 1932 elections so significant?*

KEY FIGURES

Paul von Hindenburg (1847–1934)

Although he had reluctantly taken on the office of president, he played a key role in the appointment of chancellors and government by emergency decree. He was reluctant to appoint Hitler as chancellor. His death in 1934 removed the last obstacle to Hitler becoming dictator.

Franz von Papen (1879–1969)

Papen was from an aristocratic background. He spent the First World War serving in the cavalry and as a diplomat. When he was appointed chancellor it was more because of his connections, as a friend of Hindenburg, than political ability. He was a monarchist and nationalist and was happy to see the Weimar constitution undone and rule imposed by presidential decree. He was appointed vice chancellor to Hitler, but was outmanoeuvred by him.

In the period from the dismissal of Brüning until the appointment of Hitler in January 1933, three men would play a critical role in German politics: **Paul von Hindenburg**, **Franz von Papen** and General **Kurt von Schleicher**.

With the fall of Brüning's government, it was Schleicher who used his influence with Hindenburg to get Papen appointed as chancellor. Although he was a surprising choice to many, to Schleicher he was ideal as he believed that he could influence events through him. Papen's aim was to create a more authoritarian state. The new government was a non-party government but was nicknamed the 'Cabinet of Barons' and was dominated by landowners and industrialists, many of whom were not even members of the *Reichstag*.

Papen and Schleicher also hoped to secure support from the Nazis, who agreed not to oppose the government in return for two concessions:

■ the calling of new elections to the Reichstag
■ the end of the ban on the *Sturmabteilung* (SA) and *Schutzstaffel* (SS).

Papen and Schleicher hoped that this would bring the government much-needed popularity and it was agreed that elections would be called.

The July 1932 election

The elections of July 1932 were a disaster for the democratic parties as they were able to win only 39.5 per cent of the vote, with the Nazis the big winners, gaining 230 seats and 37.3 per cent of the vote, making them the largest party. The German Communist Party (KPD) secured 89 seats and just over fourteen per cent of the vote, meaning that the extremist parties had secured over 51 per cent of the popular vote, a further indication of the decline in democracy. The election was also characterised by violence, with 86 people dying in July as a result of political fights.

Table 5.3 *Reichstag* election results, July 1932

Party	Percentage of votes	Number of seats
NSDAP	37.3	230
DNVP (German National People's Party)	5.9	37
DVP	1.2	7
Centre and Bavarian Party	15.7	97
DDP	1.0	4
SPD	21.6	133
KPD	14.3	89
Others	2.9	11

The main features of the election were:

- The Nazis were the largest party with 230 seats and 37.3 per cent of the vote.
- The vote of the DNVP fell.
- Support for the democratic DDP and DVP collapsed, as they gained just eleven seats and 2.2 per cent of the vote.

KEY FIGURE

Kurt von Schleicher (1882–1934)

Schleicher came from a noble family and became an officer in Hindenburg's regiment. He believed in the values of the army rather than the republic. Schleicher became a close confidant of both Hindenburg and his son, holding various posts which linked the army and government. He played a key role in the appointment of both Brüning and Papen, and eventually himself, as chancellors. He became worried about Nazi power and the threat of unrest in Germany and therefore tried to include the Nazis in government in an attempt to control them. He was murdered by the Nazis during the Night of the Long Knives (see pages 101–3).

SOURCE A

'Our Last Hope: Hitler.' A Nazi poster from the 1932 presidential elections.

SOURCE QUESTION

Using Source A, why might many in Germany see Hitler as their last hope?

- Support for the SPD declined to 21.6 per cent.
- Support for the KPD grew to 14.3 per cent.

Although there had been considerable violence, Papen lifted the ban on the SA and SS. He also used emergency powers to remove the socialist coalition government in Prussia (see the box below), a further step towards the abandonment of democracy as it was an arbitrary and unconstitutional act, replacing a parliamentary system with a presidential authoritarian government. The lack of resistance from the trade unions and SPD was a clear sign that democracy was in decline.

The socialist coalition government in Prussia

Papen's use of emergency powers to remove the socialist coalition government in Prussia was significant in both the long and short term. Prussia was the most important of the states within Germany and its state government had been run by a coalition of the SPD and the Centre Party, which had followed a reformist programme. However, in 1932, with the impact of the Depression, they lost their majority and there was considerable disorder in the state. Papen used Article 48 to depose the government and put it under federal control. Article 48, designed to protect democracy, had been unwittingly used to destroy it. It also had a massive impact on the left's morale and, intimidated by the army, they failed to mount an effective challenge to the decision. This had implications for the future and when Hitler came to power he used this as a precedent to overthrow other state governments.

Despite his failure to secure a majority in the elections, Papen remained as chancellor and was determined to create a more authoritarian state. However, Papen was unable to command a majority and relied on the support of the president, although he was intent on calling a fresh election in order to try and secure a majority. This failed as the opposition passed a vote of no confidence in him.

Although the Nazi Party had done well in the elections, Hitler was still left with the problem of how to translate popular support into power. He was determined to hold out to be appointed chancellor, but this was unacceptable to both Papen and Schleicher. They were willing to utilise the support of the Nazi Party in order to give the government credibility, but they were prepared to give it only limited power and influence within the cabinet. A meeting between Papen, Hindenburg and Hitler in August ended in deadlock.

It appeared as if the Nazi policy of winning power legally had failed. Modern historian Jeremy Noakes describes the period from August to December 1932 as 'the months of crisis' for the party as it led to a collapse in morale and a loss of support.

Papen's position was no better. He suffered the humiliation of a massive vote of no confidence – 512 votes to 42 – in September, which led to his dissolving the *Reichstag* and calling for new elections. The elections in November 1932 did not bring him a majority, but did weaken the Nazis' position. Their support declined, winning only 33.1 per cent of the vote and 196 seats (see Table 5.4, below).

Table 5.4 Election results November 1932

Party	Number of seats in the *Reichstag*	Percentage of the vote
KPD	100	16.9
SPD	121	20.4
DDP	2	1.0
Centre Party	70	12.0
Conservatives	11	1.9
Nationalists	52	8.3
Nazis	196	33.1

A Nazi organisation commented on the November 1932 election results:

> **SOURCE B**
>
> From a Nazi report by the Reichspropaganda-Leitung (the Propaganda Office), November 1932.
>
> *We are of the opinion that little can be salvaged by way of propaganda … New paths must be taken. Nothing more is to be done by words, placards and leaflets. Now we must act! It must not come to another election. The results could not be imagined.*

SOURCE QUESTION

Why would the writer of Source B be disappointed by the results of the November 1932 election? Why did the Nazis not want another election?

This pessimistic view was confirmed by Joseph Goebbels in the latter part of 1932:

> **SOURCE C**
>
> Extracts from Joseph Goebbels' diary in 1932.
>
> *15 Oct: Party workers become very nervous as a result of these everlasting elections. They are overworked.*
>
> *8 Dec: Severe depression prevails … financial worries render all systematic work impossible … The danger now exists of the whole Party going to pieces … Dr. Ley telephones that the situation in the Party is becoming more critical from hour to hour. Gregor Strasser's letter to the Führer resigning his office is argumentative quibbling. Treason! Treason! Treason! For hours on end the Führer walks anxiously up and down the hotel room … Once he stops and merely says: 'If the Party should ever break up, I'll make an end of things in three minutes with a revolver.'*

SOURCE QUESTION

How useful is Source C in explaining why the Nazi Party was so concerned by the November 1932 election result?

ONLINE EXTRAS

Get to grips with comparing the views of sources by completing Worksheet 14 at www.hoddereducation.co.uk/accesstohistory/extras

Despite this decline, Hitler still refused to join the government unless he was appointed chancellor.

This led to Papen considering an alternative: the establishment of a presidential dictatorship. He would dissolve the *Reichstag* and declare **martial law**. Such a plan was opposed by Schleicher, who was becoming concerned by the desperate actions of Papen. Schleicher believed that the country could slip into civil war and that the popular support for the Nazis meant that they could not be ignored.

KEY TERM

Martial law Government by the military.

This led to him informing Hindenburg that the army no longer had confidence in Papen and forced the president to demand the chancellor's resignation.

Having played a behind-the-scenes role for two years, Schleicher now took centre stage and was appointed chancellor on 21 December 1932. He hoped to establish national unity by creating a more broad-based government. This was to be achieved by:

- Appealing to some on the left through a programme of public works.
- Splitting the Nazi Party by appealing to the socialist element within it and offering Gregor Strasser the position of vice chancellor.

However, neither of these attempts succeeded. The trade unions, encouraged by the SPD, were suspicious of his motives, while the elites were unhappy about public works schemes. Initially, the appeal of Strasser appeared as if it might work, but ultimately it led to a major argument within the Nazi Party between Hitler and Strasser, with the latter forced to resign from the party.

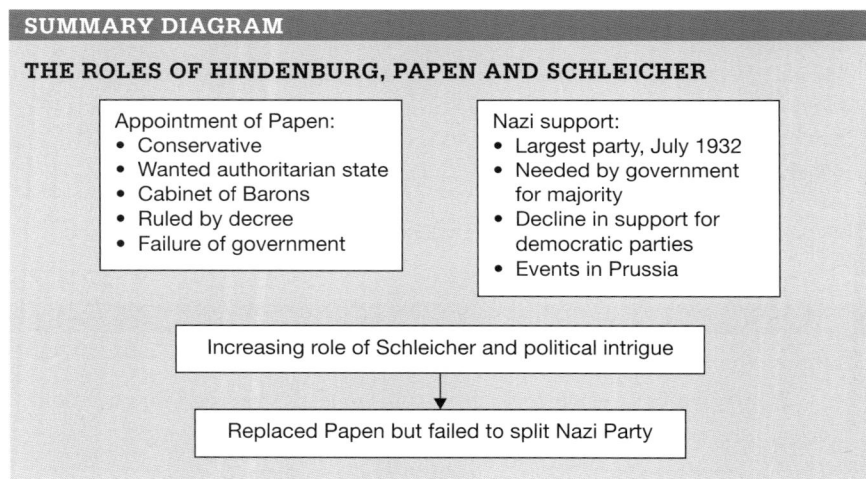

4 The collapse of Weimar democracy

- *When and why did democracy die?*

Many historians used to see the Hitler's appointment as chancellor in January 1933 as signalling the end of Weimar democracy, but as the events from 1930 to 1932 have shown, this is too simple an explanation. Weimar was already in trouble by 1930 and historians have argued that some form of authoritarian government was likely; however, this does not mean that Hitler's appointment was inevitable, as he was just one of a number of options and his appointment could have been avoided. It does raise the important question as to why Weimar democracy collapsed and there are several reasons that have been put forward to explain this:

- the hostility of Germany's vested interests
- economic problems
- limited support for the republic.

The hostility of Germany's vested interests

Germany's **elites** had been antagonistic towards the republic from the very start. They wanted to return to the pre-war authoritarian rule of the Kaiser and blamed the republic for the humiliating Treaty of Versailles. The elites played a significant role in the final collapse of the republic.

Economic problems

Throughout its existence, the republic was faced with continuous economic problems. It inherited the cost of the First World War, which was then followed by reparation payments, post-war reconstruction and the cost of welfare benefits. In 1923, the government faced the problem of hyperinflation and although that was solved relatively quickly, the period from 1924 to 1928 simply masked many underlying issues which would have dramatic consequences when the world economic crisis hit in 1929 after the Wall Street Crash.

Limited support for the republic

The republic was never able to secure widespread popular support while there was always considerable support for the political extremes which did not support democracy. This made it difficult for the republic to claim political legitimacy, which was only made worse by its links to failures such as Versailles and reparations. The political parties that supported the republic lost support and the SPD, which had been a mainstay of it, did not join the coalitions of the 1920s. As a result, many of the German population had little faith in the republic and those that did, had seen their numbers diminish over time.

The phases of the republic

The republic went through a number of phases during its life, but during each it was never able to develop and win support:

- The period from 1918 to 1919 was difficult given defeat in the war. Therefore, when it faced the problems of 1919–23 it was surprising that it survived.
- Although the period 1924–9 appeared to be a 'golden age', little was achieved and the republic was not strengthened, which made it much more difficult when crisis hit in 1929.
- The crises of 1929–33 brought an end to the republic, in part because it had never really established itself and because it lacked support.

These phases suggest that perhaps the republic never stood a chance, although some have argued that it was not until 1932 that its collapse became inevitable.

> **KEY TERM**
>
> **Elites** Conservative groups within German society who dominated the army, judiciary and civil service. Most were opposed to the republic and wanted a return to traditional, authoritarian government.

The appointment of Brüning and his system of presidential rule undermined democracy and this was soon followed by the Nazi breakthrough, which further weakened its chances. Even if the republic did not collapse until 1932, it can be argued that from the time of Brüning's appointment its chances of survival were very limited.

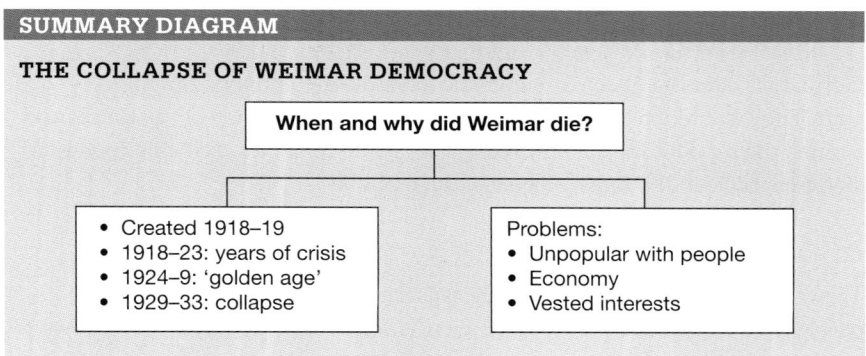

SUMMARY DIAGRAM
THE COLLAPSE OF WEIMAR DEMOCRACY

When and why did Weimar die?

- Created 1918–19
- 1918–23: years of crisis
- 1924–9: 'golden age'
- 1929–33: collapse

Problems:
- Unpopular with people
- Economy
- Vested interests

5 Political intrigue and Hitler's appointment as chancellor

■ *Why was Hitler appointed chancellor in January 1933?*

At the end of 1932 it appeared as if the Nazis' chances of gaining power had drifted away; electoral support had declined, financial support had ebbed away and morale was low. It was the actions of Papen that changed the situation. He had not forgiven Schleicher for abandoning him and was set on revenge and determined to regain office. This could be achieved only if he could convince Hindenburg that he could create a majority government. However, this could occur only with Nazi support.

Having previously despised Hitler, Hindenburg was now willing to bring him into government, believing that the Nazi threat was in decline and, therefore, would be easy to control and could be jettisoned once the Nazis had served their purpose. Papen, therefore, made contact with Nazi leaders and a meeting was held on 4 January where it was agreed that Hitler would lead a Nazi–Nationalist coalition. **Political intrigue** would dominate German politics for the rest of the month. Papen was able to gain the support of the elites, who saw this coalition as an escape from the communist threat. However, the greatest opposition to the plan was from Hindenburg. Not only did he have to be convinced to dismiss Schleicher but also to appoint Hitler.

Under pressure from his son and state secretary, Otto Meissner, and on the advice of Papen, Hindenburg was persuaded to withdraw his support from Schleicher and appoint Hitler, believing that he could be controlled and

KEY TERM

Political intrigue
Scheming and the attempt to create deals between leading politicians to ensure that their goals are achieved.

would work in the interest of the elites. The arrangement offered them mass support, an attack on the left wing and rearmament. Papen also believed that he had Hitler under control with both himself and Hugenberg in the cabinet, commenting to a friend that 'In two months we'll have pushed Hitler into a corner so hard that he'll be squeaking.' Therefore, on 30 January 1933, Hindenburg agreed to the coalition, despite his suspicions about Hitler. His appointment has been explained by historian Ian Kershaw, writing in 1991:

INTERPRETATION 3

From Ian Kershaw, *Hitler*, Longman, 1991, p. 55.

Few ... had Hitler as their first choice. But by January 1933, with other options apparently exhausted, most – with big landowners to the fore – were prepared to entertain a Hitler government. Had they opposed it, a Hitler Chancellorship would have been inconceivable. Hitler needed the elites to attain power. But by January 1933, they in turn needed Hitler as he alone could deliver the mass support required to impose a tenable authoritarian solution to Germany's crisis of capitalism and crisis of the state.

ONLINE EXTRAS WWW

Get to grips with finding out how and why different historical interpretations have been formed by historians by completing Worksheet 15 at **www.hoddereducation.co.uk/accesstohistory/extras**

Hitler had been able to triumph because the left and centre were too divided, while those on the right were willing to accept him as a partner as they believed that they could control him. Despite the election results of November 1932, there were still many ordinary Germans prepared to support the Nazis and have Hitler as their leader.

A distinguished banker comments on his views in the early 1930s:

INTERPRETATION 4

Johannes Zahn, writing in 1997, explains his feelings about the early 1930s.

You have to consider Germany's general position in 1930–33. An unemployed man either joined the Communists or became an SA man, and so business believed it was better if these people became stormtroopers as there was discipline and order. You really have to say this today, at the beginning you couldn't tell whether National Socialism was something good with a few bad side-effects, or something evil with a few good side-effects; you couldn't tell.

However, some historians have suggested that Hindenburg had a selfish motive in his decision to appoint Hitler. They have argued that, in appointing Hitler, Hindenburg hoped to avoid an investigation surrounding his Neudeck estate in East Prussia. This former family bankrupt estate had been returned to him in 1927 as a result of the *Osthilfe* (Help for the East) programme through which funds were allocated to help estates survive. However, in 1932, a *Reichstag* investigation found that some of the funds had been misused and the Neudeck estate was implicated in the scandal. However, such an interpretation seems to be unconvincing as it was only at the very end of the period that Hindenburg reluctantly agreed to appoint Hitler, as Otto Meissner, state secretary in Hindenburg's office, made clear in comments at the Nuremberg trials:

> **INTERPRETATION 5**
>
> From Otto Meissner, state secretary in Hindenburg's office, retrospective account, made to the Nuremberg Tribunal after the Second World War, 28 November 1945.
>
> *Despite Papen's persuasions, Hindenburg was extremely hesitant, until the end of January, to make Hitler Chancellor. He wanted to have Papen again as Chancellor. Papen finally won him over to Hitler with the argument that the representatives of the other right-wing parties which would belong to the government would restrict Hitler's freedom of action. In addition, Papen expressed his misgivings that, if the present opportunity were missed, a revolt of the national socialists and civil war were likely.*

SUMMARY DIAGRAM

POLITICAL INTRIGUE AND HITLER'S APPOINTMENT AS CHANCELLOR

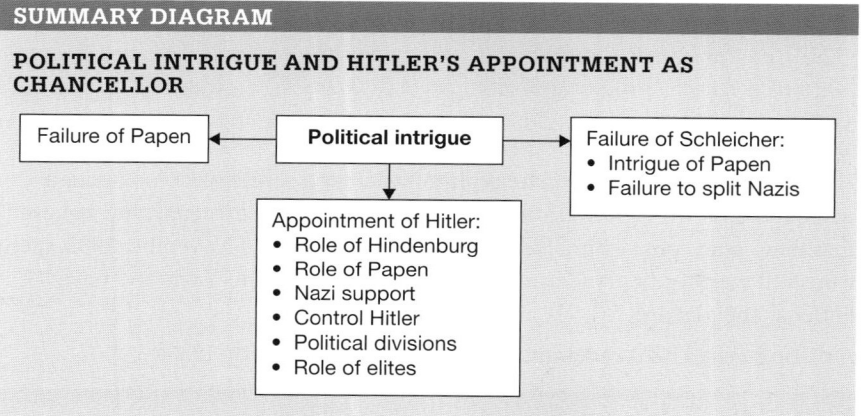

6 Key debate

■ *Was the creation of a Nazi dictatorship inevitable?*

Historians have disagreed over whether the creation of a Nazi dictatorship was the inevitable outcome considering German history. Left-wing historians argued that Germany faced a crisis of capitalism following the Wall Street Crash and as a result big business lost faith in the republic and gave its support to the Nazis who, they believed, they would be able to control and therefore secure their profits. However, there were historians such as A.J.P. Taylor, who argued in 1945 that Nazism was the natural product of German history, even going so far as to write in *The Course of German History* that 'It was no more a mistake for the German people to end up with Hitler than it is an accident when a river flows into the sea.' This view was taken even further by William Shirer in his *Rise and Fall of the Third Reich* (1960), in which he argued that the cultural and intellectual heritage of Germany and the national character of the people led to Hitler's coming to power.

Such views caused great controversy in Germany and led some German historians to focus on the developments in Europe in the period before and after the First World War. These writers, such as Ritter, focused on the decline in religion and morality, as well as the emergence of mass democracy to explain the success of Hitler. However, in the 1960s, historians such as Fritz Fischer put forward the view that German history was characterised by continuity and identified authoritarian and aggressive trends within its development, particularly from the 1850s. This *sonderweg* ('special path') or peculiar development of Germany in moving from aristocratic to democratic government was further continued in the writings of Martin Broszat (1969) and Hans Mommsen (1991) who put forward the view that conservative forces sympathised with Nazism as a way of upholding a right-wing authoritarian regime. This interpretation was challenged by Klaus Hildebrand (1985), who argued that such a view removed the central importance of Hitler from explaining the rise of Nazism. He stressed the political skills of Hitler and pointed to his ability to outmanoeuvre the political elites. More recently, in 1991, Ian Kershaw has argued that Hitler's rise to power was due to a combination of factors, including circumstances which allowed Hitler to emerge and the miscalculations of Papen and Hindenburg, which, he argued, meant that the appointment of Hitler was not inevitable, even up to the very end.

The two interpretations below further develop two of the views outlined above.

INTERPRETATION 1

From William L. Shirer, *The Rise and Fall of the Third Reich: A History of Nazi Germany*, Volume 2, Simon & Schuster, 1960, p. 93.

Acceptance of autocracy, of blind obedience, to the petty tyrants who ruled as princes, became ingrained in the German mind. The idea of democracy, or rule by parliament ... did not sprout in Germany. This political backwardness of the Germans ... set Germany apart from and behind the other countries of the West. There was no natural growth of a nation. This had to be borne in mind if one is to comprehend the disastrous road this people subsequently took and the warped state of mind which settled over it.

There thus arose quite artificially a state borne of no popular force nor even an idea except that of conquest, and held together by the absolute power of the ruler, by a narrow-minded bureaucracy which did his bidding and by a ruthlessly disciplined army ... The State, which was run with the efficiency and soullessness of a factory, became all; the people were little more than cogs in the machinery.

INTERPRETATION 2

From Ian Kershaw, *Hitler*, Longman, 1991, p. 38.

There was no inevitability about Hitler's triumph in January 1933. Five years earlier, the Nazi Party had been a fringe irritant in German politics, but no more. External events, the Young Plan to adjust German reparations payments, the Wall Street Crash and Brüning's entirely unnecessary decision to have an election in

> **ONLINE EXTRAS** WWW
>
> Test your understanding of finding evidence to support and challenge an interpretation by completing Worksheet 16 at www.hoddereducation.co.uk/accesstohistory/extras

summer 1930 – put the Nazis on the political map. Though democracy had by that time an unpromising future, a Nazi dictatorship seemed far less likely than some other form of authoritarian dictatorship or even a reversion to a Bismarckian style of government, possibly under a restored monarchy. In bringing Hitler to power, chances and conservative miscalculation played a larger role than any actions of the Nazi leader himself.

CHAPTER SUMMARY

The Great Depression had a profound political and social impact on the fragile Weimar Republic. It led to the collapse of Müller's government, which can be seen as the real end of parliamentary democracy as subsequent governments resorted to ever more desperate measures. Brüning's use of presidential decrees to rule was further evidence of the breakdown in parliamentary democracy and this policy was continued by the later chancellors, Papen and Schleicher. Members of the elites looked for alternatives to Weimar democracy and eventually they realised they would have to use the support of the popular Nazi Party. Therefore, when the governments of Papen and Schleicher collapsed, the elites persuaded Hindenburg to appoint Hitler as chancellor, hoping to use and then discard him. Under the dual challenge of the support for Nazism and the elites' dislike of democracy, the republic collapsed.

Refresher questions

Use these questions to remind yourself of the key material covered in this chapter.

1. In what ways did the economic crisis affect the lives of the German people?
2. In what ways was Weimar democracy undermined by the world economic depression?
3. Why did the economic crisis become a political crisis in 1930?
4. Why did parliamentary government decline after 1930?
5. How far was Brüning a failure?
6. To what extent can Brüning be seen as the destroyer of Weimar democracy?
7. How did Weimar governments react to the economic slump?
8. Why did the Papen and Schleicher governments fail to bring about political stability?
9. What were the alternatives to Hitler?
10. Why did Hindenburg eventually appoint Hitler as chancellor?
11. Why did Weimar collapse?
12. Why was Weimar replaced by Hitler?

Question practice: AS level

Source analysis questions

1 Using your understanding of the historical context, assess the value of these three sources to an historian studying the problems facing the Weimar Republic between 1918 and 1923.

EXAM HINT Responses should analyse and evaluate the three sources by considering the content, authorship and appropriate context of each in order to judge the value of each to an historian studying the problems facing the Weimar Republic in the years 1918–23.

SOURCE A

From Hugo Preuss, the lawyer chiefly responsible for drafting the Weimar constitution in 1919, writing on the effects of the Versailles settlement in 1923.

The German Republic was born out of terrible defeat. This cast from the first a dark shadow on the new political order, as far as national sentiment was concerned; but initially the belief still predominated that the new order was necessary for the rebirth of Germany. That is why the democratic clauses of the Weimar constitution met with relatively little resistance, despite the unrivalled severity of the armistice terms. For everyone still expected a peace settlement in accordance with Wilson's Fourteen Points, which all the fighting countries had bindingly accepted as the basis for the peace. The criminal madness of the Versailles Diktat was a shameless blow in the face to hopes of political and economic recovery. The Reich constitution was born with this curse upon it. That it did not collapse immediately under the strain is striking proof of the genuine validity of its basic principles; but its implementation and evolution were inevitably fatefully restricted.

SOURCE B

From a pamphlet issued by Social Democratic Party (SPD) members of the Weimar government, and circulated to the population of Berlin in response to the Kapp *Putsch*, March 1920.

WORKERS, PARTY COMRADES!
THE MILITARY PUTSCH HAS STARTED.
The Freikorps, fearing the command to dissolve, are trying to remove the Republic and to form a military dictatorship. The achievements of the whole year are to be smashed, your dearly bought freedom to be destroyed. Everything is at stake! The strongest counter measures are required. No factory must work while the military dictatorship of Ludendorff and Co rules. Therefore, down tools! Come out on strike! Deprive the military clique of oxygen! Fight with all means for the Republic! Put all quarrels aside. There is only one way to stop the return of the dictatorship, and that is to paralyse all economic life. No hand must move! General strike all along the line! Down with the counter-revolution!

SOURCE C

From a speech made by Franz Bumm, the health minister of the Weimar Republic, to the *Reichstag*, 20 February 1923.

Unfortunately, this picture of accelerating and shocking decline in health conditions applies to the whole Reich. In the rural areas where many self-sufficient farmers are able to feed themselves and the difficulties resulting from a great density of population do not exist, conditions seem to be better. But in the towns and in the districts with an industrial mass population, there has been a decided deterioration. Especially hard-hit are the middle-class, those living on small annuities, the widows and the pensioners, who with their modest incomes can no longer afford the most basic necessities at present day prices.

It is understandable that under such unhygienic circumstances, health levels are deteriorating ever more seriously ... we have a preliminary mortality rate for towns with 100,000 or more inhabitants. After having fallen in 1920–1, it has climbed again for the year 1921–2, rising from 12.6 to 13.4 per thousand inhabitants ... the so-called war dropsy is reappearing, which is a consequence of a bad and overly watery diet. There are increases in stomach disorders and food poisoning, which are the result of eating spoiled foods. There are complaints about the appearance of scurvy, which is a consequence of an unbalanced and improper diet. From various parts of the Reich, reports are coming in about an increase in suicides ... More and more often one finds 'old age' and 'weakness' listed in the official records on the cause of death; these are equivalent to death through hunger.

2 Using your understanding of the historical context, assess the value of these three sources to an historian studying the recovery of Weimar in the years between 1923 and 1929.

EXAM HINT Responses should analyse and evaluate the three sources by considering the content, authorship and appropriate context of each in order to judge the value of each to an historian studying the recovery of Weimar in the years between 1923 and 1929.

SOURCE A

From The Dawes Report, 1924.

We have approached our task as businessmen anxious to obtain effective results. We have been concerned with the technical, not the political aspects of the problem presented to us. The committee has had to consider to what extent the balancing of the budget and the stabilization of the currency could be re-established permanently in Germany as she actually is at the present moment, with limitations as to her fiscal rights over part of her area. We should say at the outset we have been unable to find any practical means for insuring permanent stability in the budget of currency under these conditions, and we think it unlikely that such means exist.

The task would be hopeless if the present situation in Germany accurately reflected her potential capacity. Proceeds from Germany's national production could not in that case enable her both to meet her national needs and insure payment of her foreign debts.

But Germany's growing and industrious population, her great technical skill, the wealth of her material resources, the development of her agriculture on progressive lines, her eminence in industrial science, all these factors enable us to be hopeful with regard to her future production.

SOURCE B

From Stresemann's address to the League of Nations, September 1926.

Even before her entry into the League, Germany endeavoured to promote this friendly co-operation. The action which she took and which led to the Pact of Locarno is a proof of this. The German Government is resolved to persevere unswervingly in this line of policy and is glad to see that these ideas, which at first met with lively opposition in Germany, are now becoming more and more deeply rooted in the conscience of the German people. Thus the German Government may well speak for the great majority of the German race when it declares that it will wholeheartedly devote itself to the duties devolving upon the League of Nations.

In many respects the League is the heir and executor of the treaties of 1919. Out of these treaties there have arisen in the past, I may say frankly, many differences between the League and Germany. I hope that our co-operation, within the League will make it easier in future to discuss these questions. Germany desires to co-operate on the basis of mutual confidence with all nations represented in the League.

SOURCE C

From Gilbert Parker, the American financier and the agent for reparation payments, reporting to the Reparations Commission in December 1928.

German business conditions generally appear to have righted themselves on a relatively high level of activity. A year ago, it will be recalled, German business was in the midst of a process of expansion which threatened to result in over-production in certain of the principal industries. As the year 1928 comes to a close, it appears that this over-expansion has been checked before it reached dangerous proportions, and that a condition of relative stability has now been attained. Since 1924, when stabilisation was achieved and the execution of the Experts' Plan began, Germany's reconstruction has at least kept pace with the reconstruction of Europe as a whole, and it has played an essential part in the process of European reconstruction.

3 Using your understanding of the historical context, assess the value of these three sources to an historian studying the growth of the Nazi Party between 1920 and 1930.

EXAM HINT Responses should analyse and evaluate the three sources by considering the content, authorship and appropriate context of each in order to judge the value of each to an historian studying the growth of the Nazi Party between 1920 and 1930.

SOURCE A

From a speech by Adolf Hitler, delivered in a beer cellar in Munich, October 1920.

The Nationalists on the right lack a social sense, the Socialists on the left a nationalist one. If you want to be a nationalist then come down among your people and put away your class pride. You on the left who proclaim your solidarity with the whole world, first show your solidarity with your own people – be German first and foremost. You who are real revolutionaries come over to us and fight with us for our whole nation. You who are still young and still have the fire of enthusiasm in your veins, come over to us. Join our fighting party, which pursues its aims ruthlessly, with every means, even with force! We are not a class party, but the party of honest producers. Our strength does not lie in the communist international but in our own strength, that is to say, our people!

SOURCE B

From Joseph Goebbels, writing an article for the Nazi newspaper *Der Angriff (The Attack)*, entitled 'Why do we want to join the *Reichstag*?', April 1928.

We are an anti-parliamentarian party that for good reasons rejects the Weimar constitution and its republican institutions. We enter the Reichstag to arm ourselves with democracy's weapons. If democracy is foolish enough to give us free railway passes and salaries that is its problem. We do not beg for votes. We demand conviction, devotion, and passion! A vote is only a tool for us as well as for you. We will march into the marble halls of parliament, bringing with us the revolutionary will of the broad masses from which we came, called by fate. We do not want to join this pile of manure. We are coming to shovel it out. We are coming neither as friends or neutrals. We come as enemies! As the wolf attacks the sheep, so we come. You are not amongst your friends any longer! You will not enjoy having us among you! Do not believe that running parliament is our goal.

SOURCE C

From Count Harry Kessler, writing in his diary in September 1930.

A black day for Germany. At about four o'clock I received a telegram with the election results. The Nazis have increased their representation ten fold, they have risen to 107 seats and they have thus become the second largest party in the Reichstag. The impression abroad is bound to be catastrophic and the aftermath both diplomatically and financially, will be dreadful. With some 220 deputies who now radically reject the present German state and seek to overthrow it by a revolutionary means, we are confronted with a political crisis which can only be mastered by the formation of a strong united front of all those forces which support or at least tolerate the Republic. National Socialism is the feverish symptom of the dying German middle classes, but the poison of its illness can only bring misery to Germany and Europe for decades to come.

4 Using your understanding of the historical context, assess the value of these three sources to an historian studying opposition to the Weimar Republic between 1920 and 1932.

EXAM HINT Responses should analyse and evaluate the three sources by considering the content, authorship and appropriate context of each in order to judge the value of each to an historian studying opposition to the Weimar Republic in the years 1920–32.

SOURCE A

From a pamphlet issued by Social Democratic Party (SPD) members of the Weimar government, and circulated to the population of Berlin in response to the Kapp *Putsch*, March 1920.

WORKERS, PARTY COMRADES!
THE MILITARY PUTSCH HAS STARTED.
The Freikorps, fearing the command to dissolve, are trying to remove the Republic and to form a military dictatorship. The achievements of the whole year are to be smashed, your dearly bought freedom to be destroyed. Everything is at stake! The strongest counter measures are required. No factory must work while the military dictatorship of Ludendorff and Co rules. Therefore, down tools! Come out on strike! Deprive the military clique of oxygen! Fight with all means for the Republic! Put all quarrels aside. There is only one way to stop the return of the dictatorship, and that is to paralyse all economic life. No hand must move! General strike all along the line! Down with the counter-revolution!

SOURCE B

From a speech by Adolf Hitler at his trial for treason for his involvement in the Munich *Putsch*, February 1924.

What did we try to achieve when we marched on Munich on 9th November 1923? We wanted to create in Germany the precondition which alone will make it possible for the iron grip of our enemies to be removed from us. We wanted to create order in the state. We wanted to throw out the idlers and restore economic prosperity. We wanted to re-introduce military service, which is the highest honourable duty. And now I ask you: Is what we wanted high treason? I know the verdict which you will pass. However, gentlemen, you will not pronounce judgement upon us. It is the Eternal court of History which will make its pronouncement upon the charge brought against us. That court will judge us as Germans who wanted the best for their people and their fatherland.

SOURCE C

From a letter written by leading German industrialists to President Hindenburg, November 1932.

The outcome of the Reichstag elections of the 6th November has demonstrated that the present cabinet, whose honest intentions no one amongst the German people will doubt, has failed to find sufficient support among the German people for its actual policies. We therefore humbly beg you to consider reconstituting the cabinet in a manner which would guarantee it with the greatest possible popular support. We declare ourselves to be free from any specific party-political interest. However, we recognise in the National Socialist movement, which is sweeping through our people, the beginnings of an era of rebirth for the German economy which can only be achieved by the transfer of responsibility to the leader of the largest nationalist group.

Interpretation questions

1 Historians have made different interpretations about **the Weimar Republic between 1919 and 1923**. Analyse and evaluate the two interpretations and use your understanding of the historical debate to answer the following question:

How valid is the view that the problems of the Weimar Republic in the years from 1919 to 1923 were caused by political instability?

EXAM HINT Responses should focus on the debate about the causes of instability, and consider the interpretations of this issue within the wider context of the problems facing the Weimar Republic in the period.

INTERPRETATION 1

A.J. Nicholls, in this extract from their book *Weimar and the Rise of Hitler* (Macmillan, 1968), provides a traditionalist interpretation.

The most serious problems for the Weimar Republic in the period 1919–1923 were caused by the signing of the Treaty of Versailles with the victorious allies. Just as serious as the Treaty's economic impact was the national demoralisation which the Treaty caused. Two particular issues connected with the Treaty of Versailles continued to poison the political atmosphere for many years. The first was the question of 'war guilt' and the second was the so called 'stab in the back'. The treaty cast a long shadow over the Weimar republic. It became a millstone around the neck of the young republic and wrecked the German democratic process almost from the start.

INTERPRETATION 2

G. Layton, in this extract from their book *Access to History: From Bismarck to Hitler: Germany 1890–1933* (Hodder Education, 1995), provides a revisionist interpretation.

From the start there were underlying problems with the Weimar political system which went a lot deeper than merely criticisms of the new constitutional framework on the signing of the peace treaty. From its days of origin, there was an undercurrent of anti-democratic feeling which meant that the Weimar republic was unwanted and unloved. Despite the relative success of the forces sympathetic to the republic in the Reichstag *elections in January 1919, such problems were rooted in the very nature of the political establishment. This meant that the republic was confronted by the ongoing problem of creating and maintaining government coalitions. In the years 1919–1923 the cumulative effect of these political problems created an atmosphere of ongoing political crisis and instability which reached its height in the year 1923.*

2 Historians have made different interpretations about **the Weimar Republic between 1924 and 1929**. Analyse and evaluate the two interpretations and use your understanding of the historical debate to answer the following question:

How valid is the view that in the years from 1924 to 1929 the Weimar Republic had a period of domestic success?

EXAM HINT Responses should focus on the debate about the success of Weimar in the years 1924–9, and consider the interpretations of this issue within the wider context of the Weimar Republic in the period.

INTERPRETATION 1

Golo Mann, in this extract from their book *The History of Germany Since 1789* (Praeger, 1968), provides a traditionalist interpretation.

Between 1924 and 1929 the Weimar political system functioned normally and the long-term future of the Republic looked rosy. The political violence that had characterised the period 1919–23 subsided. Germany's economic achievements after 1924 were considerable. The income of the nation returned to its pre-war levels. All the worn-out antiquated equipment was replaced. Germany had the most modern merchant fleet and the fastest railways. The workers worked well. The inventors, engineers and technicians were of high calibre. Industrial planning was magnificent and effective. If the Wall Street Crash of October 1929 had not led to a world economic depression, the Weimar Republic would have been able to win the popularity of the German people permanently.

INTERPRETATION 2

Detlev J.K. Peukert, in this extract from their book *The Weimar Republic* (Allen Lane, 1991), provides a revisionist interpretation.

The period 1924–29 provided the illusion of domestic success. These years were only successful by contrast to the periods of crisis which came before and after. The period 1924–29 was marked by a number of smaller crises that still existed. The structural problems created by the Treaty of Versailles and the establishment of the Republic had not been solved. Nor had the problems arising in the years of inflation. Tensions and frustrations were carried over into the period of so-called 'stabilisation'. The problems which arose in the period 1930–33 can be said to have been brewing in the period 1924–29. The electoral decline of the liberal parties between 1924 and 1929 was the decisive event of Weimar because it undermined the pro-Republican centre from within.

3 Historians have made different interpretations about **the rise in support for the Nazi Party between 1924 and 1933**. Analyse and evaluate the two interpretations and use your understanding of the historical debate to answer the following question:

How valid is the view that the main impact of the Depression on Germany was the collapse of democracy within the Weimar Republic in the early 1930s?

> **EXAM HINT** Responses should focus on the debate about the interpretation that the main impact of the Depression was the collapse of democracy within Germany, and consider the interpretations of this issue within the wider context of the impact of the growth of political extremism on the left and right on the Weimar Republic.

INTERPRETATION 1

Stephen J. Lee, in this extract from their book *The European Dictatorships, 1918–1945* (Methuen, 1987), provides a political interpretation.

The Depression dealt its most devastating blow to democracy in Weimar Germany. The coalition fell apart on 27th March 1930 over the question of cutting dole payments. Since the power of the Chancellor depended on the support of the Reichstag and the economic crisis had made collaboration between the political parties more difficult, the initiative now fell to President Hindenburg who had an authoritarian approach to politics. During the stable years he had no option but to play an inactive role in the manoeuvring for power between the various parties. As a result of the Depression however, from 1930 onwards, he was able to fill the vacuum left by the sudden death of consensus politics, as parliamentary democracy virtually disappeared, and Chancellors resorted increasingly to the use of Presidential decrees.

INTERPRETATION 2

E.J. Feuchtwanger, in this extract from their book *Germany 1916–1941* (Sempringham, 1997), provides a Marxist interpretation.

The Wall Street Crash of October 1929 led to unprecedented unemployment for the Weimar Republic. The decline in economic activity and rising unemployment made it increasingly difficult to balance the national budget. As the unemployed ran out of entitlement under the employment insurance scheme, they were given what was called 'crisis subvention'. When that ran out they were given local authority handouts and often they were left with nothing. Hundreds of thousands of people could not maintain the rent for their dwellings and drifted into shanty towns on the edge of the large cities. Others wandered through the countryside, with a few belongings on their back, pushing children in prams, vaguely and vainly looking for work.

4 Historians have made different interpretations about the **collapse of the Weimar Republic between 1929 and 1933**. Analyse and evaluate the two interpretations and use your understanding of the historical debate to answer the following question:

How valid is the view that Hitler was responsible for the rise to power of the Nazis by 1933?

> **EXAM HINT** Responses should focus on the debate about the interpretation that the rise to power of the Nazis was the result of the influence of Hitler, and consider the interpretations of this issue within the wider context of the impact of the policies of the Weimar government and the growing hatred of the terms of the Treaty of Versailles on the rise to power of the Nazis.

INTERPRETATION 1

Richard Overy, in this extract from their article 'Hitler' in the magazine *Modern History Review* (1989), provides a determinist interpretation.

The main reason for the growing strength of the Nazis was Hitler's appeal and the force of his personality. It was his ability to get out into Germany's provincial cities and mobilise people politically who were alienated from the established parties or who had no real experience of the democratic tradition. Hitler was not part of the traditional political classes. Hitler was a man of the people, whose own efforts, as he constantly reminded his listeners, had dragged him from local obscurity to national prominence. He promised to take the problems of his ordinary supporters and give them a national platform.

INTERPRETATION 2

Ian Kershaw, in this extract from their book *Hitler* (Longman, 1991), provides a revisionist interpretation.

There was no inevitability about Hitler's triumph in January 1933. Five years earlier, the Nazi Party had been a fringe irritant in German politics, but no more. External events, the Young Plan to adjust German reparations payments, the Wall Street Crash and Brüning's entirely unnecessary decision to have an election in summer 1930 – put the Nazis on the political map. Though democracy had by that time an unpromising future, a Nazi dictatorship seemed far less likely than some other form of authoritarian dictatorship or even a reversion to a Bismarckian style of government, possibly under a restored monarchy. In bringing Hitler to power, chances and conservative miscalculation played a larger role than any actions of the Nazi leader himself.

CHAPTER 6

Developments in Nazi control of Germany after 1933

Hitler did not have dictatorial powers when he was appointed chancellor in January 1933. However, by the summer of 1934 Germany had become a one-party state under Hitler. The Nazi state is often seen as efficient and well organised, but there were many competing forces which changed over time. Despite this, the regime was able to consolidate its position, be it through propaganda, terror or winning over the hearts and minds of the people.

This chapter will examine how Hitler was able to create a one-party state within a year of coming to power by focusing on the following themes:

- Hitler's consolidation of power 1933–4
- Propaganda
- Indoctrination and terror
- The Nazi political system
- Was Hitler a totalitarian dictator?
- Support for the regime
- Opposition and resistance

KEY DATES

1933	Jan.	Hitler appointed chancellor
	Feb.	*Reichstag* fire
	March	Elections to the *Reichstag*
		Day of Potsdam
		Enabling Act passed
		Creation of Ministry of Popular Enlightenment and Propaganda under Goebbels
	July	Establishment of a one-party state
1934	June	Night of the Long Knives
	Aug.	Death of President Hindenburg
		Office of chancellor and president combined
		Oath of loyalty taken by army
1935	May	Mass arrests by *Gestapo* of socialists and communists
1936	June	Himmler appointed chief of German police

1 Hitler's consolidation of power 1933–4

■ *How did Hitler create a dictatorship?*

When Hitler was appointed chancellor in January 1933 his power appeared to be limited. The Nazis had only three seats in the cabinet and their popular support also appeared to be in decline as they had lost seats in the November 1932 election. It therefore appeared realistic to assume, as Papen and Hindenburg

Chapter 6 Developments in Nazi control of Germany after 1933

had, that Hitler could soon be dispensed with. However, over the next eighteen months Hitler was able to transform his position and establish a powerful one-party dictatorship. More remarkably, it can be argued that this was largely achieved through legal methods.

SOURCE A

Nazi parade celebrating Hitler's appointment as chancellor near the Brandenburg Gate in Berlin during the evening of 30 January 1933.

> **SOURCE QUESTION**
> What image of Nazism is projected in the photograph in Source A?

The *Reichstag* fire

Although the Nazis were still the largest party in the *Reichstag* after the November 1932 elections, they did not have an overall majority. Hitler, therefore, persuaded Hindenburg to call fresh elections within 24 hours of his appointment as chancellor. He believed that these elections would not only increase the Nazi vote, but also his status. The Communist Party was still a major threat, and during the election campaign it was often blamed for the economic conditions within Germany. Hitler also had the advantage that his campaign was backed and partly financed by businesses who feared a growth in communist support.

However, it was the setting on fire of the *Reichstag* on 27 February by a Dutch anarchist, **Marinus van der Lubbe**, in incriminating circumstances, that aided the Nazi Party. Hitler was able to portray the communists as **anti-democratic** through their setting fire to the building that represented democracy. He also claimed that the fire was part of a communist plot to stage a takeover and

> **KEY FIGURE**
>
> **Marinus van der Lubbe (1909–34)**
>
> Dutch by birth and, according to the Nazis, a communist, he was arrested by police in the *Reichstag* after the fire had started. Hitler used this as evidence that the communists were plotting against his government. It was claimed that incendiary devices were found at the homes of many communists, along with plans for targeting public buildings. Despite Nazi claims, van der Lubbe always argued that he acted alone. Since the event there have been suggestions that the Nazis started the fire themselves, particularly as there was direct access from Göring's headquarters to the *Reichstag* building and his *Sturmabteilung* chief claimed to have started the fire.

> **KEY TERM**
>
> **Anti-democratic**
> Opposed to democracy.

[Handwritten note: Believed now that the Nazis created the fire to gain support.]

therefore, repressive measures against the communists were needed. A 'Decree for the Protection of the People and State' was signed by the president using his powers under Article 48 of the constitution the next day, and Hitler was granted emergency powers because of the apparent danger. The decree had far-reaching effects. It suspended constitutional civil rights and gave the secret police the power to hold people indefinitely in protective custody. The decree stated:

SOURCE QUESTION

According to Source B, on what grounds did the government justify its new powers?

> **SOURCE B**
>
> From the Decree of the Reich President on the Protection of the People and the State. Issued on 28 February 1933.
>
> *In virtue of Article 48, paragraph 2 of the German Constitution of the Third Reich, the following is decreed as a defensive measure against communist acts of violence endangering the state:*
>
> - *Sections 114, 115, 117, 118, 123, 124 and 153 of the Constitution of the German Reich are suspended until further notice. Therefore, restrictions on personal liberty, on the right of expression of opinion, including freedom of the press, on the right of assembly and association are permissible beyond the legal limits otherwise prescribed.*
> - *If in any German state the necessary measures for the restoration of public security and order are not taken, the Reich Government may temporarily take over the powers of the supreme authority in such a state in order to restore security.*
>
> *The decree applies from the day of publication, Berlin 28th February 1933.*

This decree would remain in force throughout the period the Third Reich was in power. Although the decree took away many civil and political liberties, it was justified by the Nazis as a response to the communist threat. The Nazis were seen by many to be acting quickly and decisively, in contrast to the old republic. The apparent threat was also used to justify the arrest of large numbers of Nazi opponents, particularly communists, which further limited opposition in the forthcoming election. Regardless of whether there had been an actual plot by the communists, the Nazis exploited the situation and used it for electoral advantage, discrediting the threat from the extreme left.

The fire created an atmosphere of fear and the election took place against a background of terror and intimidation of Nazi opponents by Hitler's private army, the *Sturmabteilung* (SA). Despite this, and a very high turnout of 88 per cent, the Nazis were still unable to secure an overall majority even though they were the largest single party. Their vote increased from 33 per cent to 44 per cent, winning 288 seats (see Table 6.1, left). However, it meant that they needed the Nationalists' support, with their 52 seats, to secure an overall majority. This result limited Hitler's freedom of action, as, in order to change the constitution and increase his power, he needed a two-thirds majority in the *Reichstag*.

Table 6.1 Election results, March 1933

Party	Seats
Nazi	288
Nationalist	52
Social Democrat	120
Communist	81
Centre Party	74
Others	32

The Enabling Act

In order to gain full control over the government and change the constitution, Hitler proposed an Enabling Act to the new *Reichstag*. The proposed Enabling Act would remove the limitations on Hitler's power. The Act would end parliamentary procedure and legislation and give full power to the chancellor and his government for four years. This meant that the dictatorship Hitler desired would be based on legality. The election result meant that Hitler would need either the abstention or support of other parties. However, this was not the only challenge facing him. At a local level, Nazi members were taking the law into their own hands and Hitler found it increasingly difficult to contain what has been called **'a revolution from below'**. This was a major concern for Hitler for two reasons:

- it threatened to destroy his image of acting legally
- it angered the conservative groups and coalition partners who supported him.

Hitler was able to successfully overcome their fears through the carefully orchestrated **Day of Potsdam**, when the *Reichstag* was opened in the presence of Hindenburg, the Kaiser's son and the army's leading generals. Such an act aligned Hitler clearly with the forces of the old, conservative Germany, rather than the radical elements of his party.

The passing of the Enabling Act on 23 March 1933 was an important development as it provided the basis of Hitler's authority in the creation of his dictatorship. The absence of the intimidated communist members of the *Reichstag* meant that Hitler was able to get the two-thirds majority he needed to change the constitution, to end parliamentary democracy and to transfer full powers to himself and his government for four years. Only the Social Democrats voted against the measure, and it was passed by 444 to 94 votes. However, the result was achieved only because of promises made to the Catholic Centre Party that he would respect the rights of the Catholic Church and uphold religious and moral values. *which he didn't do.*

> **KEY TERMS**
>
> **Revolution from below**
> The more radical elements within the Nazi Party wanted local Nazi groups to direct the revolution. This would take control away from the leadership.
>
> **Day of Potsdam**
> Ceremony for the opening of the new *Reichstag* on 21 March 1933 following the *Reichstag* fire.

Hitler was Chancellor. Not Führer until August 2nd 1934 after death of Hindenburg.

> **SOURCE QUESTION**
>
> According to Source C, in what ways did the Enabling Act increase the powers of the government?

SOURCE C

From The Enabling Act, March 1933.

Article 1. In addition to the procedure for the passage of legislation outlined in the Constitution, the Reich cabinet is also authorised to enact Laws.

Article 2. The national laws enacted by the Reich cabinet may deviate from the Constitution provided they do not affect the position of the Reichstag and Reichsrat. The powers of the President remain unaffected.

Article 3. The national laws enacted by the Reich Cabinet shall be prepared by the Chancellor and published in the official gazette. They come into effect, unless otherwise stated, upon the day following their publication.

Hitler had, within a few weeks, dismantled the Weimar constitution and was now able to create a one-party state. The passing of the Enabling Act meant that the intolerance and violence that would characterise the regime could be used as tools to govern.

The creation of the one-party state and *Gleichschaltung* (co-ordination)

The creation of the Nazi state is usually described as *Gleichschaltung*, or co-ordination, and refers to the Nazification of German society and the establishment of the dictatorship in the years 1933–4. It was put into practice at a local level – 'the revolution from below' – by the freedom given to the SA, and at a national level by the Nazi leadership –'the revolution from above'.

The idea was to merge German society with Nazi institutions and associations. This would allow the Nazi Party to control all aspects of social, cultural and educational activity. However, the first concern of the Nazi Party was political. It needed to secure its political supremacy over the federal states, trade unions and other political parties.

Federal states

Hitler's first target was the federal states. Germany had strong regional traditions which were a direct challenge to the Nazi belief in a centralised state. The process had already started with violence and intimidation. The local Nazi Party organisations aimed to dominate the states and there were outbreaks of violence as they attacked rivals. In doing so, they created widespread disorder, which the party leaders, conscious of the need to avoid being seen as revolutionary by the army (see page 102), struggled to control.

However, the situation was resolved in three stages:

- Regional parliaments were dissolved on 31 March 1933 and replaced by Nazi-dominated state governments.
- **Reich governors**, who were usually local party *Gauleiters*, were created.
- In January 1934, regional parliaments were abolished and federal government and governors were subordinated to central government.

As a result of these actions, federal government virtually disappeared.

Trade unions

The trade union movement in Germany had been strong, but its close connection with communism and socialism meant that the Nazis viewed it as a threat. Initially the unions were tricked into believing a working relationship could be established when 1 May (Labour Day) was declared a national holiday, but the next day union premises were occupied, funds seized and leaders were sent to concentration camps. This was followed by the banning of independent unions, which were replaced by the German Labour Front (DAF, see pages 159–60). However, this was more a means of controlling the workers. This, and the

> **KEY TERM**
>
> **Reich governors**
> The representatives of the Nazi government in the states following the abolition of the federalist structure of Germany.

fact that they also lost the right to negotiate wages and working conditions except through the new state organisation, meant that within a year the power of the labour movement was broken.

Political parties

The final area that the Nazi Party tackled was the existence of other political parties. As Nazism was opposed to democracy, it was never likely that it would allow the continued existence of other political parties. The Communist Party had already been banned following the *Reichstag* fire and this was followed by the Social Democrats. On 22 June 1933, the Social Democrats were banned and their assets seized. Most of the remaining major political parties, even the Nationalists, who had been in coalition with the Nazis, agreed to dissolve themselves to avoid simply being abolished. This meant that there was no opposition to the official decree, 'The Law against the Establishment of Parties' on 14 July, which declared that the Nazis were the only legal political party.

It appeared that by the end of 1933 *Gleichschaltung* was complete. However, in practice this was far from the case. The Nazis did have control in some areas but not all. In particular, the Churches (see page 142) still retained their influence, while the army and big businesses were still independent. The civil service and education had also only been partially co-ordinated with the Nazi Party and would be targeted later (see pages 115 and 134–6). Therefore, despite some successes, Nazi control was not yet complete. This was down to four main reasons:

- Hitler did not want to antagonise powerful groups, such as the army.
- He needed the support of big business for rearmament.
- He needed the support of the civil service.
- He needed to maintain support from the middle class, and this was achieved by reassuring them that traditional elements of the state were being maintained.

It was largely the need for support from these groups that resulted in the next major step of turning Germany into a one-party dictatorship. Hitler needed to reassure many of these groups that the Nazi revolution was over. However, he feared that many of the local party activists were getting out of control and that this would lose him support.

The Night of the Long Knives

Hitler's desire to control events and prevent a permanent state of revolution led to conflict with the SA, which wanted to take the process of co-ordination even further. This was a problem for the Nazi leadership as membership of the SA was growing rapidly, as Table 6.2 shows (see right).

Many of the new members were more radical and came from the working class and therefore wanted the party to pursue a more socialist path. Many of them were young and unemployed. They believed that they had helped to win

Table 6.2 SA membership 1931–4

Year	Membership
1931	100,000
1932	291,000
1933	425,000
1934	3,000,000

the battles on the streets and should now be rewarded with greater influence. Such views found support with the leader of the SA, Ernst Röhm (see page 23), who also called for a genuine 'National Socialist Revolution', criticising Hitler's approach in an interview with a local party boss in 1934. 'Adolf is a swine. He will give us all away. He only associates with the reactionaries now. Getting matey with the East Prussian generals. They're his cronies now.' Röhm made clear his determination to continue the Nazi revolution in a speech in June 1933.

> **SOURCE QUESTION**
> How useful is Source D as evidence of the aims of the SA in 1933–4?

> **ONLINE EXTRAS** WWW
> Test your understanding of the value of a source by completing Worksheet 17 at www.hoddereducation.co.uk/accesstohistory/extras

SOURCE D

An extract from a speech by Ernst Röhm, leader of the SA, June 1933.

A tremendous victory has been won, but not absolute victory! The SA and SS will not tolerate the German revolution going to sleep now or being betrayed at the half-way stage by non-combatants. There is a fantasy in the minds of some 'co-ordinated' people, and even some who call themselves National Socialists, that to keep calm is the first duty of a citizen. This is a betrayal of the German revolution. The national 'revolution' has already lasted too long. It is high time the national revolution became the National socialist one. Whether the middle class like it or not, we will continue our struggle.

Röhm also wanted to merge the SA with the army and create a people's militia, of which he would be the commander. This, and Röhm's desire for a further revolution, concerned Hitler, who was worried that Röhm's plans would alienate the army, which viewed the SA as undisciplined and too politicised, and did not want the two merged.

Although the SA, with 3 million members, was larger than the army and had helped to bring Hitler to power, the army was the only organisation that could remove him. Hitler was aware that much of the leadership was suspicious of him, but, most importantly, the army had the military skills that he would need to implement his foreign policy. The SA, on the other hand, could not match the discipline and military expertise of the army.

Reality dictated that Hitler had to support the army, but he was reluctant to fall out with his old comrade and friend, Röhm. He brought Röhm into the cabinet and organised a meeting in February 1934 between the leaders of the SA, *Schutzstaffel* (SS) and the army. However, this did not resolve the tensions as the SA continued to resent the privileged position of the army.

The situation reached crisis point in April 1934. President Hindenburg was dying and Hitler wanted to assume the role of president without an election, avoiding the possibility of a monarchical restoration. In order to achieve this, he would need the support of the army. However, in return for their support, the army commanders desired the elimination of the SA and the possibility of a second revolution. There was much to be gained from this for Hitler as:

- he would win the support of the army leadership
- he would secure his own position

- he would remove an organisation whose behaviour had become embarrassing.

It is impossible to be certain when Hitler made his decision, but it is likely that he reached an agreement with the German generals, Werner von Blomberg and Werner von Fritsch, in April 1934. However, the decision to finally make his move was probably decided in mid-June, when Papen made a speech calling for an end to the violent behaviour of the SA and criticised the policy of co-ordination. This is likely to have convinced Hitler that he needed to satisfy the conservative forces within Germany.

On 30 June 1934, the Night of the Long Knives ended the SA as a military and political force. Röhm and other leading members of the SA were shot by the SS, although the weapons and transport were provided by the army. However, it was not just the SA that was removed. Among the 200 who were killed were the former chancellor, Schleicher, and the leader of the radical socialist wing of the party, Gregor Strasser. Through this, Hitler was able to destroy the left wing of his party and the old conservative right wing of the establishment.

Hitler defended his actions in the *Reichstag* and took full responsibility, claiming that he was defending the state against a plot by Röhm.

The importance of the Night of the Long Knives

The events of 30 June marked an important development in the Nazi state:

- The radical element within the Nazi Party had been defeated and the SA virtually destroyed. The SA would play no further political role in the state, but would be limited to propaganda rallies.
- The army, and, in particular, the generals, were conciliated. They hoped that their role would increase and some generals even proposed that the army take an oath to tie Hitler and the army together. Blomberg's public vote of thanks on 1 July to Hitler for his actions showed just how close they had become. This would be consolidated further when Hindenburg died and the army took a new oath of personal loyalty to Hitler, which replaced the traditional oath of loyalty to the constitution. As historian Ian Kershaw (1998) has argued, 'Far from creating a dependence of Hitler on the army, the oath … marked the symbolic moment where the army chained itself to the Führer.'
- The event saw the emergence of the SS as a potent force. It was no longer in the shadow of the SA.
- Hitler secured his dictatorship. The acceptance of his actions meant that he had been allowed to get away with the murder of his opponents. It was a clear indication of the powers that the new regime now possessed and challenges the view that the regime was a 'legal' dictatorship. Hitler told the *Reichstag*, 'in this hour, I was responsible for the fate of the German nation and thereby the supreme judge'. It was now evident that the Nazi state was not a traditional authoritarian one, but a new personal dictatorship.

> **ONLINE EXTRAS** WWW
>
> Test your understanding of assessing the importance of events by completing Worksheet 18 at **www.hoddereducation.co.uk/accesstohistory/extras**

The death of Hindenburg

The Night of the Long Knives and the oath taken by the German armed forces meant that there remained no opposition to challenge Hitler, so when Hindenburg died aged 86 on 2 August there was no political crisis. Hitler was simply able to merge the role of president with that of chancellor and take the new, official title of Führer or leader. Any challenge to his position or the threat of a further revolution had ended.

Hitler had been able to establish his dictatorship because of a number of reasons:

- The weakness of the opposition: the left wing was destroyed with relative ease, while the right wing had never really supported the Weimar Republic and sympathised with the new regime.
- Legality: the partial use of the law justified Nazi actions and made them more difficult to resist.
- Terror: this also discouraged resistance and those who did oppose were arrested and even killed (see pages 108–10).
- Propaganda: this was used to justify the actions and to portray Hitler as acting to save Germany (see pages 104–8).
- Deception: Hitler misled powerful groups to gain their support or destroy them.

> **ONLINE EXTRAS** WWW
>
> Get to grips with planning an essay by completing Worksheet 19 at **www.hoddereducation.co.uk/accesstohistory/extras**

SUMMARY DIAGRAM

HITLER'S CONSOLIDATION OF POWER 1933–4

How was Hitler able to consolidate power?
- *Reichstag* fire
- March elections
- Enabling Act
- One-party state
- *Gleichschaltung*
- Night of the Long Knives
- Death of Hindenburg

2 Propaganda

■ *How effective was Nazi propaganda?*

The Nazis used a number of methods to maintain power and control. Propaganda and censorship were used to control what people were told and gain their support for the regime. The aim was to create a 'People's Community' or *Volksgemeinschaft*, which glorified the Aryan race and war, while spreading Nazi values. During wartime, it would be used to mobilise people, sustain morale and provide practical advice on air raids, recycling food and 'careless talk' (see page 182).

Responsibility for propaganda was given to Joseph Goebbels, who was made minister of public enlightenment and propaganda. Departments were established to run the radio, press, theatre and film. They all censored non-Nazi culture and media and promoted Nazi ideology. Both Hitler and Goebbels were experts in the use of propaganda and were determined to control all aspects of culture and use it to reinforce their power and Nazi values.

Radio

Goebbels brought broadcasting under Nazi control and created the Reich Radio Company. However, controlling the radio was of little value if people did not have the opportunity to hear the message. This was a particular problem as in 1932 only 25 per cent of Germans owned radios. In order to overcome this the government produced cheap sets – the People's Receiver – so that by the outbreak of the war in 1939, 70 per cent of the population had radios, a medium of mass communication directly under the control of the regime. The fact that radio reached people at home and in remote rural areas, along with the installation of loud speakers in factories, cafés and offices, meant that there was no escaping the Nazi message, particularly as 'radio wardens' co-ordinated listening. However, Goebbels was aware that too much political propaganda bored people; therefore, two-thirds of airtime was given over to popular songs and music. Despite this, a British journalist visiting Berlin in 1934 records the reaction of ordinary Germans to a speech made by Hitler (see Source E below).

SOURCE E

From Philip Gibbs, a British journalist, in 1934.

I remember being in a big Berlin café when it was announced that Hitler was to speak on the radio. The loudspeaker was turned on. Next to me was a group of German businessmen. They went on talking in low voices. At another table was a woman writing a letter. She went on writing. The only man who stood up was a small man with his tie creeping over his collar at the back of his neck. No-one else in the crowded café listened to Adolf Hitler.

Newspapers

Germany had over 4500 daily newspapers in 1933 and it was much harder to bring them under state control. The Nazis implemented various measures to combat this:

- Socialist and communist papers were closed down.
- The Editor's Law of 1933 made newspaper content the responsibility of the editor and he had to satisfy the requirements of the Propaganda Ministry.
- A daily press conference was held at which editors were told what to write.
- News agencies were placed under Nazi control.
- The Nazi publishing house bought up many papers, so that by 1939 it controlled two-thirds of the press.

SOURCE QUESTION

How useful is Source E as evidence of support for the Nazi regime?

ONLINE EXTRAS WWW

Get to grips with analysing the reliability of a source by completing Worksheet 20 at www.hoddereducation.co.uk/accesstohistory/extras

As a result, the press was tightly managed, but this led to a fall in the quality of journalism as writers were limited in what they could write, meaning that newspaper sales fell by ten per cent by 1939.

Drama and music

The Nazis wanted drama and music to uphold Nazi values and they exercised strict control over them. Theatres and plays had to have a licence and were subject to police supervision. They banned experimental plays and music. In music, even some works in the classical tradition were censored while jazz was forbidden as it was seen as '**degenerate**'. Music written by Jewish composers, such as Mendelssohn and Mahler, was banned and Jewish conductors and musicians were dismissed.

> **KEY TERM**
>
> **Degenerate** A term used by the Nazis to describe something of which they did not approve.

Literature, art and architecture

Writers had to be positive about Nazism, with approved themes, such as the early days of Nazism, war and expansion. The Reich Chamber of Literature listed banned books, and libraries and second-hand bookshops were raided for the prohibited books which were then burned at rallies. As a result of this policy some 2500 German writers left the country, including:

- Thomas Mann, a Nobel prize-winning novelist.
- Bertolt Brecht, a modern playwright.
- Erich Maria Remarque, a novelist who had written *All Quiet on the Western Front*, a pacifist book describing the First World War.

In terms of art, modern art was banned and modern paintings were removed from galleries, with only works that portrayed German heroes or the countryside allowed. However, many of the permitted paintings did not reflect the real world but Nazi ideology, particularly as all working artists had to become members of the Reich Culture Chamber. National and local exhibitions were organised, although the subject matter suggested by the title 'Autobahns of Adolf Hitler Through the Eyes of Art' would not suggest that it was the most exciting body of work. Nonetheless, they were often well attended, as many were curious to see the new style or because they wanted to show their support for the regime. How many people were actually exposed to Nazi art is difficult to judge, but historian Hellmut Lehmann-Haupt, in his book *Art Under a Dictatorship* (1954), argues that everyone was continually exposed to some officially sponsored form of art.

Buildings offered a more suitable form of propaganda and were seen by large numbers of people. Much effort was put into designing not just buildings but restructured cities, even at a time when resources were needed for the war effort post-1939. The vast buildings, often in a neoclassical style, served to show the supposed permanence of the Reich. Many of the new public buildings were decorated by sculptures conveying Nazi ideology. In 1934, an order was issued that public buildings should be decorated with sculptures that relayed the Nazi message.

Film

The Nazi regime exercised similar controls over the German film industry. The Reich Film Chamber was established and everyone in the movie industry had to join. The German film industry already had a high reputation and this was further enhanced by the cinematic techniques seen in the documentaries of Leni Riefenstahl, particularly *Olympia*, about the Berlin Olympics of 1936, and *Triumph of the Will*, about the Nuremberg rally of 1934. These films did much to promote nationalism. The Nazis continued to allow the cinema industry to flourish, with Goebbels realising the importance of film as a form of entertainment, and this explains why only 96 of the 1097 feature films produced between 1933 and 1945 were at the request of the Propaganda Ministry. Although there were few political films, the *Weekly Review* contained political information and had to be included in all film programmes.

Meetings and rallies

One of the most effective ways to gain support was through the mass rallies. Although those people who attended were mainly Nazi supporters, the rallies helped to reinforce their commitment to the regime. The impact of the rallies was described by historian Peter Adam in his book *Art of the Third Reich*:

> **INTERPRETATION 1**
>
> From Peter Adam, *Art of the Third Reich*, Abrams Books, 1992.
>
> *The rallies expressed power, order, solemnity. The timing of pauses and the stage management of climaxes were as important as the music and the banners. There was no casual spectator; everyone played a part. Discipline, obedience, self-sacrifice, loyalty, duty – these were the highest virtues. The individual had to enter the mass. Carefully organised, these rallies combined uniforms, mass movements, music, flags and symbols, often at night, created a feeling of wishing to belong to the movement.*

Popular rituals and festivals

The regime also attempted to create a new social ritual through things such as the Heil Hitler greeting, the Nazi salute, the **Horst Wessel anthem** and the wearing of uniforms. The most important aspect in trying to win over the public was festivals; these celebrated key dates in the Nazi year and were often associated with large-scale rallies.

A number of important days in the Nazi calendar were celebrated, when people were expected to hang out flags and parades and speeches were organised. These included:

- 30 January: Day of Seizing Power
- 24 February: Founding of the Nazi Party Day
- 16 March: War Heroes' Day
- 20 April: Hitler's birthday

KEY TERM

Horst Wessel anthem
This was a song written by a Nazi stormtrooper who was later killed in a street battle with communists. It became a Nazi marching song.

- Second Sunday in July: German Culture Day
- September: Reich Party Day
- 9 November: anniversary of the Munich *Putsch*.

The success of Nazi propaganda is very difficult to assess. Historians have previously assumed that Nazi propaganda was very effective, but recent work based on local studies has shown that the degree of success varied. It is particularly difficult to find out about people's attitudes towards the Nazi regime. Where evidence is available, it has shown that opinions varied according to the period, region, occupation and age. Some have argued that propaganda did help win the Nazis support under the Weimar Republic; it helped to create the **Hitler myth**, as seen in Robert Edwin Herzstein's 1978 book on propaganda *The War that Hitler Won*. However, Tim Mason argues that it was less successful in winning over the working classes. Meanwhile, David Welch, in his book on Nazi propaganda, *Third Reich, Politics and Propaganda* (1993), argues that it helped to strengthen overall support for Hitler, reinforcing enthusiasm for a strong leader.

KEY TERMS

Hitler myth Historian Ian Kershaw (1987) has described the 'Hitler myth'. While there were complaints about the party, local officials and policies, there was a widespread belief that Hitler was not to blame and that, as the embodiment of Germany, he stood above such matters. If only he knew what was going on, then he would step in to help his beloved people. The devotion to the leader only waned in the latter stages of the war and to that extent showed the power of the leader-orientated propaganda that portrayed him as a super-man who could solve all of Germany's problems.

Gestapo The secret state police, which played an important role in surveillance and repression.

Waffen-SS Racially 'pure' and fanatical units of the SS which were involved in the advances into eastern Europe.

SD The intelligence branch of the SS.

RSHA Reich Security Office, which brought together all police and security organisations.

New Order Used by the Nazis to describe the economic, political and racial integration of Europe under the Reich.

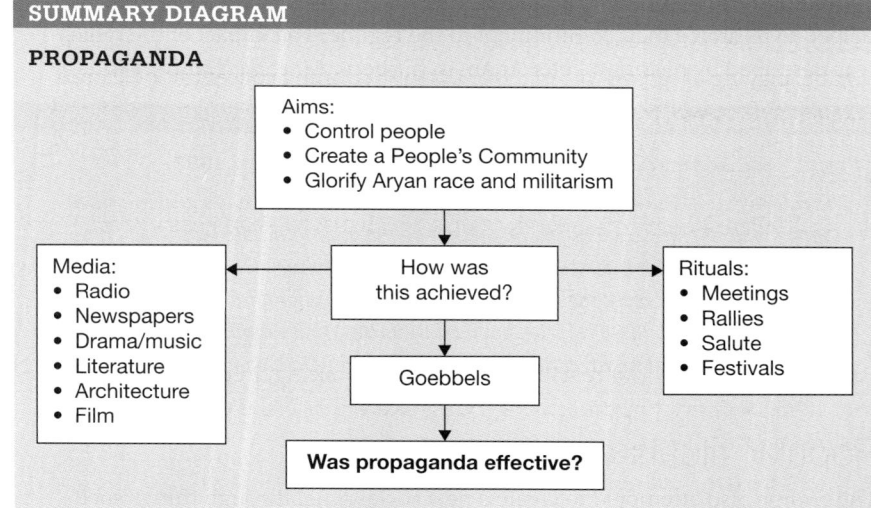

3 Indoctrination and terror

- *How important were indoctrination and terror in controlling the people?*

In order for the Nazi regime to survive, it was important that it was able to ensure obedience and eliminate its enemies. This was achieved through terror, using the courts to sentence enemies, and the SS and **Gestapo** to terrorise and intimidate people.

The courts

The courts played a significant role in enabling the regime to remove its opponents while giving the semblance of legality to Nazi actions. The new courts were under Nazi control and were therefore easily influenced to do the regime's bidding, with the People's Court trying enemies of the state. Action was also taken to extend Nazi control and influence in the pre-existing courts. Judges were instructed to issue harsher sentences for crimes as it was hoped that this would discourage others from criminal activity. New laws regarding political offences were enacted. Judges who did not carry out Nazi wishes were removed and, from 1939, judges had to study Nazi beliefs and senior court officials were replaced by Nazis. As a result, it became increasingly difficult for opponents of the regime to receive a fair trial.

The SS

The SS had been established as an elite bodyguard for Hitler in 1925. It had originally been part of the SA, but it became independent and, much more importantly, was eventually a 'state within a state', responsible only to Hitler.

The SS became a key part of the police state and was crucial in upholding the regime, playing a leading role in terror through running concentration camps and using its power of arrest and detention to hold people in 'protective custody', even after they had served official sentences imposed by the courts.

The SS included:

- the **Waffen-SS**, an armed military unit which played an increasing role in the Second World War
- the SS-Totenkopfverbande (Death's Head Units) which ran the concentration camps.

The role of the SS was far reaching and included policing, intelligence gathering, controlling security, imposing ideology, inculcating race and economic theories, and involvement in some military issues.

- In 1929, **Heinrich Himmler** became head of the SS and, in 1931, he created the **SD** – the secret intelligence wing of the SS.
- In 1934, Himmler took control of the police, including the *Gestapo* in Prussia.
- In 1935, the SS became an elite force that only Aryans could join.
- In 1936, all police and *Gestapo* powers were placed under Himmler's control.
- In 1939, all party and state police organisations were amalgamated into the **RSHA**. However, in practice, the SS was co-ordinated by Himmler's deputy, **Reinhard Heydrich**.

Himmler turned the SS into the most loyal and brutal of all the regime's agencies. However, although the basis for the SS's power had been laid, it was really due to the war and conquest of land in 1939 and the creation of the **New Order** that the Nazis imposed on occupied Europe, which meant that its power expanded and developed.

KEY FIGURES

Heinrich Himmler (1900–45)

Although involved in the Munich *Putsch*, Himmler did not join the Nazi Party until 1926, and in 1929 became head of the SS. In 1943, he was appointed Reich minister of the interior and, in 1944, commander of the reserve army and then commander in chief of the Rhine army group. In 1945, he attempted to end the war through neutral contacts in Sweden, which led to Hitler ordering his arrest, but he was captured by British troops. He killed himself before he could be tried at Nuremberg.

Reinhard Heydrich (1904–42)

Heydrich was made Himmler's deputy in 1933. He organised the deportation of Jewish people to occupied Poland and was responsible for briefing the *Einsatzgruppen* who, following the invasion of the Soviet Union in 1941, hunted down communists and Jewish people in the areas the Nazis occupied. He was assassinated by Czech resistance fighters in 1942.

The *Gestapo*

The *Gestapo* were the secret state police with a reputation for being the all-seeing and all-knowing element of the police state. This view was certainly put forward by the *Gestapo* agents themselves in order to encourage people to conform, believing that if they did not, they would be caught. The image of an organisation that would find, arrest and send opponents to concentration camps extensively prevailed at the time. However, the *Gestapo*'s actual effectiveness has to be questioned. They were only a small organisation with between 20,000 and 40,000 agents – large cities had about 4–50 agents. Many of these were no more than office workers who relied on informers or **block wardens**, of whom there were probably some 2 million nationally, for information, much of which was little more than gossip and brought few rewards for the regime. Wardens were responsible for 50 houses or apartments and ensured, for example, that Nazi flags were displayed and rallies were attended.

Given this numerical weakness, it appears unlikely that the *Gestapo* were able to impose a regime of terror, even if fear acted as a powerful deterrent. However, a study of the Rhineland has suggested that agents focused on specific enemies, such as socialists and the Jewish community, with the majority of the population accepting this persecution in return for being left alone.

Concentration camps

Concentration camps were used to question and torture, to re-educate and inflict hard labour on so-called enemies of the state. Initially, they were used in campaigns against political opponents, especially communists, trade unionists and socialists. However, several were actually closed as they were offensive to many Germans, in particular nationalists, who Hitler needed to convince that the Nazi revolution had finished. By the time Himmler took over responsibility for all concentration camps in 1934, they held only 3000 inmates.

From 1936 until the outbreak of the war, the camps housed those who did not fit into the Nazi ideal, such as **asocial people**, beggars, Romani people (sometimes called Gypsies), and even the long-term unemployed, who were considered 'workshy'. After 1942, prisoners and foreign workers were transferred to the camps as a source of forced labour and subsequently some other camps became extermination camps for Jewish people. It was during the war that the numbers within these camps grew dramatically (see Table 6.3, left).

Terror did a great deal to consolidate Hitler's power. The SS and *Gestapo* did much to break any remaining political opposition in the early years of the regime. They then moved on to deal with 'enemies' of the People's Community. Although there were few *Gestapo* agents and only six concentration camps in 1939, they acted as a warning to people because of their reputation.

> **KEY TERMS**
>
> **Block warden** A Nazi official who provided information on people in his or her neighbourhood.
>
> **Asocial people** Those who showed behaviour that was deemed unacceptable.

Table 6.3 Estimated numbers in German concentration camps 1939–45

Year	Number
September 1939	25,000
December 1942	88,000
January 1945	714,211

SUMMARY DIAGRAM
INDOCTRINATION AND TERROR

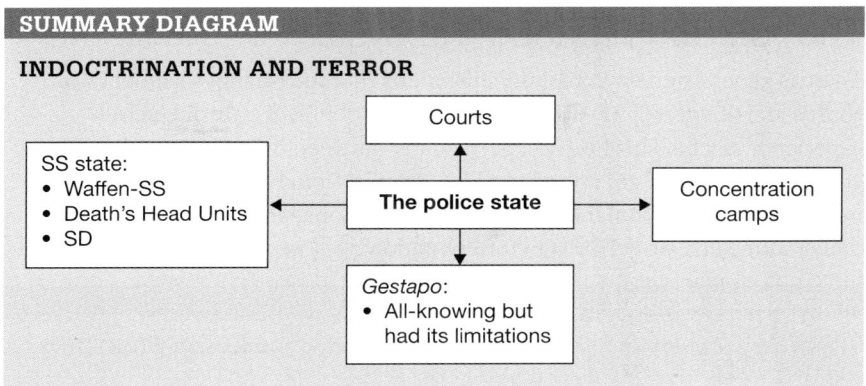

4 The Nazi political system

▪ *How were decisions taken in Nazi Germany?*

The image of the Führer, certainly from Nazi propaganda, was of an undisputed and all-powerful leader.

SOURCE F

From Nazi political theorist, E. Huber, *Verfassungsrecht des Grossdeutschen Reiches* (*Constitutional Law of the Greater German Reich*), Hanseatische Verlagsanstalt, 1939.

We must not speak of 'state power' but of 'Führer power'. For it is not the state as an impersonal entity which is the source of political power, but rather political power is given to the Führer as the executor of the nation's common will. 'Führer power' is comprehensive and total.

SOURCE QUESTION

Using the information in this section, how far do you agree with the view expressed in Source F?

Germany was a one-party state, led by Hitler. With the death of Hindenburg, Hitler had combined the offices of president and chancellor and was also head of the armed forces. Although Hitler gave the impression of being a charismatic and dynamic leader, this image has been questioned by some historians who have argued that he was actually quite lazy, leaving subordinates to do most of the work. Others have contended that there were only a few issues, such as architecture or foreign policy, that really interested Hitler. Therefore, although the image that was presented by the Nazi Party was of an all-powerful dictator, Hitler did not co-ordinate the government, which in practice was rather confused, with decisions often based on informal conversations rather than a clear plan. Despite the destruction of opponents there were still rival power structures that overlapped and only added to the confusion. There was rivalry within and between the various factions of the Nazi Party and state, such as the ministries, civil service and the SS. Some historians have claimed that Hitler did this deliberately to encourage competition between individuals and departments, thus preventing opposition to him from forming.

The role of Hitler and the system of government

There is general agreement among historians that the Nazi government was confused. Hitler certainly did not help the situation. Not only did he lack experience, but also his lifestyle, particularly his sleeping pattern (which was to go to bed late and to get up late) and his absence from Berlin for long periods, made effective government difficult. Hitler's personal assistant describes his daily routine and work habits in Interpretation 2 below.

> **INTERPRETATION 2**
>
> From Fritz Wiedemann, *The Man Who Wanted to Command*, Blick + Bild Verlag, 1964.
>
> *Hitler normally appeared before lunch. He disliked the study of documents. I have sometimes secured decisions from him without his ever asking to see the relevant files. He took the view that many things sorted themselves out on their own if one did not interfere. He let people tell him the things he wanted to hear, everything else he rejected. One still sometimes hears the view that Hitler would have done the right thing if people surrounding him had not kept him wrongly informed.*

Hitler wanted to give the impression of being all-powerful and this meant that many were frightened to make decisions without his approval. It was also seemingly impossible for an individual to control all areas of government, but Hitler also failed to co-ordinate it. As there was no clear and established system for cabinet government in the Third Reich, it meant that government and law emerged in a very haphazard form.

> **INTERPRETATION 3**
>
> From Carl Schmitt, a constitutional lawyer, and Ernst von Weizsäcker, diplomat, quoted in Jeremy Noakes and Geoffrey Pridham, editors, *Nazism 1919–1945, Volume 2: State, Economy and Society 1933–39*, Exeter University Press, 1984, p. 197.
>
> *Ministerial skill consisted in making the most of a favourable hour or minute when Hitler made a decision, this often taking the form of a remark thrown out casually, which then went its way as an 'order of the Führer'.*

Hitler played a limited role in day-to-day government. His absences, lifestyle, unwillingness to make decisions and lack of contact with ministers meant that they had to try and determine his actual wishes. This process was known as **'working towards the Führer'**, which resulted in further contradictions.

> **SOURCE G**
>
> From a speech written by Werner Willikens, state secretary in the Food Ministry, 1934.
>
> *The Führer can hardly dictate from above everything which he intends to achieve. Everyone with a part in the new Germany has worked best when he has, so to speak, worked towards the Führer. It is the duty of everybody to try to work towards*

KEY TERM

Working towards the Führer A situation in which Hitler's followers carried out what they presumed to be his intentions. In this way, others took responsibility for trying to determine what the Führer wanted.

SOURCE QUESTION

How useful is Source G as evidence of Hitler's style of government?

ONLINE EXTRAS WWW

Test your understanding of the value of a source by completing Worksheet 21 at www.hoddereducation.co.uk/accesstohistory/extras

the Führer along the lines he would wish. Those who make mistakes will notice it soon enough. But anyone who really works towards the Führer along the Führer's lines and towards his goal will certainly one day have the finest reward in the confirmation of their work as law.

The haphazard state of the government was made worse by Hitler's dislike of paperwork and committee meetings and the decline in the role of the cabinet, which met 72 times in 1933 but only four in 1936. This approach invited, as the historian Ian Kershaw has argued, initiatives from below provided they were broadly in line with Hitler's actual goals. Such an approach led to the radicalisation of policy, seen most clearly in the policy of terror, **genocide** and foreign policy.

> **KEY TERM**
>
> **Genocide**
> The extermination of a whole race.

Hitler's relationship with the German people

It was his relationship with the German people that was the basis of Hitler's power. He claimed that he alone knew what *they* wanted and could fulfil their needs; his will was absolute because it was the will of the people. This meant that his power was not simply based on his position within government, but on his mission. Much of this belief and acceptance was the result of the weak Weimar government and humiliations that had preceded him. The German people wanted a messiah and in Hitler they believed that they had found one. The Nazi Party had been built on the principle of *Führerprinzip*, which was now applied to all of Germany. Hitler's successful policies and propaganda helped to create a charismatic leadership which was sustained by the Hitler myth. This image of his power has been examined in detail by Ian Kershaw in *The Hitler Myth* (2001), where he explains the support gained as a result of the myth and its impact (see Interpretation 4, below).

> **INTERPRETATION 4**
>
> From Ian Kershaw, *The Hitler Myth: Image and Reality in the Third Reich*, Oxford University Press, 2001, pp. 1 and 171.
>
> *Although the extremes of the personality cult had probably gripped only a minority of the population ... elements of the personality cult had attained far wider resonance and ... affected the vast majority of the population ... Hitler stood for at least some things they admired, and for many had become the symbol and embodiment of the national revival which the Third Reich had in many respects been perceived to accomplish.*
>
> *The adulation of Hitler by millions of Germans who might otherwise have been only marginally committed to Nazism meant that the person of the Führer, as the focal point of basic consensus, formed a crucial integratory force in the Nazi system of rule.*
>
> *Most important of all, Hitler's huge platform of popularity made his own power position ever more unassailable, providing the foundation for the selective radicalisation process in the Third Reich by which his personal ideological obsessions became translated into attainable reality.*

Administration and the traditional power structures

Although Germany was, at least in theory, a powerful centralised state during Nazi rule, this was not always true in practice. There were limits to Nazi power, as established institutions remained, and there were divisions within the actual party itself.

When Hitler took power, he kept most of the existing structures of the republic, even if some became unimportant. Similarly, most officials from the Second Reich who had stayed in power under Weimar were happy to continue to work for the new regime.

The bureaucracy of the state was already established and had effective and experienced staff. The old institutions were, therefore, not destroyed and the civil servants who ran these bodies, being often conservative in outlook, were happy to remain in post. The same was true of the judiciary. However, this situation created conflict, overlap and confusion within party organisations. This was particularly the case with the SS, which was strictly a party organisation but in practice had police powers and ran alongside state organisations. Similarly, the Hitler Youth was a party organisation but took on some functions of the state, with membership being made compulsory from 1939.

The *Reichstag*

The Enabling Act had given legislative powers to Hitler and the *Reichstag* would pass only seven more laws. The Enabling Act was renewed every four years, with the *Reichstag* itself seldom meeting and, when it did meet, it was usually to applaud the speeches of Nazi leaders.

The cabinet

The cabinet remained, but as with the *Reichstag* it largely lost its role. Hitler did not view it as important since decisions were increasingly made on an individual basis, often depending on who had access to the Führer. Laws were issued through Hitler rather than the cabinet, having been drawn up by the Reich Chancellery.

The Reich Chancellery

This was the central administrative body as laws and decrees were drawn up by its officials. Its role was to co-ordinate government, but it found this increasingly difficult because of the growing number of institutions. Government ministries, such as economics, found themselves under pressure from Nazi institutions with the Four Year Plan (see page 156).

Civil service

Most civil servants who had worked for the republic continued in their jobs, with only five per cent removed under the Law for the Restoration of the Civil Service in 1933. It was further Nazified as more Nazis took up jobs in the civil service and other civil servants thought it best to join the party. However, by the late 1930s it was less important as other agencies had been established which bypassed the ministries.

Local government

This was taken over by centrally appointed officials, and state governments became the agents of central government with real power in the hands of the Reich governor.

The judiciary

With the establishment of new courts, such as the special courts or the People's Courts, which allowed the Nazis to circumvent the established system, the judiciary faced interference. Most importantly, the SS–police system was arbitrary and acted as if it was above the law. Therefore, although the judiciary continued to function, its role was limited.

The role of the Nazi Party

The Nazi Party itself was not designed to govern but to attract support and, as Table 6.4 shows (see right), this was achieved.

Once in power, the party needed to find a new role. Although it was based on the principles of hierarchy and *Führerprinzip*, this did not lead to effective government. It was the *Gauleiters* who were dominant in the regions and their main concern was to preserve their interests and, therefore, they often resisted both the state and party institutions. However, after 1938, there were attempts to increase party influence as the deputy Führer, **Rudolf Hess**, insisted that all civil servants had to be party members. Supervision of party members was also increased and **Martin Bormann** created the Department for Internal Party Affairs to discipline the party structure and the Department for Affairs of State, which aimed to secure party supremacy over the state.

The conflict and overlap between the state and party created confusion as their relationship was never clarified. As a result, government was not the well-ordered system that Nazi propaganda portrayed.

By 1939, the party had strengthened its position. However, it always had to compete with established institutions and divisions within the party. The influence of the *Gauleiters* further weakened its position. Moreover, some of the party members who gained power abused it and many Germans resented them, suggesting that while Hitler remained popular, the Nazi Party was not.

Table 6.4 Growth in party membership

Year	Membership
1933	850,000
1935	2,500,000
1943	6,500,000

KEY FIGURES

Rudolf Hess (1894–1987)

Hess was an early member of the party, secretary to Hitler and his deputy from 1933 to 1941. During this period, Hess was completely loyal and, with Bormann, helped to develop the party bureaucracy. However, he betrayed Hitler in 1941 and flew to Scotland on his own initiative to try and negotiate peace; he was arrested and jailed. At the Nuremberg trials he was sentenced to life in prison.

Martin Bormann (1900–45)

Bormann was *Gauleiter* in Thuringia and chief of staff to Hess. He became head of the party chancellery in 1941 and Hitler's secretary in 1943.

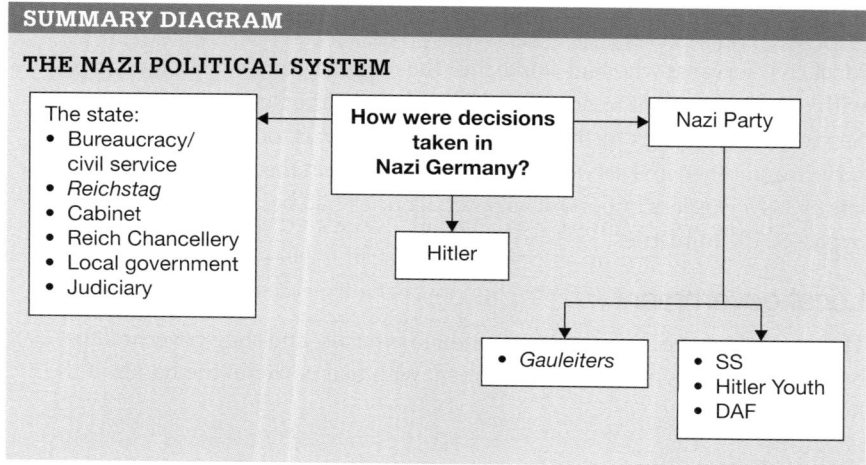

SUMMARY DIAGRAM

THE NAZI POLITICAL SYSTEM

5 Was Hitler a totalitarian dictator?

■ *How powerful was Hitler?*

By August 1934, Hitler had consolidated his position and begun to construct a totalitarian regime. Traditional interpretations have viewed Hitler as a strong leader, alongside the likes of Joseph Stalin in the USSR, who made all the decisions which were then implemented by disciplined subordinates. However, since the 1960s, more detailed studies have been made of the operation of the Nazi system of government and these have challenged the traditional view. They led to the Nazi regime's being viewed as having a **feudal structure**, with Hitler as a weak dictator who was scarcely involved in government directives, allowing others to make decisions as he was unwilling to make them. More recent work, particularly by Ian Kershaw, puts forward a more complex picture, arguing that elements of both views are correct. Kershaw considers that Hitler was the key activator, with policy reflecting his vision for Germany. However, Kershaw also argues that Hitler did not initiate specific policies, even if he legitimised them. This contention suggests that his subordinates worked along the lines they believed he would have wished and that nothing would have been done without his central ideas. Hitler was, therefore, crucial, but as there was a set of central ideas, he did not need to send out constant directives. The lack of opposition meant that when he did intervene he was unchallenged.

In spite of a lack of opposition, the regime did not have total control. The regime was, at least at the start of the period, heavily dependent on support from the army and industrial elites, meaning that the Nazis did not attempt to dominate them. This was clearly seen in the Night of the Long Knives in 1934, when the

> **KEY TERM**
>
> **Feudal structure** This term has been used to describe the dominance of Nazi leaders who were at the head of agencies. These leaders owed ultimate loyalty to Hitler, but that did not stop them building up their own power. It also led to quarrels between them, which Hitler viewed as a good thing as it diluted any threat to him.

SA was purged to satisfy the army and more conservative elements in Germany (see pages 101–3).

It could be argued that in the years 1936–8 the situation changed. Hitler's position became stronger because of the growing power of the SS, which lessened his need to compromise. Chapter 8 will consider how the Four Year Plan in 1936 reduced the power of the industrial elite (see page 156). The position of the army was also weakened in 1938 with the removal of some generals after the criticism of foreign policy by Blomberg and Fritsch. Therefore, by 1938 the influence of potential opponents had been reduced. This would continue in the war years as the SS gained even more power, leading some historians to speak of the emergence of the SS state.

Propaganda also helped to create the impression that Hitler was all-powerful, but, as pages 112–13 have shown, there was a lack of planning and direction from the Führer. This created tensions and rivalry within the government, with leading Nazis often in conflict with each other in order to protect their own empires. There were also personality clashes between figures such as Göring and Goebbels.

However, despite all these clashes and weaknesses, the importance of Hitler should not be ignored. He had created the party and the major developments did follow his wishes. The regime was built on the principle of authoritarian leadership. It was, after all, Hitler's ideology that created the most distinctive features of the regime:

- in foreign policy, it was his drive for German expansion and dominance
- in social policy he wanted to create a racially pure state
- politically he wanted a one-party state.

Conclusion: where did power reside in the Third Reich?

Historians have questioned the efficiency of the state, undermining the traditional image of an effective, totalitarian state. The machinery of government was a raft of overlapping bodies and institutions, leading historians to use the terms **polycratic**, feudal and chaotic to describe it.

Kershaw has tried to explain the situation in his book *The Nazi Dictatorship*, first published in 1985 (see Interpretation 5, below):

> **KEY TERM**
>
> **Polycratic** Used to describe the many different bodies in the state. Often, Nazi institutions overlapped with existing ministries and Hitler even set up more to deal with problems that arose.

INTERPRETATION 5

From Ian Kershaw, *The Nazi Dictatorship: Problems and Perspectives of Interpretation*, Bloomsbury Revelations, 2015, pp. 88 and 98–9.

The dissolution of the government into a multiplicity of competing and non-coordinated ministries, party offices, and hybrid agencies all claiming to interpret the Führer's will. Hand in hand with this development went the growing autonomy of the Führer-authority itself, detaching itself and isolating from any framework of corporate government and correspondingly subject to increasing delusions of grandeur and diminishing sense of reality.

The overall structure of government was reduced to a shambles of constantly shifting power-bases or warring factions.

Evidence suggests that the regime was polycratic rather than totalitarian, but this has resulted in historians asking why the structure was so chaotic. Further debate has ensued among historians between the intentionalist and structuralist groups. According to the intentionalist argument, individuals played a key role in shaping and explaining events as they had the power and influence to bring about their aims. On the other hand, structuralists argue that changes came about because of broader developments, such as the economic or political structure of society.

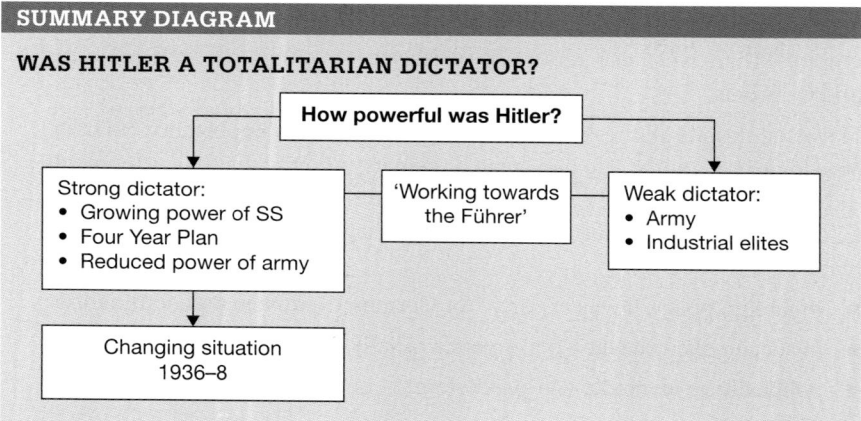

6 Support for the regime

■ *Why was there support for the Nazi regime?*

Not only is it difficult to ascertain the amount of support for the regime, but historians also offer a number of different explanations as to why the Nazis were able to maintain themselves in power from 1933 to 1945. The Nazis won considerable endorsement in elections in 1932 and 1933, some of the backing being gained through intimidation, but other support being achieved through the benefits they offered to ordinary Germans. In particular, they promised many of the unemployed jobs (see page 58) and historian Hans Rothfels, in *The German Opposition to Hitler* (1961), argues that many supported Hitler out of the 'necessity of economic existence which since inflation had been reduced to bare subsistence' and that the Nazis were able to exploit the economic situation through propaganda. That alone was enough to secure their support, while others backed the regime because they saw it as strong and a restoration of national pride after the humiliation of the Weimar Republic. A study of Northeim, a small country town in northern Germany, by W.S. Allen in the 1960s, where he interviewed many who had lived there in the 1920s and 1930s, supports this interpretation. A Northeim resident commented that, 'those who joined did so because they were for social justice, or against unemployment'. Local studies have also shown that very few people joined the party because of their anti-Semitic policies (see page 64).

However, other historians, such as Ian Kershaw in *The Hitler Myth: Image and Reality in the Third Reich* (1994), suggest that Hitler's leadership was crucial in sustaining support, arguing that 'The Hitler myth secured the loyalty to the regime of even those who opposed the Nazi movement itself. Millions of ordinary Germans believed that the Führer would certainly right all the wrongs in Nazi Germany.' Many accounts have stressed the role of terror in limiting opposition, but Eric Johnson, in *Nazi Terror: Gestapo, Jews and Ordinary Germans* (1999), states that 'most Germans suffered not at all, from terror'. Even if they did not suffer from terror, it is possible to suggest, as Ralph Flenly does in *Modern German History* (1991), that 'the long tradition of obedience to authority and the retarded development of political and civil freedom undoubtedly played their part. So too did the divided state of the political parties under Weimar.' The wide-ranging explanations for support for the regime suggest that no one reason explains why the regime was able to consolidate its position, and there remains considerable debate as to the extent of popular backing and why so many were willing to conform, although regional studies suggest that it was a balance between repression and genuinely popular support.

The horrors of the regime, particularly during the Second World War, make it more difficult to understand why people continued to back the regime or saw the benefits of it, but it is the benefits that stand out in personal accounts from the period, as shown in Interpretation 6 below.

INTERPRETATION 6

From Laurence Rees, *The Nazis: A Warning from History*, The New Press, 1997.

Neither a study of the documents nor the opinions of academics enabled me to understand how it was possible before World War II, to actually like living in Nazi Germany. But after listening to witness after witness, not hardline committed Nazis, tell us how positive their experiences had been, a glimmer of understanding emerged. If you have lived through times of chaos and humiliation, you welcome order and security. If the price of that is 'a little evil', then you put up with it.

This view is further supported by George Clare, a Holocaust survivor, who stated in a television programme in 1989 that 'With all the successes Hitler had, Germany was actually a wonderful place to be alive, unless you were Jewish, you had strong political convictions either as a socialist or a communist, or you believed in individuality and the freedom of the individual; but that is never the majority of any people.'

SUMMARY DIAGRAM
SUPPORT FOR THE REGIME

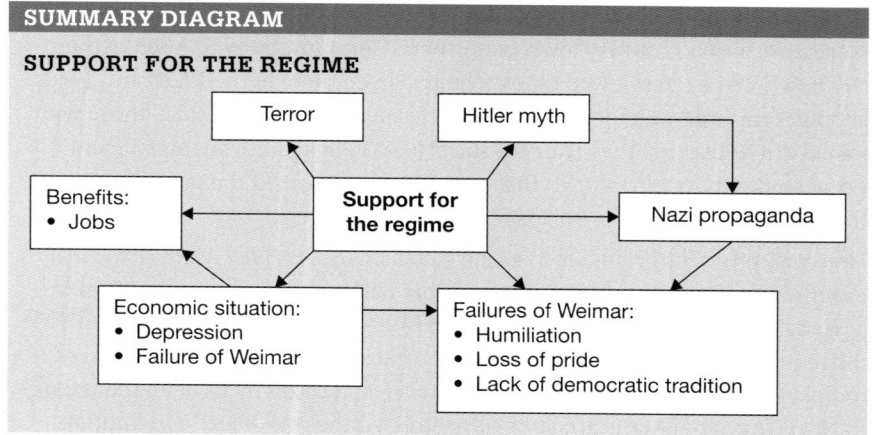

7 Opposition and resistance

■ *Why was there so little opposition to the Nazi regime?*

The fear and terror created by the SS (see page 109) did much to limit opposition to the Nazis. However, despite the dangers, there were those who were willing to resist the regime. Some of the opposition was little more than private grumbling to friends or family, or simply refusing to greet someone with 'Heil Hitler'. There were others who became involved in the underground resistance or actively opposed the regime and then, particularly as defeat in the war became almost inevitable, attempted to overthrow it.

Opposition to Hitler

It would be difficult to argue that there was significant opposition to Hitler and the Nazi regime since most of the population appeared to support it, even in the final weeks of the war. There were a number of reasons why opposition was limited, most of which are developed in other sections of this book:

- Terror (see pages 108–11). Despite the limitations to terror, many people were frightened by the prospect of the *Gestapo* and concentration camps and, therefore, chose to conform.
- The economic miracle (see pages 149–53). The Nazis provided most people with jobs and, therefore, many were prepared to accept Nazi measures and unpopular policies.
- The Nazis abandoned or hid unpopular policies. After the criticism that followed *Kristallnacht* (see pages 129–30) and the euthanasia campaign (see page 133), the policies were either suspended or carried out in secret.
- Opposition was divided (see Table 6.5, pages 121–2).

The methods adopted by these groups and the lack of co-ordinated planning and action resulted in individual acts of resistance rather than the significant opposition needed to topple the regime. Hitler's success in 1934 with the Night of the Long Knives showed that he could quite literally get away with murder and still maintain support. The regime's successful foreign policies and its achievement in reducing unemployment also made it difficult for opponents to gain support. It took the pressure of military defeat before there was any substantial or co-ordinated attempt at resistance.

Table 6.5 Groups who opposed the Nazi regime and their reasons and effectiveness

Group	Aims and actions	How effective?
Communists	They had most of their support in the industrial areas of large cities. They produced pamphlets attacking the Nazis. Most important was the Red Orchestra, a spy network that sent information to the Soviet Union	Their impact was limited as the leadership had been arrested after the *Reichstag* fire. Pamphlets had little impact and many communists were more concerned with simply avoiding arrest. The *Gestapo* infiltrated their network with informers, making it difficult for them to operate
Social Democrats	They also had support among the working class, and like the communists, had been banned as a political party but retained some underground activity. They produced pamphlets attacking the regime, but their leaders were arrested. There was an underground organisation run by the exiled party from Prague which gathered information and spread discontent	Their impact was limited as, like the communists, much of the leadership had been arrested and the party banned. They did not cooperate with the communists and this weakened left-wing opposition. Many were simply concerned with self-preservation
Trade unionists	They had support among the working class and factory workers. However, they had been weakened by arrests in 1933–4. Despite the arrests, there were strikes in 1935–6 with a working-class identity allowing opposition to survive	Industrial action was not effective and they had been weakened following arrests in 1933–4 and the establishment of the German Labour Front to replace independent unions
Churches	There were criticisms of some Nazi policies from the pulpits of both Protestant and Catholic Churches (see page 143). In 1941, the Bishop of Münster, **Clemens von Galen**, condemned **euthanasia**	Most were pragmatic in their response in order to preserve religious practices. Although Galen's attack on euthanasia did result in a temporary suspension, Churches did not provide effective opposition as many lower level clergy who did speak out against the regime were sent to camps

continued

KEY FIGURE

Clemens von Galen (1878–1946)

Galen was Bishop of Münster from 1933. He was a conservative nationalist and a strong anti-communist, but had doubts about Nazi policies. In 1941, he gave three sermons attacking euthanasia. His attacks were so powerful that the regime did not arrest him and the programme was stopped.

KEY TERM

Euthanasia Nazi programme of killing those too ill, old or handicapped to work, known to the party as 'useless mouths'.

Group	Aims and actions	How effective?
Youth	There were some who did not enjoy the activities of the Hitler Youth or resented the loss of their freedom. A number of groups were established, largely during the war, which included the Swing Youth, Edelweiss Pirates, Roving Dudes and the Navajos. They often just behaved in an anti-social manner, but this mostly just involved playing dance and jazz music. However, they disliked the military activities of the Hitler Youth and there were some attacks on its members	The actual opposition was limited. There were some attacks on the members of the Hitler Youth and *Gestapo* offices, but little of significance. Many simply wanted to listen to music and disliked the military emphasis of the Hitler Youth
Students	The White Rose, a student group in Munich, issued pamphlets condemning the values of the Nazi regime	They had minimal impact and the leaders of the White Rose were arrested, tortured and beheaded
Conservatives	There was some opposition from those who had previously been members of the civil service in the Weimar period and disliked the regime's more radical policies. The Kreisau Circle included officers, aristocrats, academics and churchmen. They drew up plans for post-Nazi Germany	There were pacifists within the group who were opposed to a coup to overthrow the regime. Although conservatives shared information, they took little direct action before the war. Resistance really only developed late on, and it was difficult to organise and plan as they feared arrest
Military	There were a number among the commanders and high-ranking officers who resented Hitler's background. Opposition was slow to develop due to the army oath (see page 103) and early military success during the war. However, army support for Hitler declined after defeat at Stalingrad in 1943. Some commanders began to conspire, and this culminated in the **July Bomb Plot** under Stauffenberg in 1944 (see pages 186–7)	The July Bomb Plot failed and officers were slow to act, allowing Hitler to regain control. About 5000 members of the resistance were killed afterwards

KEY TERM

July Bomb Plot
An attempt to assassinate Hitler on 20 July 1944. It involved both civilian resistance figures and army officers, including Colonel von Stauffenberg. He placed a bomb in a meeting room, but it was moved before the meeting and that probably saved Hitler's life. In the confusion afterwards, supporters of Hitler were able to arrest the conspirators.

The treatment of opponents

The lack of opposition to the Nazis, particularly in the period from 1933 to 1939, suggests that the treatment of opponents who were caught did much to dissuade others. The regime was built on a system of surveillance and censorship and was supported by extensive propaganda (see pages 104–8), all of which had an impact on limiting those who openly opposed the Nazis. Opponents were also aware that individual actions, no matter how heroic, would have little impact. This limited the numbers willing to resist. People were very conscious that the state had the ability to destroy people's lives, or at least make them very difficult through arrests, torture and routine brutality. The wearing down and demoralising of opponents in the camps made many powerless or unwilling to continue to resist if they were released. Although concentration camps may have played a role in reducing opposition, the numbers imprisoned fell away after 1933–4 and there were many Germans who agreed with their use, so the victims often gained little sympathy.

ONLINE EXTRAS WWW

Get to grips with evaluating a range of factors as to why the Nazis were able to control Germany by completing Worksheet 22 at **www.hoddereducation.co.uk/accesstohistory/extras**

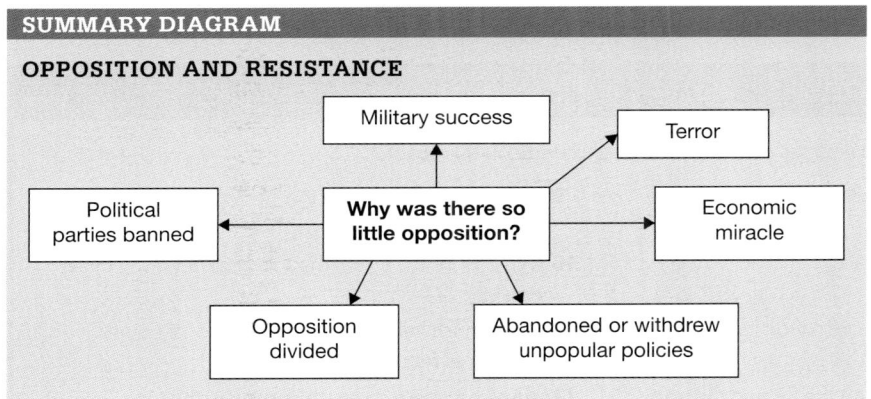

SUMMARY DIAGRAM

OPPOSITION AND RESISTANCE

CHAPTER SUMMARY

When Hitler was appointed chancellor in January 1933, he did not have dictatorial powers, but within two months he had introduced the Enabling Act which allowed this to be achieved. In the period between March 1933 and August 1934, he extended these powers, destroying trade unions and other political parties while also bringing the federal states under his control. Although there were other forces, such as the army, that could challenge him, they were won over by his destruction of the SA in the Night of the Long Knives. Hitler's regime has been seen as all-powerful, yet his lifestyle and chaotic and overlapping nature of government institutions meant that in reality this was not the case. However, Hitler's use of terror, censorship and propaganda created an atmosphere of fear that sustained the regime and led to people accepting Nazi policies. Opposition was weak and divided following the destruction of other political parties and trade unions, making his task that much easier, particularly as many were willing to turn a blind eye to the evil as he had provided jobs and promised economic recovery.

Refresher questions

Use these questions to remind yourself of the key material covered in this chapter.

1. How did the Nazis use the *Reichstag* fire to consolidate their power?
2. What was the importance of the Enabling Act of March 1933?
3. What was the extent of co-ordination by the end of 1933?
4. Why did the conflict between the SA and the army come to a head?
5. Who gained by the Night of the Long Knives?
6. How effective was Nazi propaganda?
7. To what extent did the Nazis change German culture?
8. Why did the SS become so powerful?
9. How much control did the *Gestapo* have over people?
10. What were the strengths and weaknesses of Hitler as leader?
11. How much influence did the traditional power structures retain?
12. Why was there so much overlap in the administration of the state?
13. Was the Nazi dictatorship efficient?
14. How much opposition was there to the Nazi regime?
15. Why was opposition ineffective?

CHAPTER 7
Nazi racial, social and religious policies 1933–45

The Nazi regime aimed to establish *Volksgemeinschaft*, which would transform German society and overcome old divisions of class, race, religion and politics. The Nazis wanted to create a new sense of national identity by encouraging people to work together.

This chapter will examine the impact of these policies and the attempts to create a *Volksgemeinschaft* by focusing on the following themes:

- Nazi racial ideology
- Anti-Semitism
- Policies towards 'asocials'
- Social policies
- Workers
- The Churches
- The effectiveness of *Volksgemeinschaft*

KEY DATES

1933	April	First official boycott of Jewish shops and businesses	1938	Sept.	Start of the euthanasia campaign
	May	Confessional Church established	1941	Aug.	Bishop Galen's sermon against euthanasia
	June	Women offered interest-free loans to marry and give up work		Sept.	All Jewish people forced to wear a Yellow Star of David
	July	Concordat signed with the papacy	1942	Jan.	Wannsee Conference co-ordinated Final Solution to the 'Jewish problem'
1934	Jan.	Proportion of girls allowed to enter higher education limited		Spring	Extermination facilities set up at Auschwitz, Sobibor and Treblinka
1935	Sept.	Nuremberg race laws introduced	1943	Feb.	Start of sending Germany's Romani population to Auschwitz
	Dec.	Introduction of *Lebensborn* to 'improve racial quality'			
1938	Nov.	*Kristallnacht*			
	Dec.	Decree for 'The Struggle Against the Gypsy Plague'			

1 Nazi racial ideology

■ *What were Nazi racial beliefs?*

Nazi ideology that developed in the 1920s was based on three key elements:
- race
- nationalism
- authoritarianism.

Other doctrines, such as communism, were rejected and replaced by the concept of *Volksgemeinschaft*, or a People's Community. The idea was to create a society built on the concepts of race and struggle, bringing together traditional German values and a new ideology. At the centre of this was the idea of a 'racially pure' state, which would therefore mean the exclusion of some from the People's Community. Those excluded were deemed 'biologically inferior' and were seen to be of a lesser racial value.

This ideology was based on Social Darwinism and the concept of the 'survival of the fittest'. The Nazis believed:

- Aryans (*Herrenvolk*) were the superior race because of their intelligence, hard work and willingness to make sacrifices for the nation.
- Germany had lost the First World War because of weak people, so they had to be removed.
- Mixing with **Untermenschen** had 'contaminated' the Aryans and this led to the Nazi belief in **eugenics**. To achieve racial purity, selective breeding and the removal of 'undesirables' was needed.

The 'undesirables' did not fit the ideal image of the German peasant working on the soil, seen in the concept of '**Blood and Soil**'. The 'undesirables' covered all ethnicities, such as Romani people, Slavs and Jewish people, but it also included those who were physically and mentally disabled. Those who were considered undesirable were to be discriminated against and persecuted throughout the period from 1933 to 1945.

However, Nazi policies towards such groups were not consistent. In part, this was because there was opposition within the Reich to some of the actions. It should be remembered that many of those who had voted for the Nazis had done so not because of the Nazis' racial beliefs but because of issues such as unemployment, desire for a strong government or fear of communism.

> **KEY TERMS**
>
> **Untermenschen** Sub-human or racially inferior people.
>
> **Eugenics** A programme to genetically improve the race.
>
> **Blood and soil** (*Blut und Boden*.) A romantic nationalist ideal which glorified the rural role of peasants.

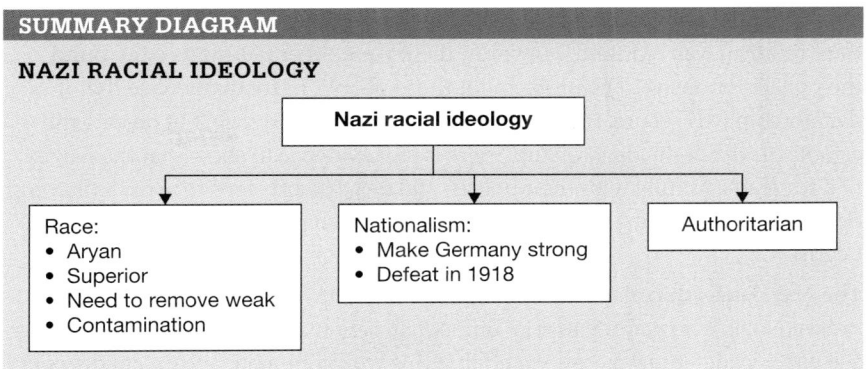

SUMMARY DIAGRAM
NAZI RACIAL IDEOLOGY

2 Anti-Semitism

■ *In what ways did Nazi anti-Semitic policies change?*

At the heart of the Nazi social policy was the issue of race, particularly anti-Semitism, which was probably the most consistent of Hitler's beliefs. It would lead to a series of laws, violence, and ultimately genocide and the Holocaust (see Chapter 9).

Anti-Semitism was not new. Jewish people had been discriminated against in medieval Europe, often being blamed for events such as the **Black Death** and used as scapegoats when things went wrong. During the nineteenth century, right-wing nationalism had given further impetus to anti-Semitism in many European states and its appeal grew, particularly in Germany in the aftermath of the First World War, with the Jewish community blamed by some for Germany's defeat and the humiliation of Versailles. This led to the emergence of a number of racist political parties, of which the Nazis were one.

Hitler was able to exploit growing anti-Semitism and turn it into a racial ideology of hatred. Although some people have argued that it was this that helped to bring him to power, most historians would now contend that it was issues such as unemployment that played the central role. Evidence for this view is supported by a 1934 survey in which, when people were asked why they joined the Nazi Party, some 60 per cent did not mention anti-Semitism.

It has been claimed that policies towards the Jewish community were gradual and that the early moves of the Nazis gave no indication of the violence to which Jewish people were subjected during the Second World War (see Chapter 9). There were some Germans who agreed that legal discrimination against the Jewish population was no more than they deserved. These people accepted some of the Nazis' arguments that Jewish citizens had been to blame for Germany's defeat in the First World War or were considered to be making vast profits while ordinary hard-working Germans suffered from the Depression. Others were receptive to Nazi propaganda that asserted that mixing with 'sub-humans'

KEY TERM

Black Death A disease that struck Europe during the fourteenth century and killed about a third of the population. It was carried by fleas on rats, but this was not understood at the time and a variety of prejudiced theories were offered, including blaming the Jewish community.

had weakened the German race, and that for Germany to achieve racial purity their removal was required. However, there were other Germans who found the policies offensive. The problem for these people, particularly once the dictatorship was secure, was how to register their abhorrence. But despite the establishment of the dictatorship, there is still evidence to show that the Nazis had to tread carefully with their policies, take backward steps to avoid inflaming opinion and only embark on the genocide of Jewish people once the war had begun.

The Nazi leadership also faced a problem from within as there were many radical Nazis who wanted to take immediate action against Jewish people, while the party leadership was concerned that this would escalate and create disquiet. There were, therefore, a number of issues that had to be taken into consideration in the development of their policies.

Policies and actions towards the Jewish community

A lack of consistency is seen in the early days of Nazi power regarding racial policy. At first, Hitler did not issue any directives and it was violence from the members of the *Sturmabteilung* (SA) against individual Jewish people and their property that forced him into action as the government feared that it would damage their reputation abroad.

> **KEY TERM**
>
> **Boycott** Refusal to deal commercially with someone; in this case, refusing to use Jewish owned shops.

In order to control the violence, Hitler announced a one-day **boycott** of Jewish businesses on 1 April 1933, with members of the SA positioned outside shops to persuade people not to use them. However, this boycott was not popular and also caused bad publicity abroad. As a result, the policy was abandoned. Instead, Hitler attempted to appease the radicals by expelling Jewish individuals from the civil service, with the Law for the Restoration of the Professional Civil Service on 7 April. He also expelled Jewish people from universities and journalism.

The Nuremberg laws

Although the Night of the Long Knives (see pages 101–3) went some way to removing the radical elements within the Nazi Party, by the summer of 1935 there was further widespread violence against Jewish people and local party activists wanted further action taken against them. However, Hitler was concerned that the regime was losing support at home and that attacks on the Jewish population would negatively affect international opinion. It was only at the last minute that he decided to announce, at Nuremberg, measures to regularise the status of Jewish people in Germany by removing their citizenship rights.

In issuing the Nuremberg laws, Hitler had hoped to satisfy radical elements within the Nazi Party and put an end to the violence. The laws ensured that anti-Semitism became more embedded in German society and led to Jewish people being increasingly discriminated against. They were often banned from places such as restaurants or swimming pools. Sexual relationships between Germans and Jewish individuals resulted in prosecution in special courts and new forms of public humiliation. This was reinforced by propaganda and indoctrination. Posters and signs appeared claiming 'Jews are not wanted here', a number of newspapers, such as *Der Stürmer*, were openly anti-Semitic and films such as *The Eternal Jew* were released.

However, this policy came to a temporary halt in 1936. This was for two reasons. First, Berlin hosted the 1936 Olympics and the regime wanted to avoid international condemnation by putting across a positive message about Nazi Germany, showing that it was tolerant and unified. Second, conservatives within the regime were still able to exert a restraining influence, with ministers, such as Schacht, arguing that anti-Semitic action would have a detrimental impact on the economy.

Kristallnacht

In 1938, action against the Jewish population intensified. Once again, party activists demanded more radical action. In this, they were aided by Göring, who wanted to confiscate Jewish assets to help pay for rearmament. This pressure, reinforced by increased nationalist feeling within the country, was encouraged by the **Anschluss** with Austria and growing tensions over the Sudentenland. The rising likelihood of war encouraged many to demand that Jewish people, whom they saw as 'the enemy within', be removed.

This culminated in a violent attack, or pogrom, on 9–10 November, which was known as *Kristallnacht*, or the Night of Broken Glass, because of all the smashed windows. This appeared to replicate the large-scale attack there had been on Jewish people in Vienna in March following the *Anschluss*. The attack spread through Germany and resulted in the destruction of Jewish homes, businesses and synagogues, and the deaths of over 100 Jewish people, while some 20,000 were taken to concentration camps. It was claimed by the Nazis that the actions were a 'spontaneous' response to the murder of Ernst vom Rath, a German diplomat in Paris, by a young Jewish man, Herschel Grynszpan.

> **KEY TERM**
>
> **Anschluss** The union of Germany and Austria. Although the population of Austria was German, the Treaty of Versailles outlawed the union of the two countries.

SOURCE A

From a press statement about the events of *Kristallnacht* by Joseph Goebbels, 10 November 1938.

The justifiable and understandable indignation of the German people at the cowardly murder of a German diplomat in Paris was widely displayed last night. In numerous towns and villages of the Reich, reprisals were carried out against Jewish buildings and places of business. The whole population is now firmly asked to abstain from all further action of whatever nature against the Jews. The final reply to the Jewish outrage in Paris will be given to the Jews by legal means.

> **SOURCE QUESTION**
>
> What is the purpose of Goebbels' press statement in Source A?

> **ONLINE EXTRAS** **WWW**
>
> Test your understanding of analysing sources by completing Worksheet 23 at **www.hoddereducation.co.uk/accesstohistory/extras**

There is, however, much debate as to attitudes towards the Jewish population in Germany at this time.

SOURCE QUESTION

How useful is Source B as evidence for attitudes towards the Jewish people in Germany?

SOURCE B

An extract from a report by the Social Democratic Party in exile, December 1938.

The broad mass of the people has not condoned the destruction, but we should nevertheless not overlook the fact that there are people among the working class who do not defend the Jews. There are certain circles where you are not very popular if you speak disparagingly about recent incidents … Berlin: the population's attitude was not fully unanimous … If there has been any speaking out in the Reich against the Jewish pogroms, the excesses of arson and looting, it has been in Hamburg and the neighbouring Elbe district. People from Hamburg are not generally anti-Semitic, and the Hamburg Jews have been assimilated far more than Jews in other parts of the Reich.

Rather than the murder of Ernest vom Rath, it was more likely that it was other events that led to *Kristallnacht*. In particular, Goebbels wanted to win back Hitler's favour following his affair with a Czech actress. It was probably this that led to the co-ordination of persecution, thus destroying any claim that it was spontaneous. There is little doubt that the event marked a turning point in the treatment of Jewish people.

The Jewish community was fined for the damage caused by *Kristallnacht* and the pogrom was soon followed by a series of anti-Jewish laws (see Table 7.1, below). The situation developed in the next year with further attacks as Jewish people were forced out of their jobs and had their remaining assets seized.

Table 7.1 Major laws targeted at the Jewish people 1933–9

Date	Law
7 April 1933	Law for the Restoration of the Professional Civil Service. Jewish workers were excluded from the civil service
4 October 1933	Law for the exclusion of Jewish journalists
5 September 1935	The Nuremberg race laws
	Reich Citizenship Act: 'A citizen of the Reich is a subject who is only of German or kindred blood.' As a result, Jewish people lost their citizenship in Germany
	Law for the Protection of German Blood and Honour. Marriage and extramarital relations between Jewish individuals and Germans were forbidden
5 July 1938	Decree prohibiting Jewish doctors from practising medicine
28 October 1938	Decree to expel 17,000 Polish Jews resident in Germany
15 November 1938	Decree to exclude Jewish pupils from schools and universities
3 December 1938	Decree for compulsory closure and sale of all Jewish businesses
1 September 1939	Decree introducing curfew for the Jewish population

Emigration

The establishment of the Central Office for Jewish Emigration in Vienna, following the *Anschluss*, led to an addition to Jewish policy: forced emigration, with the most common destinations being Palestine, Britain and the USA. This office was set up to force Jewish people to emigrate and used money from the seizure of Jewish goods to fund it.

The office was headed by Adolf Eichmann; under him, some 45,000 Jewish people left within six months. The success of the policy led to the creation of the Reich Central Office for Jewish Emigration being established in 1939. As a result of the establishment of these two offices, it is estimated that half the Jewish population had left before the war.

It has been argued that from November 1938, with the events of *Kristallnacht*, the fate of Jewish people was sealed. On 12 November, Göring claimed that Hitler had written a letter informing him that 'the Jewish question be now once and for all co-ordinated and solved one way or another'. Despite this, Hitler claimed to foreign diplomats that he was preventing a massacre of Jewish people. However, comments he made in 1939 made it clear what Jewish people could expect. He told the Czech foreign minister that he would 'destroy the Jews', while he made his famous speech to the *Reichstag* in January 1939 in which he stated that if war broke out it would result in the 'annihilation of the Jewish race in Europe'.

Historians have long argued over the meaning of these words, but even if their meaning is clear, an analysis of the anti-Semitic measures that were brought in between 1933 and 1939 would suggest that there was no clear plan or policy. The measures against the Jewish population appear to be responses to demands from radical elements within the party and this goes a long way to explaining their haphazard nature. However, there is little doubt that Hitler harboured a deep hatred of Jewish people and had considered violent action but was constrained by circumstances before 1938.

Hitler's anti-Semitism was apparent in his early speeches and programmatic statements in the 1920s and, most noticeably, in *Mein Kampf*. Anti-Semitism was central to his conception of the *Volksgemeinschaft*. Yet the *Volksgemeinschaft* could not simply be created by laws from above; the German people had to be actively persuaded to exclude the Jewish community from the national community. After 1938, however, there does appear to have been a clear change in policy, with a more radical approach, which would reach its culmination during the Second World War (see Chapter 9).

ONLINE EXTRAS **WWW**

Get to grips with constructing a balanced argument by completing Worksheet 24 at **www.hoddereducation.co.uk/accesstohistory/extras**

SUMMARY DIAGRAM

ANTI-SEMITISM

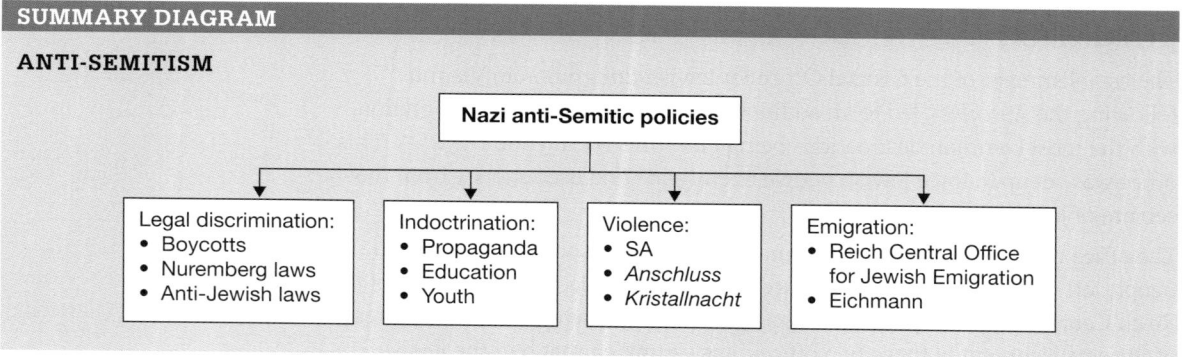

3 Policies towards 'asocials'

■ *Who were the 'asocials' in Nazi Germany?*

The term 'asocial' was used to describe anyone who did not conform to the Nazi ideal and whose behaviour was, therefore, seen as unacceptable, and those who did not carry out their duties to the national community. 'Asocials' included alcoholics, criminals, homeless people and those unwilling to work. There was also one other racial group that was persecuted: the Romani people (sometimes called Gypsies).

Many of these groups were rounded up and organised into a compulsory workforce or, if they were viewed as disorderly, imprisoned, while some even had medical experiments performed on them or were sterilised.

Policy towards the Romani people

The Nazis subjected the Romani people to persecution. Not only were they viewed as outsiders, but they were also seen as non-Aryan and work-shy, and, therefore, did not fit the Nazi ideal. There had been considerable hostility towards the Romani people during the Weimar period and in 1929 the Central Office for the Fight against the Gypsies had been established.

Once the Nazis were in power, Romani people were subject to similar policies as Jewish people, as can be seen in Table 7.2 (below).

Table 7.2 Nazi policies towards Gypsies 1935–9

Year	Policy
1935	Gypsies had to comply with the Nuremberg race laws and were banned from marrying or having sexual relations with Germans
1938	Decree for the Struggle Against the Gypsy Plague. Gypsies had to register to ensure there was racial separation
1939	With the outbreak of war, 30,000 Gypsies were deported to special sites in Poland

Policies towards 'asocial' groups

A series of laws were passed to deal with various 'asocial' groups:

- The Sterilisation Law of 1933. The Law for the Prevention of Hereditary Diseased Offspring allowed the 'simple-minded', 'chronic alcoholics' and sufferers of schizophrenia, hereditary blindness and deafness to be sterilised. From about 1934, some 350,000 men were sterilised.
- The Law against Dangerous Habitual Criminals was introduced in 1933. This introduced compulsory castration for some sexual offenders and indefinite sentences or incarceration in concentration camps for repeat offenders.
- Male homosexuality was already illegal before 1933, but persecution increased with the establishment of a department within the *Gestapo* to deal with homosexuals. Some 50,000 male homosexuals were arrested; however, lesbianism was not made illegal.
- By 1936, the work-shy, homeless people, prostitutes, homosexuals and juvenile delinquents were being sent to concentration camps.
- The euthanasia campaign was launched in 1939. There were existing laws for the safeguarding of the health of the nation by sterilisation of those who were mentally ill, but in 1939 there was an increase in this policy by allowing the killing of those affected to be organised by a special government department. Popular unrest about the disappearance of relatives meant that the programme was halted, but it did resume more covertly. The experience of legalised murder informed the policy of racial genocide during the war.

Although Jewish and Romani people were at the centre of the racial campaign of the regime, other groups, such as male homosexuals, who did not fit the Nazi ideal were also persecuted, even if there was little co-ordination or direction to the policies.

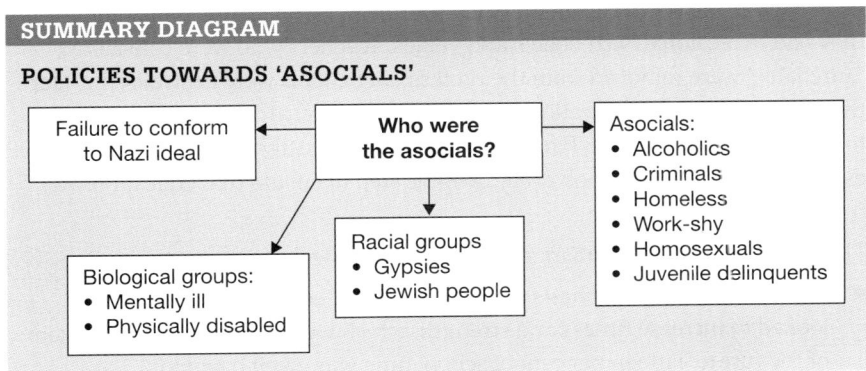

4 Social policies

■ *How successful were Nazi social policies?*

Hitler claimed that National Socialism aimed to transform German society and establish a *Volksgemeinschaft*. The concept of *Volksgemeinschaft* is very difficult to define, but the essential aim was to remove old divisions caused by class, politics and religion and create a new national identity where people would work together. This new society would be built on the Nazi ideals of race and struggle, uniting traditional German values with this new ideology. This was to be achieved by focusing on groups such as young people and women.

Young people

The youth were the future of the 'Thousand-Year Reich' that Hitler intended to establish. The Nazi policies aimed to **indoctrinate** the young in Nazi ideals and to consolidate the regime so that its survival would not be challenged. Hitler himself summed up the importance of the young in 1933 (see Source C, below).

> **KEY TERM**
>
> **Indoctrinate** To impose a set of beliefs.

> **SOURCE QUESTION**
>
> What is the message of Source C?

SOURCE C

From a speech by Hitler, 6 November 1933.

When an opponent declares, 'I will not come over to your side', I calmly say, 'Your child belongs to us already. What are you? You will pass on. Your descendants, however, now stand in the new camp. In a short time they will know nothing else but this new community.'

This indoctrination was to be achieved not only through the education system, but also through the development of Nazi organisations.

Education

In order to bring about the changes the regime wanted, teachers were told that they had to reinforce Nazi beliefs and values. Teachers who were considered 'unreliable' were removed from the profession. Schools were centralised under the Reich Ministry of Education, Culture and Science, and head teachers had to be members of the Nazi Party. A National Socialist Teachers' League was established as the party took every possible step to ensure that education was firmly under its control.

The curriculum was also changed to reflect Nazi ideology:

- There was greater emphasis placed on physical education as the regime looked to increase fitness and strength, which were essential in the soldiers of the future. Fifteen per cent of school time was given over to it.
- There was greater emphasis on German history, which was used to stress German nationalism and heroism.
- Biology was used to reinforce Nazi racial policy.
- German language and literature were studied to create a feeling of being German and create a martial and nationalist spirit.

- Religious studies was removed from the curriculum because the subject did not uphold Nazi values.

The Nazis also brought in new types of schools to produce a new elite. The aim of these establishments was to prepare the best of Germany's youth for leading the regime. The emphasis was again on physical fitness and political indoctrination. The new schools consisted of:

- *Napolas* or National Political Educational Institutions, 21 of which were established.
- Adolf Hitler Schools run by the Hitler Youth, ten of which were established.
- *Ordensburgen*, for boys of college age.

It is very difficult to assess the impact of these changes. However, it can be argued that the teaching profession certainly felt under pressure to conform and this is probably reflected in the rising number of teacher vacancies. Standards within education, particularly among the academic subjects, fell as physical education dominated the curriculum. The changes may have appealed to the less academic, but the curriculum was certainly less challenging for the more able. It is also difficult to assess the impact of such changes as the regime was in power for only twelve years and the desired results of the changes would have taken much longer to be noticeable.

Hitler Youth

The term Hitler Youth is used to describe a range of youth groups in Germany, not just the *Hitler-Jugend*. Germany had a long tradition of youth groups and it is therefore not surprising that the Nazi groups were able to attract members.

SOURCE D

From a report by the Social Democratic Party in Exile (SOPADE), 1934.

Youth is still in favour of the system: the novelty, the drill, the uniform, the camp life, the fact that school and the parental home take a back seat compared to the community of young people – all that is marvelous. Many believe that they will find job opportunities through the persecution of Jews and Marxists. For the first time, peasant youth is associated with the State through the SA and the Hitler Youth. Young workers also join in: one day socialism may come; one is simply trying to achieve it in a new way. The new generation has never had much use for education and reading. Now nothing is demanded of them; on the contrary, knowledge is publicly condemned. The chaps are so fanaticized that they believe in nothing but their Hitler.

SOURCE QUESTION

How useful is Source D as evidence as to why many young people were attracted to the Hitler Youth?

ONLINE EXTRAS

Test your understanding of the value of a source by completing Worksheet 25 at **www.hoddereducation. co.uk/accesstohistory/extras**

As with education, the Nazis wanted to use the youth groups to indoctrinate the young. It appears that the potential for success was there as membership rose from just one per cent of the youth in 1933 to 60 per cent by 1936, before becoming compulsory in 1939. The position of the Nazi youth groups was also strengthened by abolishing all other youth groups, except the Catholic Youth Movement.

> **SOURCE QUESTION**
>
> In what ways could the poster in Source E be seen as effective propaganda for the Nazis?

SOURCE E

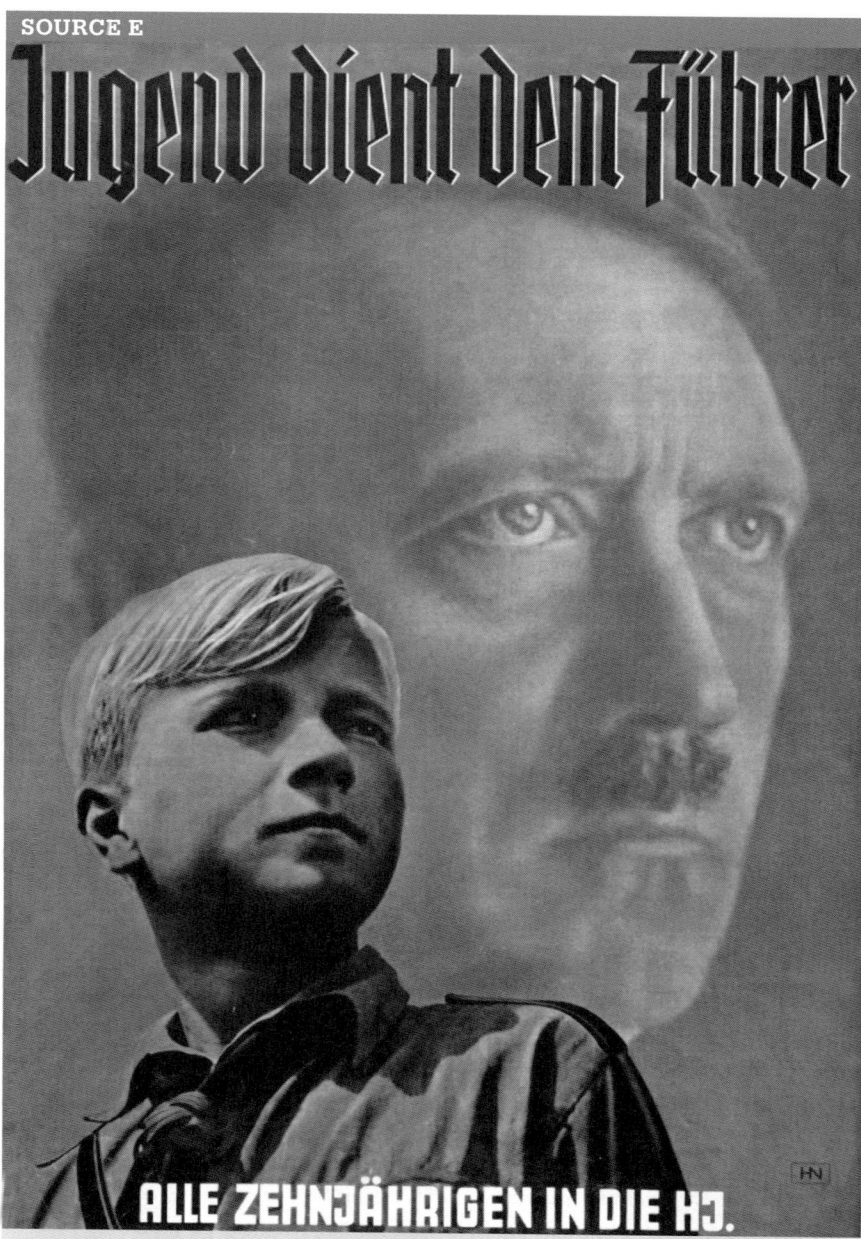

'Youth serves the Führer! All ten-year-olds join the Hitler Youth!' A Nazi propaganda poster of 1940.

The range of activities varied for boys and girls, but within all four groups political indoctrination was important, with an emphasis on the greatness of the Führer and German patriotism. In the boys' organisations the emphasis was on preparing them for a military life with large amounts of physical and military-style activities. In the girls' organisations, although they were very austere and involved uniforms and marching, the emphasis was on preparing them for their domestic role as mothers.

Table 7.3 The Nazi youth groups

Age range	Male	Female
10–14	*Deutsches Jungvolk* (German Young People)	*Jungmädelbund* (Young Girls' League)
14–18	*Hitler-Jugend* (Hitler Youth)	*Bund Deutscher Mädel* (League of German Girls)

As with education, it is difficult to assess the impact of the groups, but at best it appears to have been mixed. Many, particularly those from poorer backgrounds, enjoyed the camping and sporting activities, as they had often not been away from their neighbourhoods before. However, organisation and leadership were often poor. This was made worse by the rapid expansion in numbers joining and the increasing military emphasis and discipline. The compulsory nature of the movement was also resented by some and led to disillusionment among many. Some of the young simply ignored the indoctrination, but enjoyed other different aspects, and others formed alternative groups.

Alternative youth groups

Although limited in their appeal and membership, the two most notable non-Nazi organisations were the Swing Youth and Edelweiss Pirates, the latter being centred on the Rhineland and the Ruhr. Both were hostile to the ethos of the Hitler Youth and provide a clear indication that the regimentation and military drill associated with the Hitler Youth was not universally popular.

Recent research suggests that, by 1939, there were quite large pockets of resentment, with many young people not won over. Alienation and dissent grew and this was seen even more clearly in the war years (see page 185). However, this should not be overemphasised as many still saw the Hitler Youth as providing them with opportunities and the chance to play a role in the new Germany.

Women

Under the Weimar government there had been a change in social attitudes and women had been freed from a lot of the restrictions they had faced in the pre-war years. Many had taken up employment opportunities. At the same time, the birth rate within Germany had also fallen. The Nazi view of women was in complete contrast to the Weimar period and the aim of Nazi policies was to reverse both of these trends. Women stood to lose many of the gains that they had made during the Weimar period.

Nazi view of women

The Nazis believed that a woman's place was at home and that she should fulfil a completely different role to that of men, and that it was the state's responsibility to ensure that this happened. She was expected to have a large family, not only to increase the population, but also to provide soldiers. Women were to have completely different roles to men, summed up by the three Ks, '*Kinder, Kuche, Kirche*' – children, kitchen and church.

> **ONLINE EXTRAS** WWW
>
> Test your understanding of Nazi education policy by completing Worksheet 26 at **www.hoddereducation.co.uk/accesstohistory/extras**

Although such views might appear to undermine the gains that women had made since the First World War, it must be remembered that they were not unusual at the time. Other European countries were also trying to increase their birth rate and were rewarding women for having large families. It might also be argued that the importance given to motherhood enhanced the status of women; however, they were denied many other opportunities, particularly in the field of employment.

The ideal Nazi woman

Women were also expected to live up to the Nazi ideal and become perfect mothers. Not only were they not to go to work, but, in order to produce healthy children, they were encouraged not to diet excessively, to be fit and healthy and not smoke. The Nazis even gave instructions as to how they should dress – without make-up, in full skirts and flat shoes. It was also emphasised that they should be good cooks.

Nazi policies and their success

The aim of reducing the number of women in employment was, at first, quite successful. Married women were prevented from entering many of the professions between 1933 and 1936, while the number of girls allowed to enter higher education was limited in 1934 and further reduced in 1937. Grammar school education was abolished for girls and they were forbidden to study Latin, which was a requirement to enter university. As a result of these policies, professional middle-class women and ambitious girls found their opportunities for advancement and fulfilment reduced.

Incentives were also offered to persuade women to give up work and return to the home to fulfil the Nazi ideal. In June 1933, interest-free loans were offered to women to marry and give up work. At the same time, labour exchanges were encouraged to discriminate in favour of men. As a result of these policies, the percentage of women in employment fell from 37 per cent in 1932 to 31 per cent by 1937, but this may have been inevitable as male unemployment was the Nazis' major concern and this fell from an all-time high in 1932 to virtually full employment by 1937–8.

To further emphasise the importance of motherhood, a propaganda campaign was launched with the slogan 'I have donated a child to the Führer', and rewards such as the Mother's Cross were implemented. These were medals given out in bronze, silver and gold depending on the number of children a woman had borne. Attempts to increase the population were also implemented with the introduction of strict anti-abortion laws and limited contraception, as well as maternity benefits and family allowance. However, the campaign to increase the population reached its culmination with the introduction of the policy of *Lebensborn* ('fount of life') in 1935. Under this policy, unmarried mothers of 'good racial background' were to be cared for, and Aryan girls were to made pregnant by members of the *Schutzstaffel* (SS).

These policies did not result in a significant increase in the birth rate between 1933 and 1939. Access to artificial forms of contraception was restricted but married couples continued to make use of natural forms of contraception. This is reflected in the low number of births per marriage – only around two births per marriage as opposed to the four desired by the regime. However, more people did get married, probably because of the improving economic conditions, and this helped to increase the birth rate.

After 1937 policies changed because:

- there was a labour shortage
- the Four Year Plan (see pages 156–7) exacerbated the situation.

Women were now encouraged to work in factories and were also allowed to re-enter their professions. This can be seen in the increase in the number of female doctors. The total number of working women rose from 5.7 million in 1937 to 7.1 million in 1939. However, this change in policy had been forced on the Nazis because of their obsession with rearmament and not because there was any real change in attitude towards women. This increase in women at work would continue during the war, when even greater labour shortages were faced, so that by 1942, women made up 52 per cent of the labour force.

In terms of growing the birth rate the policies had, at best, limited success. This is clearly illustrated in the work of historian Michael Burleigh, who argues in *The Third Reich: A New History* (2000) that 'although there was an appreciable short-lived increase in the birth of third or fourth children, the absence of a commensurate public housing policy did little to affect the secular drift towards nuclear families'. Although there was a modest increase in the birth rate, the regime failed to get the four children from each marriage that it wanted. How far this limited success was due to Nazi policies or propaganda is debatable and could be due to other factors such as the improving economy.

Nazi women's organisations

Although women were excluded from government, two women's organisations within the party were established that provided some limited employment opportunities. These were:

- the National Socialist Womanhood
- the German Women's Enterprise.

They ran Mothers' Schools, which offered courses in household management and motherhood skills. There was also a Women's Section within the Labour Front, which did the same. Women's organisations were used to propagate anti-feminist ideology through a range of cultural, educational and social programmes. Attempts within the National Socialist Womanhood to increase opportunities for women resulted in its organisers being discredited.

Conclusion

Historians have been very critical of policies that reduced the status of women. Changes in society and the increasing employment of women meant that Nazi views were out of touch with reality and became increasingly contradictory. However, Tim Mason argues that Nazi policies towards women were not unpopular with them, suggesting in *Women in Germany 1925–40: Family, Welfare and Work* (1995) that women were actually pleased to stay at home rather than work in factories, claiming that 'the overtly anti-feminist policies of the regime after 1933 were at least partially successful, in that they secured the approval, perhaps gratitude, of many German people, men and women alike; partially successful too in blocking and turning back the social, economic and educational pressures which had led towards emancipation in the preceding decades'.

The Nazis viewed women as different from, not inferior to men, and claimed that there were many positive features of their policies that made their lives easier. However, many historians, such as Claudia Koonz, are highly critical of Nazi policies towards women. Koonz also argues that women were just as guilty as anyone in ignoring the horrors of the regime, claiming in *Mothers in the Fatherland: Women, the Family and Nazi Politics* (1988), that 'Mothers and wives made a vital contribution to Nazi power by preserving the illusion of love in an environment of hatred … Nazi women, no less than men, destroyed ethical vision, debased humane traditions, and rendered decent people helpless.'

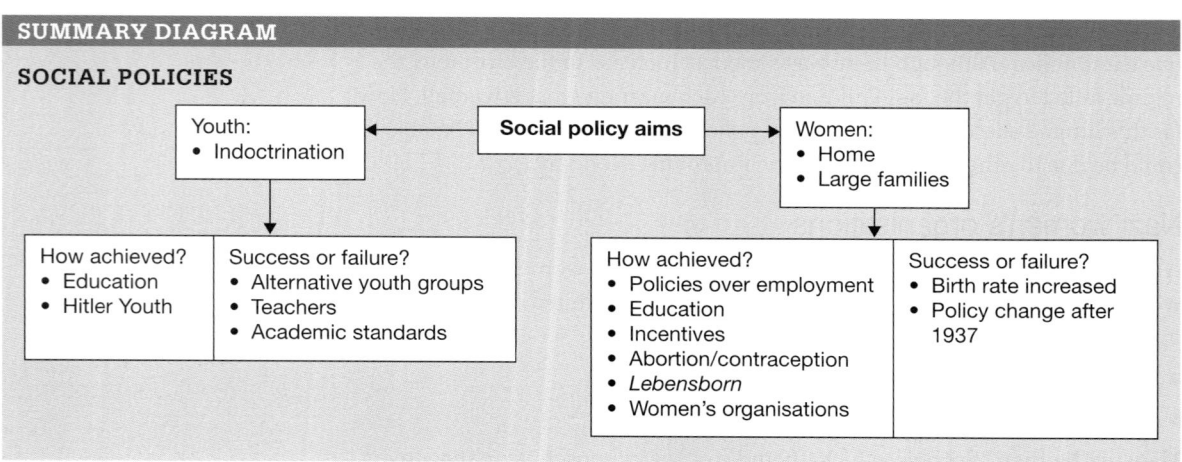

SUMMARY DIAGRAM

SOCIAL POLICIES

5 Workers

▪ *To what extent did workers benefit from Nazi rule?*

When the Nazis came to power in 1933, the main concern of German workers was unemployment. In many ways the Nazis were able to solve that problem (see page 151), but the effects of their policies varied considerably for different groups.

Industrial workers

The working class made up the largest social group in Germany, representing nearly half of the population. Workers had also been hardest hit by the Depression, with many losing their jobs. Despite this, the Nazis could not count on their support as many industrial workers had traditionally voted for the Communist Party (KPD) or the Social Democratic Party (SPD).

Although the Nazis closed down the trade unions (see page 100), they also provided many workers with labour, which allowed them to provide for their families. However, this labour was often in government programmes, which had poor pay and conditions, and if the unemployed refused the work they did not get the benefits. Even those who found employment also discovered that real wages were slow to recover and working hours were often longer.

The abolition of free trade unions meant that workers lost the right of industrial bargaining and the government and management were able to control pay rises and limit workers' freedom of movement. Nazi control was further ensured with the creation of the German Labour Front (DAF, see pages 159–60) which replaced independent unions and was made mandatory for workers.

Wages and conditions

It is difficult to assess the impact of the regime on workers. Those who worked in the armaments industries were better off than those who worked in the consumer industries. When workers did see a rise in take-home pay it was often because they had done overtime, with the average working week officially increasing from 43 hours in 1933 to 47 in 1939. Workers were certainly better off than they had been on the dole, with take-home pay in 1936 on average some 35 marks per week higher than the dole. However, Richard Grunberger argues in his book, *A Social History of the Third Reich* (1971), that hourly wages increased by only one per cent per year under Nazi rule. It actually took until 1938 for the average worker's real wages to pass the 1929 level. This meant that with deductions for membership of the DAF, **Winterhilfe** and **NSV** contributions, as well as insurance and tax, workers were actually worse off.

A similar pattern can be seen when examining food consumption among working-class families. This saw a drop in quality and more emphasis on cheaper staple foods, such as rye bread and potatoes, while meat and dairy consumption declined dramatically. There was also little investment in housing

> **KEY TERMS**
>
> **Winterhilfe** Winter relief: a scheme to provide extra help for the unemployed during winter months. Money for it was raised by donations resulting from the savings made by eating a 'one-pot' meal on a Sunday once a month.
>
> **NSV** National Socialist Welfare Organisation: this oversaw the expansion of welfare facilities, such as rural health clinics and improved childcare, leading to a reduction in infant mortality.

for ordinary people, which may also have played a role in why some were reluctant to have large families.

It is clear that, on the whole, workers lost freedom but gained some improved facilities. Their political power certainly declined with the abolition of free trade unions and political parties. In 1935, all workers were issued with a workbook, which was needed when seeking employment, and then in 1938, the government took powers to direct workers to wherever they were needed. For many, the most important benefit of Nazi rule was gaining a job, but, although more were employed, this was in part the result of removing women and Jewish workers from the workforce, and male conscription to the army and the **Reich Labour Service (RAD)**.

> **KEY TERMS**
>
> **Reich Labour Service (RAD)** Introduced in 1935, it required young men to do six months' unpaid work, usually in military construction projects, before joining up for military service.
>
> **Pastors** Ministers in charge of a church or congregation.
>
> **Confessional Church** Established in 1934 in opposition to the Reich Church, the Confessional Church upheld traditional Protestant beliefs and rejected Nazi distortions.
>
> **Reichskonkordat** An agreement between the Nazi state and the Catholic Church signed in July 1933.

SUMMARY DIAGRAM

WORKERS

Workers

Gains:
- Jobs
- DAF
- Facilities at work

Losses:
- Poor pay/conditions
- End of free trade unions
- Longer working hours
- Contributions
- Food consumption
- Workbook

6 The Churches

■ *How successful was Nazi policy towards the Churches?*

Nazi ideology, with its emphasis on violence, war and strength, was a direct challenge to Christian ideals of peace, love and protecting the weak in society. Christianity, therefore, presented a problem for the Nazi regime, particularly as Jesus was Jewish rather than Aryan and this went against the ideals of the People's Community. Moreover, many Germans had strong Christian beliefs and, therefore, might be less willing to support the regime.

Protestant Churches

Despite their religious beliefs, many Protestants were willing to support the Nazis because of their family values. A number of **pastors** spoke in favour of the Nazis, encouraged their congregation to vote for them and were willing to allow their churches to be used as Nazi bases. There were many different Protestant

Churches and Hitler wanted to co-ordinate and control them. A united Reich Church was established in 1933 under Ludwig Müller, a fanatical Nazi.

However, Nazi policies gradually resulted in the alienation of many Protestants and in 1934, two Protestant bishops were arrested for opposing the Reich Church. As a result, other pastors established the **Confessional Church**, which was independent of the state, under the leadership of **Martin Niemoller**, and attracted the support of 7000 out of 17,000 pastors. Such support for Niemoller provides evidence of the ineffectiveness of Nazi policies when deeply held religious traditional beliefs were threatened.

Catholic Church

Hitler was concerned by the potential threat posed by the Catholic Church as its followers might put loyalty to the pope before that of the state. However, he did not want to provoke a conflict and, at the same time, the Catholic Church was concerned to preserve its independence. The Church therefore signed the *Reichskonkordat* with the state in July 1933. This appeared to guarantee religious freedom:

- The Church could run itself and appoint its own ministers.
- Parents were able to request Catholic schools for their children.
- In return for the Church keeping out of politics, the Nazis agreed not to interfere with the legal and property rights of the Church.

Opposition from the Churches

Despite the *Reichskonkordat*, the Nazis did interfere in the Catholic Church. The Nazis embarked on a series of policies to undermine the Churches with the Ministry of Church Affairs led by **Hanns Kerrl** introducing the following measures:

- it closed some Church schools
- crucifixes were removed from school walls and replaced with swastikas
- nativity plays and carols were banned
- there were attacks on the Catholic Youth Movement
- pastors and priests were arrested
- Church funds were confiscated.

Although this weakened the Churches, it did not destroy opposition from them, and even the papacy criticised the regime in an encyclical called 'With Burning Concern' which was read out in every Catholic Church on Palm Sunday in 1937. Individual clergy who spoke out against the regime, such as Niemoller and **Dietrich Bonhoeffer**, were sent to concentration camps to silence them. But the popularity of such individuals made it difficult for the Nazis to do any more, as was seen when Bishop Galen's attack on euthanasia led to its suspension (see page 121).

> **KEY FIGURES**
>
> **Martin Niemoller (1892–1984)**
> Niemoller led the Confessional Church. He was a nationalist and had formerly been a U-boat commander before becoming a pastor. He had doubts about the Nazi regime and was a co-founder of the Confessional Church. He criticised the regime in his sermons and was arrested and sent to concentration camps until the end of the war.
>
> **Hanns Kerrl (1887–1941)**
> He was minister of Church affairs from 1935 to 1941, but was increasingly marginalised by more extreme Nazis. When he died of natural causes in 1941 he was not replaced.
>
> **Dietrich Bonhoeffer (1906–45)**
> Bonhoeffer was an academic and pastor who joined the Confessional Church in 1940. He also became involved in political opposition and was in contact with the conservative Kreisau Circle (see page 122). He was banned from preaching because of his criticism of the regime, but he continued to help Jewish people emigrate and worked with the resistance movement until he was arrested by the *Gestapo* in 1943 and eventually murdered in Flossenburg concentration camp.

The German Faith Movement

The regime also attempted to establish an alternative to Christianity, the German Faith Movement, which was non-Christian and based on the beliefs of Germans in ancient history. It was based on four key themes:

- A belief in the superiority of the Germanic races and opposition to the Jewish community.
- The replacement of Christian ceremonies, such as marriage, with pagan versions.
- A rejection of Christian ethics of mercy and forgiveness.
- A belief in the cult of Hitler's personality.

Even more than the Nazi policy towards the Churches, the Faith Movement was a failure as only five per cent of Germans ever joined it.

It was only after military success in the war during 1939–40 that the regime was confident enough to persecute the Churches. Monasteries were closed, Church property was attacked and Church activities were restricted. However, while the Churches were constrained, they were not destroyed. The regime was still reluctant to attack the Churches because it wanted to avoid unrest; the Nazis were aware that religious beliefs were strong in Germany and they did not want to provoke problems. Moreover, after 1942, the Churches played an important role in supporting the population after bombing raids. As a result, the regime could not afford to alienate the Churches as they played a valuable role in maintaining morale at home.

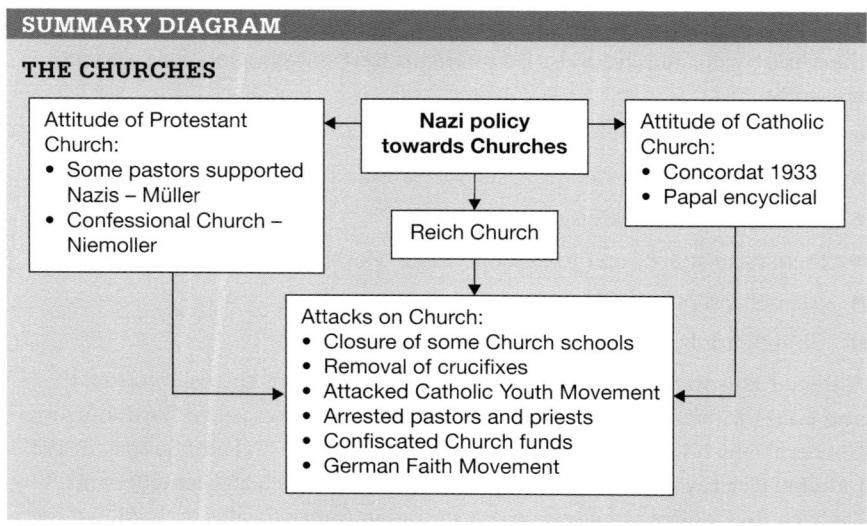

7 The effectiveness of *Volksgemeinschaft*

■ *How far did the Nazis succeed in creating a* Volksgemeinschaft?

It appears that by the mid-1930s Hitler was popular with the people and many Germans viewed the regime in a positive light. There were many features of the regime that appealed to people, and schemes such as *Winterhilfe* helped to create a sense of community and working together for the common good. However, in making any assessment, we have to balance the image created by propaganda with the reality. For example, although *Winterhilfe* was supposed to be a voluntary scheme, there was considerable pressure put on people to contribute. *Gestapo* reports indicate that there was grumbling at Nazi officials and there is evidence to suggest that the government was concerned as to how people would react if living standards fell because of the emphasis on rearmament. The Nazis' reluctance to implement or continue policies such as euthanasia also indicates that they had not won over the hearts and minds of the majority. This is seen even more clearly in the hesitancy of the Nazis' policy towards the Churches. This lack of support would become even more apparent when the war started to progress badly from 1943 onwards.

The limitations of the success are explained in Benjamin Sax and Dieter Kuntz's work of 1992 (see Interpretation 1, below).

INTERPRETATION 1

From Benjamin Sax and Dieter Kuntz, *Inside Hitler's Germany: Documentary History of Life in the Third Reich*, D.C. Heath & Co., 1992, p. 183.

During the 1930s the Nazi dictatorship only partially realized National Socialist ideology. … These failures resulted both from inner contradictions within the ideology itself and from the tremendous gap between National Socialist ideals and the realities of German society. … Nazi policy often ignored the great difficulties confronting modern industrial societies, and it therefore failed to create a Volksgemeinschaft.

The view that *Volksgemeinschaft* failed to be achieved is reinforced by both Michael Hughes in his work of 1988 and Ian Kershaw in his book, first published in 1985. However, the two historians do place different emphasis on the success and failures of Nazi policies, as the extracts in Interpretation 2 and 3 show (see page 146).

INTERPRETATION 2

From Michael Hughes, *Nationalism and Society: Germany, 1800–1945*, Hodder Arnold, 1988, p. 214.

The greatest success of the National Socialist regime was in its propaganda. Large numbers of Germans became convinced as a result of Goebbels' efforts that they did live in a genuine **Volksgemeinschaft**. *This was increased by symbolic devices such as the cheap Volkswagen car and Volksempfanger radio receiver, putting what had previously been luxury goods within the reach of ordinary Germans, and party-encouraged mass participation in the* **Winterhilfe** *social welfare scheme. The reality was very different. The promise of a 'national revolution', the creation of a classless Germany with equality of opportunity for all and new criteria of worth to the nation, was not fulfilled.*

The impression of a kind of compulsory national unity was achieved by institutions such as the Labour Service, eventually obligatory for all young Germans, and the process known as 'standardisation' (**Gleichschaltung**). *Under this a large number of National Socialist organisations were given monopoly powers within their own field and membership of such bodies was usually compulsory for people engaged in a given profession, as was involvement in organised activities, a false air of unity could be created.*

The only aspect of **Volkisch** *nationalism which was realised was the elimination of the Jews.*

INTERPRETATION 3

From Ian Kershaw, *The Nazi Dictatorship: Problems and Perspectives of Interpretation*, Bloomsbury Revelations, 2015, pp. 206–7.

Recent research which paints an extremely complex picture of social behaviour and attitudes in the Third Reich, suggests strongly that it is easy to exaggerate the nature of changes in values and attitudes under Nazism, and that here too there can be no suggestion of Nazism having effected a social revolution ... There was some penetration of Nazi values and attitudes [but] the regime's social propaganda made little serious dent in the traditional class loyalties, particularly among older industrial workers.

The hold of the Church and clergy over the population, especially in the country areas, was often strengthened rather than weakened by the 'Church struggle' ... Nazi policy failed categorically to break down religious allegiance. Even in their attempt to inculcate the German people with racial, eugenic, and social Darwinist values the Nazis, it appears, had only limited success.

Much suggests that the Nazis made their greatest impact on young Germans ... but even here, the regime had only partial success ... signs of conflict, tension and opposition within certain sections of German youth were already apparent by the later 1930s and increased in the war years, suggesting that the Nazis had been only temporarily successful in winning over, mobilising and integrating young Germans.

The view that the Third Reich was a totalitarian regime that modernised Germany has been undermined. However, there is still much debate as to how far most Germans took in the Nazi view of the *Volksgemeinschaft*.

ONLINE EXTRAS

Get to grips with weighing up the success and failure of *Volksgemeinschaft* by completing Worksheet 27 at **www.hoddereducation. co.uk/accesstohistory/extras**

SUMMARY DIAGRAM

THE EFFECTIVENESS OF *VOLKSGEMEINSCHAFT*

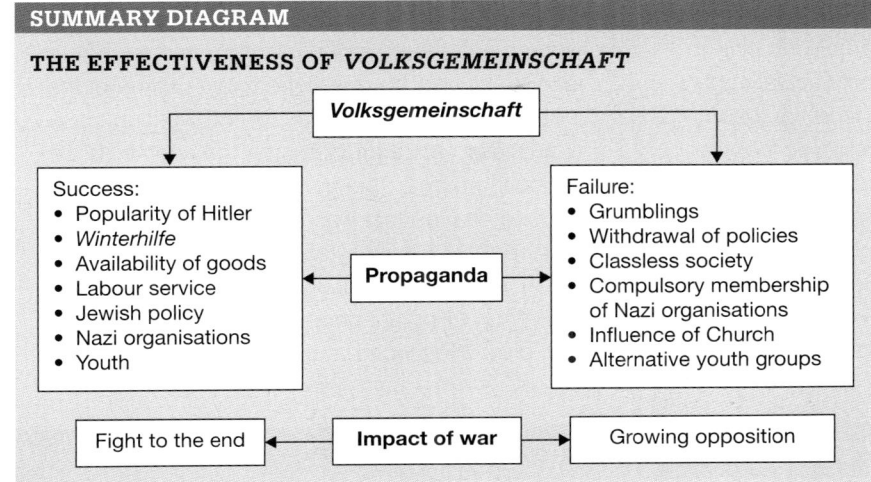

CHAPTER SUMMARY

Volksgemeinschaft was an ambitious plan to change German society, but its actual impact over such a short period of time has been questioned. Although Hitler enjoyed popular support, particularly in the years up to 1943, *Volksgemeinschaft* failed to create a new and lasting German or Nazi culture. The position and influence of the traditional German Churches was not really challenged by the German Faith Movement. The impact of the policies on both women and the young, particularly in the long term, must also be questioned. Even some of the initial benefits, such as jobs for the working class, would later create problems for the regime as the economic realities became apparent. However, the one change that was clear was the Nazis' racial policy and their treatment of non-Aryans, which went from gradualism to radicalism as Jewish and Romani people, 'asocials' and those with disabilities faced a growing intolerance.

Refresher questions

Use these questions to remind yourself of the key material covered in this chapter.

1 What was the basis of Nazi racial ideology?
2 In what ways could Nazi policy towards Jewish people be described as 'gradualist'?
3 Why did Nazi policy towards Jewish people become radical after 1938?
4 Who were the 'asocials' in Nazi Germany?
5 Why were the 'asocials' persecuted?
6 How did the Nazis aim to transform German society?
7 How was education used to indoctrinate the young?
8 How successful was the education policy in indoctrinating the young?
9 How successful was the Hitler Youth in making the young conform?
10 What was the aim of the Nazi policy towards women?
11 How successful was the Nazi policy towards women?
12 What problems faced the Nazis in trying to gain the support of the workers?
13 What were the main features of Nazi policy towards the workers and was it successful?
14 How did Nazi policy towards the Churches change?
15 How successful was Nazi policy towards the Church?
16 How successful was the policy of *Volksgemeinschaft*?

CHAPTER 8

Nazi economic policy 1933–45

On Hitler's appointment as chancellor in January 1933 there were nearly 6 million unemployed, but by 1939 there was a labour shortage. This transformation helps to explain Hitler's popularity, but also suggests that in the pre-war years his economic policy was a success. Although the reduction of unemployment was important, a bigger concern for Hitler was to prepare the country for war.

This chapter will examine how effective Hitler was in achieving these aims by focusing on the following themes:

- The performance of the economy 1933–9
- The wartime economy
- The role of individuals
- Trade unions
- Conclusion: Nazi economic policy

KEY DATES

1933	May	Creation of the German Labour Front (DAF)
	Nov.	Creation of the Strength Through Joy movement
1934	Sept.	New Plan introduced
1935	June	Reich Labour Service for all men aged 19–25
1936	Oct.	Four Year Plan introduced

1938		DAF organised the Volkswagen car scheme
1939	Dec.	War economy decrees
1941	Dec.	Rationalisation Decree
1942	Feb.	Speer appointed minister of armaments
1943	Feb.	Goebbels' 'Total War' speech

1 The performance of the economy 1933–9

▪ *How well did the German economy perform in the period from 1933 to 1939?*

One of the most important reasons for the increase in support for the Nazis from 1929 was the economic situation, particularly the high level of unemployment. There is little doubt that when the Nazis came to power economic issues were a major problem:

- Six million people were unemployed.
- Industrial production had returned to the levels of the 1890s.
- The agricultural sector was depressed.

However, by 1933, the worst of the Great Depression was over and there were already signs of recovery. Hitler was able to build on the public works schemes of Schleicher and was helped financially with the end of reparations in 1932. The Depression and early Nazi action against trade unions also meant that demands for higher wages were silenced. In many ways, the economic position was not as bleak as it had been, and the success of Nazi policies should be judged in this context.

Economic recovery

Hitler was aware that the survival and stability of his regime depended to a large extent on bringing Germany out of the Depression. He had promised in 1933 to solve the unemployment problem within four years. In this, he was helped by the fact that the Depression had reached its lowest point in the winter of 1932–3 and from then on the trade cycle began to improve. A central part of his plan was public works schemes which involved public investment, led in most part by the state, which would stimulate demand and raise national income. One billion Reichsmarks were invested in such schemes, which saw the building of roads, canals and houses. The car industry was encouraged with tax concessions, which resulted in a 40 per cent increase in production. Rearmament (see pages 152–3) also helped. This was soon followed by the introduction of

SOURCE QUESTION

In what ways do you think that the photograph in Source A could be seen as propaganda?

SOURCE A

The first *autobahn* was instigated by the mayor of Cologne, Konrad Adenauer. The stretch of motorway from Cologne to Bonn was opened in 1932. A further 3000 km (1900 miles) of motorway roads were developed in the 1930s. They served as an economic stimulus, but were also politically used as a propagandist tool. Their military value has been doubted.

conscription in 1935, which assisted in absorbing a large number of young unemployed men. The government also continued the **Voluntary Labour Service**, which also facilitated in removing young people from the labour market and, by 1935, employed some 500,000 men. But perhaps the most significant measure was the Law for the Reduction of Unemployment, which succeeded in removing some women from the labour market by offering loans to those about to marry if they gave up their jobs.

The government tripled public investment between 1933 and 1936 and increased government expenditure by some 70 per cent. By 1936, with the economic recovery well under way, the government was able to place greater emphasis on rearmament.

Table 8.1 Public investment and expenditure in billions of Reichsmark 1928–36

	1928	1932	1933	1934	1935	1936
Total public investment	6.6	2.2	2.5	4.6	6.4	8.1
Total government expenditure	11.7	8.6	9.4	12.8	13.9	15.8

Table 8.2 Public expenditure by category in billions of Reichsmark 1928–36

Category	1928	1932	1933	1934	1935	1936
Construction	2.7	0.9	1.7	3.5	4.9	5.4
Rearmament	0.7	0.7	1.8	3.0	5.4	10.2
Transportation	2.6	0.8	1.3	1.8	2.1	2.4

> **KEY TERMS**
> **Voluntary Labour Service** Established by Brüning in 1931. It was a state-sponsored employment organisation that provided services to civic and land improvement projects. By 1932, it had enrolled some 300,000 men.
>
> **Reich Food Estate** Government body responsible for everything involved in agricultural production. It fixed prices, regulated supplies and even decided what fertilisers and seeds were to be used. It also secured protection from the selling of foreign food supplies in Germany.

The recovery was also helped by the policies towards small businesses and farmers, both groups having been badly hit by the Depression. However, this was also a politically astute move as both of these groups had provided large numbers of loyal supporters of the regime. The policies included:

- Subsidies for farmers from the **Reich Food Estate**.
- Tariffs on imported food stuffs to protect German farmers.
- The Reich Entailed Farm Law, which gave small farmers greater security of tenure and helped to reduce their debts.
- Grants for house repairs.

These strategies appear to show a success as there was a dramatic fall in unemployment, such that, by 1938, there was virtually full employment. From the peak of 6 million in January 1932, unemployment had declined to 1.6 million by 1936, a welcome development for those who had been out of work and admired by other nations where unemployment was a problem. However, there are a number of limitations to this view. Although unemployment had fallen to 2.5 million by 1934, it did not fall again until 1936, following the introduction of conscription and rearmament in 1935. Much of the work, such as the Reich Labour Service, in which 18–25-year-old men had to do six months' work service, was not only badly paid but involved hard labour, often in poor conditions. Therefore, although the statistics suggest that the problem of unemployment was solved, they do not take account of the human effects.

Despite this, the government argued that economic policies in the years 1933–5 were a success.

> **SOURCE QUESTION**
>
> According to Hitler in Source B, what challenges did the Nazis face in restoring the German economy?

> **SOURCE B**
>
> From a speech by Hitler to the *Reichstag*, 21 May 1935.
>
> *What we have achieved in two and a half years in the way of a planned provision of labour, a planned regulation of the market, a planned control of prices and wages, was considered a few years ago to be absolutely impossible. We only succeeded because behind these apparently dead economic measures we had the living energies of the whole nation. We had, however, first to create a number of technical and psychological conditions before we could carry out this purpose. In order to guarantee the functioning of the national economy it was necessary first of all to put a stop to the everlasting fluctuation of wages and prices. It was further necessary to remove the conditions giving rise to interference which did not spring from higher national economic necessities, to destroy the class organisations of both camps which lived on the politics of wages and prices. The destruction of the Trade Unions, both of employers and employees, which were based on the class struggle demanded a similar removal of the political parties which were maintained by these groups of interest, which interest in return supported them.*

> **ONLINE EXTRAS** WWW
>
> Get to grips with source evaluation by completing Worksheet 28 at www.hoddereducation.co.uk/accesstohistory/extras

The revival of the economy caused concerns because it also led to a balance of trade deficit, with Germany importing more than it was exporting. As a result, gold and foreign currency reserves fell. Measures were taken by Hjalmar Schacht with the New Plan (see pages 155–6) of 1934, but growing demand still meant that imports were high.

Rearmament

There are a number of issues that have to be considered when comparing German preparedness for war:

- Was it that economic problems caused by rearmament forced Germany into a war in 1939 before it was ready?
- Was the economy simply not ready for war?
- Was it ready for a different type of war?

Conscription, or compulsory military service, reintroduced in 1935, had certainly helped to reduce unemployment levels, but rearmament, which involved one-quarter of the workforce, created a number of economic problems. There were still severe strains due to a budget deficit and balance of payments problems. Schacht wanted to encourage exports and slow the spending on armaments, but this was unacceptable to the armed forces and Nazi leaders. This raised the issue of the '**guns or butter?**' debate: should the economy focus on rearmament or consumer goods? It also resulted in Göring being put in charge of a new economic organisation, the Office of the Four Year Plan (see pages 156–7).

From 1936, with the Four Year Plan, the main emphasis of the German economy was undoubtedly armaments production. This is clear from Table 8.3 (see page 153), which compares Germany with other powers. However, the guns

> **KEY TERM**
>
> **Guns or butter?**
> A phrase used to describe the debate as to whether Germany should focus on rearmament (guns) or consumer goods (butter).

Table 8.3 Gross national product (GNP) and military expenditure in Germany, USA and Britain 1929–45 (in billions of specified currencies)

Year	Germany			USA			Britain		
	GNP (RM)	Military expenditure (RM)	GNP (%)	GNP ($)	Military expenditure ($)	GNP (%)	National income (£)	Military expenditure (£)	National income (%)
1929	89	0.8	1	104	0.7	1	4.2	0.1	2
1932	58	0.8	1	59	0.6	1	–	0.1	–
1934	67	4.1	6	65	0.7	1	3.9	0.1	3
1936	83	10.8	13	83	0.9	1	4.4	0.2	5
1938	105	17.2	17	85	1.0	1	4.8	0.4	8
1940	141	53.0	38	101	2.2	2	6.0	3.2	53
1942	165	91.0	55	159	49.6	31	7.5	4.8	64
1943	184	112.0	61	193	80.4	42	8.0	5.0	63

before butter deliberation is evidence that the Nazis were unable to subordinate all areas to armaments. The debate over priorities also provides further evidence that Hitler was not the all-powerful dictator who could subordinate everything to his personal wishes.

On the surface, it would appear that Nazi economic policy was a success in the years before the war. Unemployment was dramatically reduced and Germany's economic strength meant that when war did break out in 1939 the nation was able to dominate Europe. However, despite this military success, some historians, such as Richard Overy in *The Nazi Economic Recovery 1932–38* (1992), argue that the emphasis on rearmament had a considerable impact on the economy, suggesting that 'the switch to war preparation did not produce any real crisis in the economy before September 1939, but it did increasingly compromise the achievements already made'. This view has been taken further by Jeremy Noakes and Geoffrey Pridham in *Nazism 1918–1945, Volume 2: State, Economy and Society* (1984), where they posit that with the economy increasingly geared towards war it was heading towards a crisis: 'the cracks in an economy which was operating beyond its capacity were beginning to show. Although the use of the term "crisis" to describe the German economy in 1939 may be an overstatement, it was already clear to the regime's leaders that a serious economic crisis was just around the corner.' Tim Mason (1993) has gone even further and states that the strain was evident as early as 1937 and that the economy was in danger of expanding too quickly. Mason suggests that there was significant social discontent among the workforce, and it was this that pushed Hitler to war in 1939. This view has caused much controversy and Overy argues that rather than being pushed into war, Hitler stumbled unintentionally into it. He claims that Hitler did not envisage a major conflict until 1943 and that economic preparations were geared to that date, with earlier conflicts supposed to be purely local and, therefore, it should not be a surprise that Germany was not ready for war in 1939 as it had not planned for it at that time.

ONLINE EXTRAS **WWW**

Get to grips with the success and failure of Nazi economic policy in the years before the Second World War by completing Worksheet 29 at **www.hoddereducation.co.uk/accesstohistory/extras**

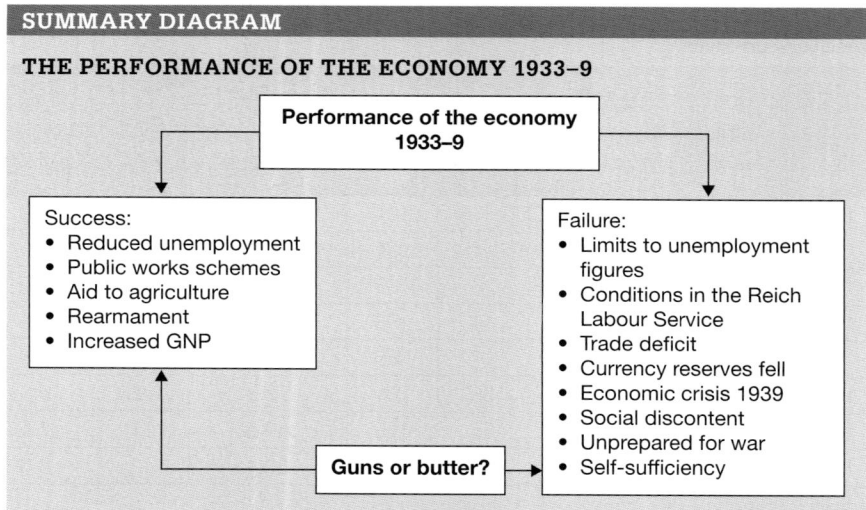

SUMMARY DIAGRAM

THE PERFORMANCE OF THE ECONOMY 1933–9

Performance of the economy 1933–9

Success:
- Reduced unemployment
- Public works schemes
- Aid to agriculture
- Rearmament
- Increased GNP

Failure:
- Limits to unemployment figures
- Conditions in the Reich Labour Service
- Trade deficit
- Currency reserves fell
- Economic crisis 1939
- Social discontent
- Unprepared for war
- Self-sufficiency

Guns or butter?

2 The wartime economy

■ *How well did the German economy perform during the war?*

The economy was being prepared for a major war in the 1940s. Hitler was strengthening Germany through the *Anschluss* and the take-over of Czechoslovakia, (see pages 166–8), which brought him further resources and raw materials. However, the invasion of Poland in 1939 changed the situation. Hitler had expected it to lead to no more than a local war, but it caused a major war for which Germany was not prepared.

In response, Hitler ordered a massive economic mobilisation for war. However, there was still a shortage of war supplies, seen most clearly in Germany's inability to replace the planes it lost in the Battle of Britain in 1940, which was crucial in its failure to defeat Britain. Even as late as 1941, when Germany invaded the Soviet Union, one-third of its troops had inadequate equipment. Therefore, for the first two years of the war the economy was unable to meet the military needs of the country. In part, the Germans were able to overcome this problem as the success of **Blitzkrieg** meant that they could take resources from conquered lands.

The nature of the war changed when the German advance was halted at Moscow and Stalingrad (present-day Volgograd). From then on, the war became a drain on the economy. It led to a major economic organisational change. Göring's bureaucracy had failed and he was replaced, initially by **Fritz Todt**, but after his death by **Albert Speer**, and it was under him that the economy was more effectively organised to cope with Total War (see page 172).

Under Speer, there was a great increase in output, even though it coincided with the massive Allied aerial bombardment. Some historians have used this to argue

> **KEY TERM**
>
> **Blitzkrieg** 'Lightning war'. The strategy used by Hitler in 1939–40 to avoid the static war of 1914–18. It used dive-bombers, paratroopers and motorised infantry to ensure that there was a rapid advance.

> **KEY FIGURES**
>
> **Fritz Todt (1891–1942)**
>
> He was responsible for the building of the *autobahns* in the 1930s. In 1940 he was appointed minister of armaments, which led to clashes with Göring. He was killed in a plane crash in 1942.
>
> **Albert Speer (1905–81)**
>
> He was a close friend of Hitler's and became his architect. He replaced Todt as minister of armaments in 1942. Speer increased the production of armaments. At the Nuremberg trials, he was sentenced to twenty years' imprisonment.

that the bombing campaign was a failure, but historian Richard Overy considers that it should be seen as evidence of the success of Speer. Overy has even suggested that if it had not been for the bombing campaign, Germany might have outproduced the USSR and Britain together. It was only when the military situation deteriorated in 1945 that the German economy was unable to support the war.

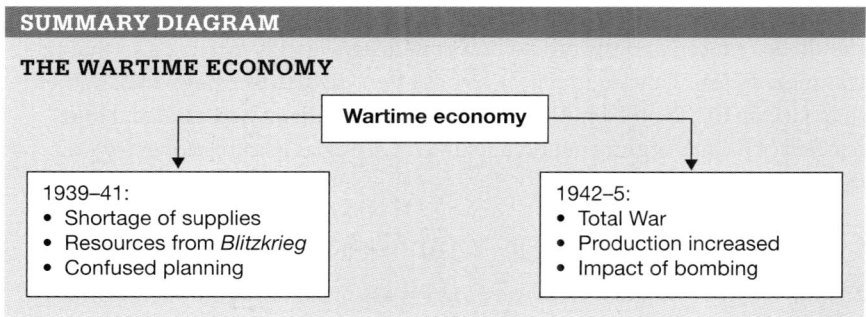

3 The role of individuals

■ *How successful were key individuals in achieving their economic aims?*

Schacht and the New Plan

To help with the economic recovery after the Great Depression, Hjalmar Schacht (see page 34), the president of the Reichsbank from 1933 to 1939, was appointed as minister of economics from 1934 to 1937. In order to bring about recovery, he encouraged heavy state spending, following a policy of deficit financing which resulted in government spending rising by 70 per cent in the period from 1933 to 1936. Although this and the accompanying public works schemes did lead to a fall in unemployment, it was also accompanied by a balance of trade deficit as Germany was importing more raw materials and failing to increase its exports, which resulted in a shortage of money.

The New Plan was introduced by Schacht in September 1934. The main features of this were:

- The government took control over all trade, tariffs, capital and currency exchange.
- The government could decide which imports to allow, with priority given to those needed by **heavy industry**.
- **Bilateral trade treaties** were signed, particularly with south-east Europe and South America, through which German purchases were paid in Reichsmarks, which the countries then had to use to buy German goods.

> **KEY TERMS**
>
> **Heavy industry** The manufacture of large products, often through several processes and in large factories, usually associated with the production of coal, iron and steel.
>
> **Bilateral trade treaties** A trade agreement between two countries.

The rapid increase in spending created the prospect of inflation, but this was avoided through the introduction of *Mefo* bills. These were credit notes to pay manufacturers of military equipment and were guaranteed by the government as payment for goods. The bills were used to raise funds by offering a four per cent interest rate with banks forced to invest in them. This policy also helped to disguise government spending. However, despite the raising of funds for rearmament, the demand this created for imports meant that the balance of payments problem was worsening. Schacht argued that arms expenditure should be reduced and the production of industrial goods increased so that there was more to sell. This led to the 'guns or butter?' debate (see page 152). Rather than face up to the problems that increasing rearmament had created, Hitler rejected Schacht's argument and appointed Göring as commissioner for raw materials and currency.

Göring and the Four Year Plan

The aims of the Four Year Plan were to increase armaments production, make Germany ready for war in four years and also achieve autarky, so that Germany was producing its own food and industrial goods. In order to achieve this, the Four Year Plan set out to increase agricultural and industrial production, develop **ersatz** products (such as artificial rubber from acetylene to replace imports) and use coal to produce oil, and regulate imports and exports so that armaments were favoured over agriculture. However, the production of oil was not a success as it took six tons of coal to produce a ton of oil.

As head of the plan, Göring presided over a new organisation, which, typically for Nazi Germany, cut across other economic ministries. The Office of the Four Year Plan issued regulations which controlled:

- foreign exchange
- labour
- raw materials
- prices.

It was, therefore, able to create a managed economy, with the government setting targets for private industry.

The emphasis within the economy appeared to make it clear that Hitler was moving towards creating a **Total War** economy and that he was contemplating large-scale rather than localised war. Göring was given responsibility for rearmament, with the result that Schacht resigned in November 1937.

One of the aims of the Four Year Plan was to increase production in key war industries, such as synthetic rubber, fuel, oil and iron ore. Large plants were built in order to achieve this and, in 1938, after the *Anschluss*, Austrian companies were taken over. This was followed by a takeover of the **Škoda Works** in the **Sudetenland**, after annexation. As a result, industrial production rose, and at a considerable rate in some industries, such as aluminium. However, most targets were not met, particularly for oil and rubber, and the demands of the armed

> **KEY TERMS**
>
> **Ersatz** Substitute.
>
> **Total War** A war that involves the whole population, both economically and militarily.
>
> **Škoda Works** An armaments factory in the Sudetenland region.
>
> **Sudetenland** A largely German-speaking region of Czechoslovakia, which was annexed by Germany in 1938.

forces were not satisfied. This meant that by 1939, when war broke out, Germany still relied on foreign supplies for one-third of its raw materials and therefore, although the economy was dominated by preparations for war, it was not ready for Total War. The success or otherwise of the policy can be seen in Tables 8.4 and 8.5 below.

Table 8.4 Figures from the Four Year Plan

Commodity	Output (in thousands of tons)			Four Year Plan target
	1936	1938	1942	
Oil	1,790	2,340	6,260	13,830
Aluminium	98	166	260	273
Artificial rubber	1	5	96	120
Nitrogen	770	914	930	1,040
Explosives	18	45	300	323
Steel	19,216	22,656	20,480	24,000
Iron ore	2,255	3,360	4,137	5,549
Lignite	161,382	194,985	245,918	240,500
Hard coal	158,400	186,186	166,059	213,000

The production of aluminium and explosives expanded considerably, while the target for lignite (a type of low-quality coal) was met. However, Table 8.4 shows that it fell well short in the crucial areas of oil and rubber, while armament production also failed to reach the target (see pages 158 and 172). Perhaps the clearest indication that the plan failed was that when war broke out Germany still depended on foreign supplies for one-third of its raw materials.

> **ONLINE EXTRAS** WWW
>
> Get to grips with turning assertion into argument by completing Worksheet 30 at **www.hoddereducation.co.uk/accesstohistory/extras**

Table 8.5 Percentage of major foodstuffs produced within Germany 1927–39

Foodstuff	1927–8	1933–4	1938–9
Grain	79	99	115
Potatoes	96	100	100
Vegetables	84	90	91
Meat	91	98	97
Fats	44	53	57
All food	68	80	83

Speer

The appointment of Speer as minister of armaments, following the death of Todt in 1942, marked a significant turning point in the development of the economy. His close relationship with Hitler allowed him to cut through many interests and implement his programme of what he called 'industrial self-responsibility'. This allowed far greater mass production as controls and constraints on business were relaxed. A Central Planning Board was set up in April 1942 and this was supported by a number of committees, each of which dealt with a specific area of the economy. Industrialists were encouraged to join his ministerial team, while military personnel were excluded from the production process. Speer simply co-ordinated the process and ensured that a more efficient exploitation of resources and manpower was in place.

Although the concept of Total War is often associated with Goebbels' speech in February 1943, following the surrender at Stalingrad (see page 175), the real transformation had actually begun much earlier and was due to Speer. His success can be seen in Tables 8.6 and 8.7 below.

Table 8.6 Number of tanks produced by Germany, Britain, USA and USSR 1940–5

Year	Germany	Britain	USA	USSR
1940	1,600	1,400	300	2,800
1941	3,800	4,800	4,100	6,400
1942	6,300	8,600	25,000	24,700
1943	12,100	7,500	29,500	24,000
1944	19,000	4,600	17,600	29,000
1945	3,900	–	12,000	15,400

Table 8.7 Number of aircraft produced by Germany, Britain, USA and USSR 1940–5

Year	Germany	Britain	USA	USSR
1940	10,200	15,000	6,100	7,000
1941	11,000	20,100	19,400	125,000
1942	14,200	23,600	47,800	26,000
1943	25,200	26,200	85,900	37,000
1944	39,600	26,500	96,300	40,000
1945	–	12,100	46,000	35,000

Despite this dramatic improvement in production levels, it could be argued that Germany had the capacity to produce even more, but Speer constantly faced a struggle with *Gauleiters* and the *Schutzstaffel* (SS), particularly in exploiting the conquered lands.

ONLINE EXTRAS WWW

Get to grips with weighing up evidence on Nazi economic policy during the Second World War by completing Worksheet 31 at www.hoddereducation.co.uk/accesstohistory/extras

---

SUMMARY DIAGRAM

THE ROLE OF INDIVIDUALS

Schacht:
- New plan
- *Mefo* bills
- Bilateral treaties
- Public works
- Deficit financing

Göring:
- Four Year Plan
- Rearmament
- Autarky
- Total War economy

Speer:
- Central Planning Board
- Co-ordination
- Total War

4 Trade unions

■ *To what extent did workers lose out by the abolition of trade unions?*

The trade union movement within Germany was strong, with large-scale membership and close links to both socialism and Catholicism. It was hostile to Nazism and was, therefore, seen as a threat to the stability of the state.

The banning of trade unions

Despite being a powerful force in Germany, trade union influence and power was destroyed by May 1933, just a few months after the Nazis came to power. Trade unions had already been weakened by the Depression, which had led to a fall in membership, and many workers were more concerned about keeping their jobs.

The Nazis were able to exploit this weakness and the unions' initial hope that they would be able to work with the new government. The government, perhaps surprisingly, declared 1 May, which was the traditional day to celebrate international socialist labour, a national holiday. This helped to convince the unions that there might be the opportunity to build a working relationship with the Nazis. However, it left them unprepared for the events that followed. On 2 May 1933, union offices were occupied, funds seized and many union leaders sent to concentration camps.

These events were then followed, as part of the process of *Gleichschaltung* (see page 100), by the banning of independent trade unions and their replacement by the German Labour Front (DAF).

The German Labour Front (DAF)

In place of the trade unions, workers had to join the DAF under the leadership of **Robert Ley**. This became the largest Nazi organisation, with membership rising from 5 million in 1933 to 22 million in 1939. Although workers did not have to join, it was advisable to do so. Its role was outlined in a government statement in November 1933 (see Source C, below).

> **SOURCE C**
>
> From a government statement on the role of the DAF, November 1933.
>
> *The German Labour Front is the organisation for all working people without reference to their economic and social position. Within it workers will stand side by side with employers, no longer separated into groups and associations which serve to maintain special economic or social distinctions or interest.*
>
> *In accordance with the will of our Führer, Adolf Hitler, the German Labour Front is not the place for deciding the material questions of daily working life. The high aim of the Labour Front is to educate all Germans who are at work to support the National Socialist State and to indoctrinate them in the National Socialist mentality.*

KEY FIGURE

Robert Ley (1890–1945)

Ley had trained as a chemist and worked for IG Farben. He was leader of the DAF but became an alcoholic and lost support during the war.

ONLINE EXTRAS

Test your understanding of the value of a source by completing Worksheet 32 at **www.hoddereducation. co.uk/accesstohistory/extras**

SOURCE QUESTION

What is the purpose of Source C? How useful is it as evidence of the aims of the DAF?

The DAF was responsible for nearly all areas of work, including:
- working hours and wages
- training schemes for apprentices
- supervising working conditions through the Beauty of Labour (a propaganda campaign focusing on clean work environments)
- the provision of meals for workers
- dealing with industrial unrest, absenteeism and strikes
- ensuring that rents for housing remained stable.

Strength Through Joy

Aware of the need to win the support of the workers, another offshoot of the DAF, the 'Strength Through Joy' (KdF or *Kraft durch Freude*) movement, was established, which offered workers sports facilities, cultural visits and holidays. This was a state welfare organisation introduced to gain the support of workers and improve conditions and morale in the workplace. Although the number of holidays taken by its members rose from 2.3 million in 1934 to over 10 million in 1938, these were really only available to loyal workers and were therefore limited in their impact. Perhaps the most striking example of the limits to the benefits is the opportunity that workers were given to start paying towards the purchase of the 'People's Car', the Volkswagen. Many workers did contribute, but no cars were actually delivered.

Table 8.8 Official figures for participants in Strength Through Joy activities in 1938

Activity	Number of participants
Cruises	131,623
Hikes	1,937,850
Other holidays	8,259,238
Films	857,402
Exhibitions	1,595,516
Concerts	2,515,598
Operas	6,639,067
Theatre	7,478,633
Variety shows	7,980,973
Popular entertainments	13,660,015
Various sports	22,379,631
Other activities	13,776,791

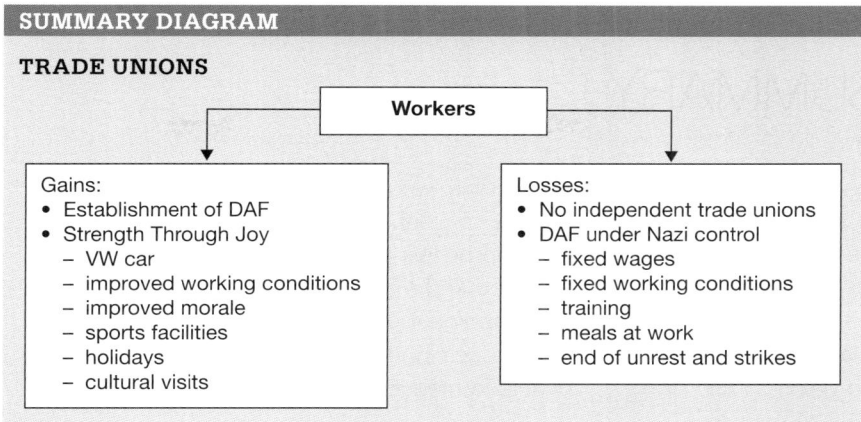

5 Conclusion: Nazi economic policy

■ *How successful was the Nazi economic policy?*

It is difficult to assess the success or otherwise of Nazi economic policy, as much depends on the criteria against which it is judged. On the one hand, in the period to 1939, the regime had been able to virtually eradicate unemployment, which had been one of Hitler's promises. However, it was achieved only because one-quarter of the workforce was employed in rearmament. In terms of preparing Germany for war, which had been the main aim from 1936, it had failed to reach the full-scale mobilisation needed for Total War, but that was because large-scale war was not planned until 1943. Certainly, vast amounts had been spent on rearmament, with some seventeen per cent of Germany's GNP going on military expenditure in 1938–9, compared to just eight per cent in Britain. However, these large amounts had created other economic problems, such as production bottlenecks, competition for scarce resources, labour shortages, a lack of foreign exchange to pay for imports and a growing danger of inflation. There had certainly been an increase in the production of goods, such as synthetic rubber, fuel oil and iron ore, aided by the taking over of the Škoda Works. However, despite the increase, production targets were not met and imports were still needed, which continued to drain the financial resources of the country. Whether Germany was ready for a short war is a matter for debate, but it was certainly not ready for the war it actually had to fight.

At first, the war economy was not effectively mobilised, but under Speer, production levels increased quite dramatically. However, there were still problems of labour and resource shortages and the economy, therefore, failed to meet the production levels of some of its enemies. This was not helped by the Allied aerial bombing campaign (see pages 182–4), which resulted in resources having to be diverted to build anti-aircraft installations.

CHAPTER SUMMARY

In many ways, it does appear as if the Nazi economic policy was a success as full employment was achieved and the nation's economic strength was considerably built up, allowing early successes in the war. This also helped to make Hitler popular. However, the recovery had already started before Hitler came to power, suggesting that he was not fully responsible, while the policy of rearmament had serious consequences, with most German people failing to benefit from the growth. Autarky was not achieved and many resources were wasted until Speer reorganised and rationalised the system. Despite gearing the economy to war, it was still unable to meet Germany's needs.

Refresher questions

Use these questions to remind yourself of the key material covered in this chapter.

1 Why was the German economy able to recover in the early 1930s?
2 What role was played by public works schemes in the recovery?
3 What was the impact of rearmament on the economy?
4 What was the impact of the war on economic growth?
5 How did Schacht's policies stimulate the economy?
6 How did Schacht attempt to deal with the balance of payments problem?
7 What were the main aims of the Four Year Plan?
8 How successful was the policy of autarky?
9 What were the main achievements of Speer's economic policy?
10 Why did the Nazis consider trade unions a threat?
11 Was the regime able to win the support of workers?
12 What were the losses for the workers as a result of the DAF?
13 Did the workers benefit through Strength Through Joy?

CHAPTER 9

Nazi foreign policy and the Second World War 1933–45

The early years of the Second World War were militarily successful for Germany, with most of western Europe occupied and major advances into the Soviet Union. The economy was bolstered by these wars of conquest and the successes brought further support for the regime. However, the advances eastwards also brought large numbers of Jewish people under Nazi control and resulted in a change of policy as resettlement was no longer a realistic option. This ultimately led to the Final Solution.

This chapter will focus on the aims of German foreign policy and how they were put into practice, and the impact of the Second World War, by focusing on the following themes:

- The aims of Nazi foreign policy to 1939
- The outbreak of war
- German success in western Europe
- The turning point of the Second World War
- The Wannsee Conference (1942) and the Final Solution
- The defeat of Germany
- The impact of war on society

KEY DATES

1936	March	German troops occupied the demilitarised Rhineland
1937	Nov.	Hossbach Memorandum
1938	March	*Anschluss* with Austria
	Sept.	Sudetenland given to Germany
1939	March	Czechs bullied into accepting takeover of Bohemia-Moravia
	Aug.	Nazi–Soviet Pact
	Sept.	Outbreak of Second World War, Germany invaded Poland
1940	April	Germany occupied Denmark and conquered Norway
	May	Germany invaded Netherlands, Belgium and France
	Aug.–Sept.	Germany planned to invade Britain, but defeated in the Battle of Britain
1941	April	Germany invaded Yugoslavia and Greece
	June–Dec.	Germany invaded USSR but halted at Moscow and Leningrad
	Aug.	Bishop Galen's sermon against euthanasia
1942	Jan.	Wannsee Conference co-ordinated Final Solution for the 'Jewish problem'
	May	German offensive at Stalingrad
1944	June	Allies launched D-Day
	July	Stauffenberg Plot
	Nov.	Execution of Edelweiss Pirates in Cologne
1945	Feb.	Yalta Conference
	April	Suicide of Hitler
	May	Surrender of Germany
	Aug.	Potsdam Conference

1 The aims of Nazi foreign policy to 1939

■ *What were the aims of Nazi foreign policy in the period from 1933 to 1939?*

There has been a great deal of debate among historians as to Hitler's foreign policy aims and the extent to which his two books, *Mein Kampf* (*My Struggle*, 1925) and *Zweites Buch* (*Second Book*, 1928), express his ambitions. It can be argued that further evidence of the aims can be seen in both the 1936 'Secret Memorandum' on the Four Year Plan and his 1937 'Hossbach Memorandum' recording Hitler's speech at a meeting in Berlin between his key military and political figures.

In *Mein Kampf* there were few foreign policy references, but Hitler did call for the acquisition of new land for the excess population, which should be gained in the east at the expense of Russia. However, these ideas were developed more in *Zweites Buch* where there was a much greater stress on the need for *Lebensraum* in the east. There was also an explanation as to why Hitler thought that Britain would not oppose Germany in Europe, suggesting that Germany was not a threat to the British Empire. Instead, he saw a final struggle between a German-dominated Europe and the USA.

Hitler's Secret Memorandum in 1936 justified the massive rearmament programme which was to be continued, despite the economic problems that Germany faced, to prepare the country for war in four years' time. In it, he argued that the menace of the USSR meant that German rearmament was essential (see Source A, below).

SOURCE QUESTION

Looking at Source A, what was the purpose of the Secret Memorandum?

SOURCE A

From Hitler's Secret Memorandum on autarky, August 1936.

The crisis cannot and will not fail to occur, and Germany has the duty of securing her existence by every means in the face of this catastrophe. For a victory of Bolshevism over Germany would lead not to a Versailles Treaty but to the final destruction, indeed to the annihilation, of the German people. In the face of the necessity of warding off this danger, all other considerations must recede into the background as completely irrelevant.

By the time of the Hossbach Memorandum a year later in 1937, there were severe tensions with Schacht, who was critical of the excessive resources directed towards rearmament. Hitler used this speech to his generals to argue that rather than cutting back there needed to be an even more aggressive approach to foreign policy. He argued that Germany needed to solve the problem of *Lebensraum* by 1943–5, although there was no specific mention of war with the USSR. Hitler's speech was poorly received, with the result that most of his audience were replaced, but many historians believe that the Hossbach Memorandum does provide a clear indication of his longer-term foreign policy intentions.

> **SOURCE B**
>
> From the Hossbach Memorandum, 1937.
>
> *The aim of German policy was to make secure and to preserve the racial community and to enlarge it. It was therefore a question of space ... Before turning to the question of solving the need for space, it had to be considered whether a solution holding promise for the future was to be reached by means of autarky or by means of increased participation in the world economy ...*
>
> *German policy had to reckon with two hate-inspired antagonists, Britain and France, to whom a German colossus in the centre of Europe was a thorn in the flesh, and both countries were opposed to any further strengthening of Germany's position either in Europe or overseas ... Germany's problem could only be solved by means of force, and this was never without attendant risk ...*
>
> *For the improvement of our political and military position our first objective, in the event of being embroiled in war, must be to overthrow Czechoslovakia and Austria simultaneously in order to remove the threat from our flank in any possible operation against the West.*

SOURCE QUESTION

How useful to the historian is Source B as evidence of Nazi plans?

ONLINE EXTRAS WWW

Get to grips with analysing sources by completing Worksheet 33 at **www.hoddereducation.co.uk/accesstohistory/extras**

However, it should be remembered that the Hossbach Memorandum is not an official document but was based on notes that Colonel Hossbach took at the meeting and wrote up five days later. Hossbach had been responsible for taking the official minutes of the meeting, but this document was never shown to Hitler. Although the original disappeared, various copies were used at the Nuremberg trials as evidence of planned Nazi aggression.

Historians have also questioned the extent to which Hitler had a masterplan for war, with Hugh Trevor-Roper (1953) suggesting that the Führer was able to control the events that led to his desired war in 1939. Such a view was challenged by A.J.P. Taylor (1964), who posits that Hitler did not have clear aims and was a pragmatist who took advantage of events as they developed. More recently, a compromise position has emerged, put forward by Alan Bullock (1967), which argues that although Hitler had an overall aim, he was willing to be flexible, and this has become the accepted standpoint.

There is little doubt that Hitler wanted war; he prepared Germany for it, believing that nations, like animals, had to fight for survival. In Hitler's mind, Germany was engaged in an all-out struggle with Jewish Bolshevism, but he intended this major conflict to take place between 1943 and 1945. He believed that by this time, Germany would have been strengthened by a series of victories in short, localised conflicts. Rearmament would be at its peak, whereas his opponents would be less prepared. Such an interpretation does appear to be supported by the following developments.

Occupying the Rhineland

The initial objectives certainly seem to have been to secure areas which were populated by German speakers or where Hitler could claim that he was only taking back land that was rightly Germany's. He was also cautious in the early years as Germany was still weak militarily and did not want to provoke the west.

However, public opinion in the west wanted to avoid military conflict and Hitler was able to exploit this. It was this that allowed him to reoccupy the Rhineland in March 1936. It also allowed Hitler to achieve one of his objectives by securing Germany's border against France and giving him greater assertion in the east. The remilitarisation also supports the argument that although this was part of his overall plan, he was an opportunist. Hitler's original plan had been to remilitarise the Rhineland in 1937, but the international situation in 1936, with Mussolini's actions in Abyssinia (see the box below) and Britain and France quarrelling over their response, created a distraction that he was able to exploit. France asked Britain for assurances of support over the Rhineland, but Britain refused to give them.

Not only did the success strengthen Hitler's position and prestige at home, but smaller nations felt that they could no longer trust Britain and France and it encouraged them to be conciliatory towards Germany.

Mussolini's actions in Abyssinia

Italian forces had been defeated by Abyssinian forces at Adowa in 1896. Mussolini saw an invasion of Abyssinia as an opportunity for revenge and the chance to create an East African empire which would detract from problems at home. A border incident at Wal-Wal in 1935 provided the pretext for an Italian invasion. It took Italian forces some eighteen months to subdue the kingdom, despite the League of Nations failing to help Abyssinia.

Anschluss

Success over the Rhineland encouraged Hitler to look again to Austria. There had been a failed Austrian Nazi coup in 1934. However, Hitler saw his chance to increase Nazi influence. In 1936, an Austro-German agreement had increased Nazi influence, with the National Opposition (Austrian Nazis) given a role in government. By 1938, the Austrian economy was in a weak position, not having recovered from the Depression, and Austria saw the advantage of joining a prosperous Germany.

Soundings from the western powers suggested that they would not object to closer links between Austria and Germany. As a result, Hitler encouraged Austrian Nazis to stir up trouble. As intended, this provoked the Austrian government, which took action to restore order and gave Germany a pretext for intervention. The annexation of Austria had always been an aim, as historian Alan Bullock makes clear in Interpretation 1 on page 167.

> **INTERPRETATION 1**
>
> From Alan Bullock, 'Hitler and the Origins of the Second World War', *Proceedings of the British Academy, LIII*, Oxford University Press, 1968, pp. 272–3.
>
> *The Anschluss seems to me to provide, almost in caricature, a striking example of that extraordinary combination of consistency in aim, calculation and patience in preparation with opportunism, impulse and improvisation in execution which I regard as characteristic of Hitler's policy.*
>
> *The aim in this case was never in doubt; the demand for the incorporation of Austria in the Reich appears on the first page of* **Mein Kampf**.

When German troops entered Austria on 12 March 1938 there was no resistance and Hitler was well received. Therefore, he decided to go further than just securing a satellite government; he absorbed Austria into Germany and thus overturned one of the key terms of the Treaty of Versailles, which had forbidden *Anschluss*.

This was a crucial preliminary to further eastward expansion, and, as Christopher Thorne writes in his 1973 book, *The Approach of War 1938–1939*, it also showed 'the easy triumphs that could be achieved by ruthless pressure and swift action against a critical but passive Europe'.

Czechoslovakia

Czechoslovakia was destroyed by Nazi Germany in two moves. The first used the argument of the Sudetenland Germans' right to self-determination in order to undermine the Czech state and make it defenceless. Once it was defenceless, Hitler could then conquer the rest of it. His policy was once again made that much easier by the attitude of the western powers. Britain was determined to avoid war and the British prime minister, **Neville Chamberlain**, did not view Czechoslovakia as important, considering the transfer of the Sudetenland, which contained some 3 million Germans, to Germany as reasonable. France, although it was allied to the Czech state, followed Britain's lead and accepted the agreement to transfer it to Germany in order to avoid war.

In the summer of 1938, a propaganda campaign by Hitler against the Czechs over the treatment of the German minority within their borders created tensions over the possibility of war. This persuaded France to encourage Britain to find a solution to avoid conflict. Chamberlain was able to reach an agreement with Hitler by which the Czechs would give up all areas where there were more than a 50 per cent German population. The Czech state was pressured into accepting this, but Hitler, seeing his opportunity, increased his demands. He now demanded all of the Sudetenland by 1 October. In order to avoid the possibility of a conflict for which they were poorly prepared, Britain and France persuaded the Italian dictator, Mussolini, to agree to a conference to discuss the issue. This led to Germany gaining all of the Sudetenland without having to fight, as Britain

KEY FIGURE

Neville Chamberlain (1869–1940)

He is closely associated with the policy of appeasement, which, his critics argue, involved surrendering to German demands, while his defenders argue that it was the only realistic policy given the state of British defences and public opposition to another war.

was unwilling to go to war over it and France was reluctant to act on its own. Their inaction provided Hitler with further evidence of the weakness of the west.

Having been thwarted in his desire for war, Hitler drew up plans to take the rest of Czechoslovakia. This marked a new departure for Hitler as, for the first time, it involved the conquest of non-German territory. Troops entered Prague on 15 March 1939 and incorporated Bohemia-Moravia into the Reich. The following day, Slovakia asked for German protection and troops were sent in to establish a satellite state, while the Hungarians took over Ruthenia.

Once again, the German Reich had been able to expand its territory without a war, but Hitler's actions did weaken the view in Britain and France that his demands were moderate and that he could be trusted. However, the inaction of the west also worried the USSR, which began to look for further ways to protect itself.

Poland and the Nazi–Soviet Pact

With the annexation of Czechoslovakia, it was obvious that Germany's next target was Poland. Almost immediately after the taking of Czechoslovakia, Hitler demanded that Lithuania returned Memel, which had been lost by Germany as a result of the Treaty of Versailles. Lithuania was forced to agree and, at the same time, Hitler began to exert pressure on Poland, claiming that Germans there were being mistreated and demanding the return of Danzig (the present-day port of Gdańsk in Poland).

Poland was unwilling to give in, particularly after Chamberlain gave Poland a guarantee to protect its integrity if it was attacked, at the end of March 1939. This angered Hitler as it reduced his chances of being able to pressurise Poland into agreeing to his demand. However, Hitler was convinced that despite talks between Britain, France and the USSR, they would still not intervene. Nevertheless, he wanted to avoid a repetition of the First World War where Germany was forced to fight a war on two fronts, in both the east and west. As a result, he developed contacts with the USSR.

Hitler believed that circumstances for an invasion of Poland were more favourable in 1939 than they would be in two or three years. His view was based on his belief that it would be only a localised war, with Britain and France, despite their hard words, not intervening. However, much to the shock of the world, he also concluded a treaty with the Soviet Union, even though he had always despised both Jewish communism and the Slavic nation. The agreement meant not only was the prospect of war on two fronts avoided, but Hitler also hoped it would further discourage French and British intervention, while securing vital raw materials from the USSR to help Germany overcome its rearmament problems.

The Nazi–Soviet Pact, signed in August 1939, allowed Hitler to invade Poland on 1 September, confident that it would be a short, victorious war with the west keeping out. However, Britain and France ultimately did declare war against Germany, although Poland was still defeated despite valiant resistance.

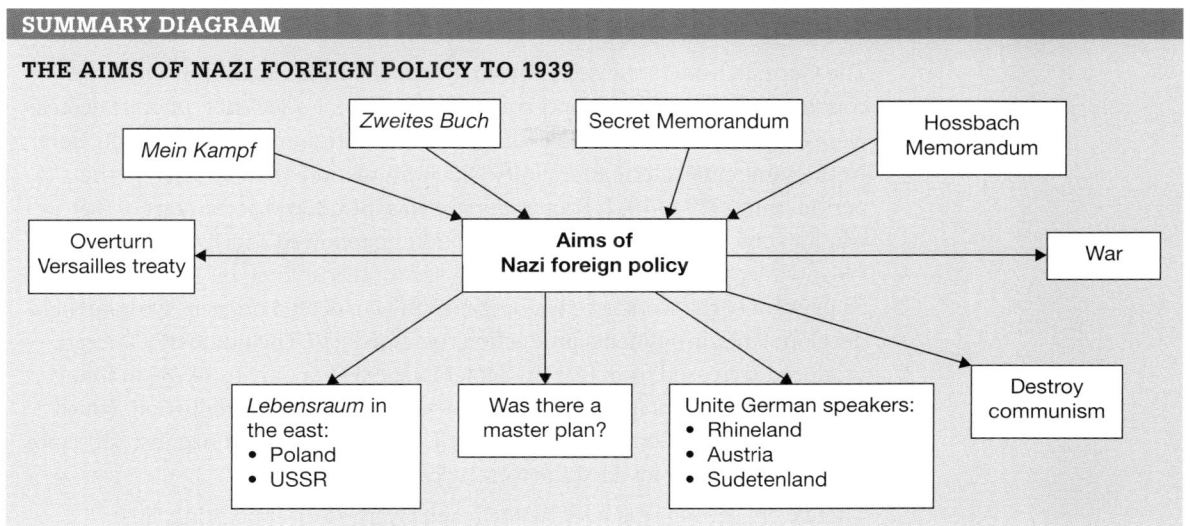

2 The outbreak of war

■ *How effectively did the German economy meet the challenges of war?*

On 1 September 1939, German forces invaded western Poland and on 17 September the USSR invaded eastern Poland. The war was over by 6 October. Polish forces were encircled. Despite the use of aircraft and tanks, the war was not predominantly won by *Blitzkrieg* but by more traditional tactics of infantry; encircling Polish forces which had been weakened by aerial bombing and the use of tanks. The Poles had expected help from their French and British allies in the form of attacks on the western front. This would have made the Germans withdraw some of their forces from Poland to counter the attack in the west, but help did not materialise.

Despite the victory against Poland, the German army was in desperate need of tanks and ammunition. Some historians think that these shortages were the reason why the German invasion of France was delayed for seven months, as Germany lacked the necessary resources to confront the much more powerful French army.

The reorganisation of the economy to meet Total War

German victories at the start of the war, achieved partly as a result of *Blitzkrieg*, gave the impression that the economy had not been overstrained. This view has been used by historians to explain why there was only partial economic mobilisation until 1942. Yet, as we saw in Chapter 8, other historians have argued that the German economy faced problems even before the war began.

The war economy

The German leaders wanted to avoid the problems that had confronted the country during the First World War and, therefore, a series of economic decrees were issued in December 1939 outlining vast programmes for war production. At the same time, German military expenditure more than doubled in the period from 1939 to 1941. Food rationing was introduced at the start of the war for some products, while clothes rationing followed a few months later. Meanwhile, the labour force was mobilised for war so that, by 1941, some 55 per cent of the workforce was engaged in war-related projects. Despite these developments, armaments production remained low. The number of aircraft produced increased from 8290 in September 1939 but only to 10,780 in June 1941. Such a disappointing increase was also seen in tank production, which meant that when Germany invaded the USSR in June 1941 it had just 800 more tanks than when it invaded the west in 1940.

There were several reasons why the results were so disappointing. First, production was hit by inefficiency and poor co-ordination. Some of this was the result of war being declared in 1939 when a number of key projects were not due to be finished until 1942. This failure to increase production was made worse by the lack of central control. There were numerous agencies, including the ministries of armaments, economics, labour and finance, which continued to function in their own way and often had different interests and demands. When corruption and the infighting between Nazi officials is added to this list, it is hardly surprising that the attempts to increase production were largely a failure. This problem is made even more evident if one considers the groups responsible for armaments: the Office of the Four Year Plan, the *Schutzstaffel* (SS) and the various branches of the armed forces. The armed forces wanted high-quality armaments to be produced, which took time, and this resulted in Germany failing to achieve the required levels of output by the time the invasion of the USSR began.

Germany also faced a labour shortage. In May 1939, before the war had started, 24.5 million men were employed in industrial production, but by 1940, that had fallen to just 20.5 million as some 4 million had been called up to fight in the armed forces. In an attempt to overcome this, Germany forcibly recruited foreign workers from both southern and central Europe. This would become even more important as the war progressed, but it created further problems. The foreign slaves had to be policed to ensure that they worked and that there was no undesirable racial contact between German and non-German workers. This policing absorbed even more of the potential workforce. There were also attempts to overcome the problem by calling up women into the workforce despite the regime's reluctance to do this. Even as early as September 1939, single women made up over 37 per cent of the labour force, a figure initially much higher than that in Britain. However, unlike Britain, Germany did not mobilise its married women in such numbers. Hitler repeatedly vetoed plans to conscript married German women, as he felt this would damage soldiers' morale. There was an attempt by the Reich Labour Ministry in the spring of 1940 to introduce female conscription for single women, but that caused unpopularity and was another reason why foreign labour was used. There were concerns within the regime that in order to maintain morale the armed forces needed to know that wives and girlfriends were being properly looked after. Many in government were concerned that if they were not, then there would be a repeat of 1918 and a collapse of morale at home. This was to be avoided at all costs.

The failure to mobilise adequately at the start of the war is made even clearer by comparing the percentage of gross domestic product (GDP) of Germany spent on the military with that of Britain, as can be seen in Table 9.1 (below).

Table 9.1 Percentage of GDP on military expenditure

Year	Germany	Britain
1937	13	7
1938	17	8
1939	23	22
1940	38	53
1941	47	60

Although Britain had lagged considerably behind Germany in the years prior to the outbreak of war, it soon caught up and then overtook Germany in its armaments production.

Rationing

Rationing was introduced early in the war, with many more items rationed than in Britain. However, the result was that two out of five Germans actually ate more healthily than before the war, although the diet was very monotonous and the amount of meat and dairy produce was limited. Clothes were also rationed, as was soap, while toilet paper was not available and hot water was allowed only two days a week. As the early years of the war went well, goods produced in Germany were bolstered by large amounts of plundered items from the conquered countries, even though much of this went to high-ranking party officials.

The Russian campaign of 1941 accustomed many to seeing injured soldiers on the streets of Germany. The German leaders were concerned that food rationing would undermine confidence in the regime, and, therefore, food allowances were increased at Christmas 1942. However, with the declaration of Total War in 1943, everything was geared to the conflict. Sweetshops were closed even though they often sold food as well. In August 1943, clothes rationing was ended but that was only because the government had stopped the manufacture of civilian clothes.

As defeat became more likely, government became more chaotic. Ration cards were no longer honoured. Instead, people had to rely on the black market for goods.

Goebbels, Speer and Total War

Production difficulties were a big problem by 1941. By the end of that year, Germany was at war with Britain and its empire, the USSR and the USA. However, armaments production was lower than that of Britain. As a result, Hitler issued the '**Rationalisation Decree**' in December 1941, which was intended to reform the economy and eliminate waste. More importantly, in February 1942, Albert Speer was appointed minister of armaments. He was able to use his close relationship with Hitler to cut through conflicting interests and implement industrial self-responsibility, which relaxed previous controls and constraints placed on businesses to fulfil Nazi wishes, to ensure mass production. A Central Planning Board was established in April 1942 and this was supported by a range of committees to represent different parts of the economy. Speer was now able to co-ordinate production and ensure that resources were properly exploited. This included the introduction of a number of policies:

- Using concentration camp prisoners as workers.
- Employing women in armaments factories.
- Ending the conscription into the armed forces of skilled workers.
- Eliminating professional sport and closing magazines and businesses that were not essential to the war.

It was only after the surrender of the German army at **Stalingrad** in February 1943 that Goebbels called for Total War in a famous speech in Berlin. The Nazis had avoided this, but now the total commitment of all human and material resources in the nation to waging war was official policy.

At first, Speer's policy appeared to be successful as, within his first six months in office, tank production rose by 25 per cent, ammunition by 97 per cent and total arms production by 59 per cent. As a result, by 1944, there had been a threefold increase in war materials when compared with 1942. However, despite these encouraging figures, the economy could have produced even more. Speer was handicapped by a number of factors, including:

- The influence of party *Gauleiters* (see page 170) at a local level, as they were able to prevent Speer's orders from being carried out.
- The SS exploited conquered lands for personal gain rather than the benefit of the war economy.
- Conquered territories were plundered rather than exploited.
- The impact of Allied bombing (see pages 182–4), which prevented Germany from increasing arms production further and also caused the diversion of resources to the construction of anti-aircraft sites.

The result was that Germany was unable to meet the demands of Total War and although production levels peaked in August 1944, these were below their full potential.

> **KEY TERMS**
>
> **Rationalisation Decree** A decree issued by Hitler to eliminate waste and ensure that resources were used in a more efficient way. Committees were established with responsibility for producing a particular class of weapon or equipment.
>
> **Stalingrad** The initial invasion of Russia in 1941 failed to take Moscow and Leningrad. The strategy for 1942 was to thrust into the south of Russia but the attack was held up at Stalingrad by very determined Soviet opposition. A long siege developed in the winter of 1942–3. Facing bitter winter conditions and shortage of supplies, the Germans surrendered in February 1943. This was the beginning of the end of German advances and one of the great turning points of the war.

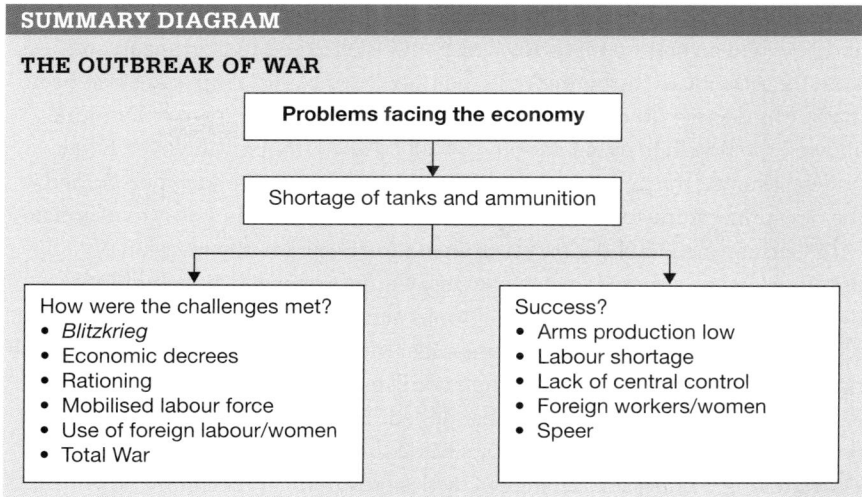

3 German success in western Europe

■ *Why was Germany successful in its invasion of western Europe?*

Hitler's aim was to defeat France and force Britain to surrender before turning east and attacking the USSR.

Despite these plans, the initial attack in the west was on Norway. This region was of vital importance to Germany as iron ore supplies from Sweden passed through neutral Norway. The first move was to occupy Denmark in April 1940, which, as it had few defences, was unable to resist. Norway was then attacked over two weeks and this not only secured iron ore supplies but gave Germany an Atlantic base. Although Norway was important to the Allied cause, there was little that Britain or France could do as it would have weakened their forces in France.

Hitler then turned his attention to Belgium and the Netherlands. Once again these were conquered with relative ease; the Netherlands fell in five days, Belgium in eighteen. Both countries had small armies and air forces and relied on rivers and canals for defences, which proved to be inadequate against the German forces.

Hitler finally turned his attention to France. It might have been expected that France would provide a much sterner test, but it fell within a month. This was in part due to a defeatist attitude but also because of ineffective French preparation over many years and a reliance on the **Maginot Line**, which was simply evaded by the German forces. The north and west of the country were occupied while a collaborationist French government was established in the south at Vichy.

KEY TERM

Maginot Line French defence fortifications built along the Franco-German border by the French during the 1930s. They were supposed to be impenetrable, but the Germans simply bypassed them.

KEY FIGURE

Winston Churchill (1876–1965)

Churchill had been both a Conservative and Liberal MP and held a variety of posts in government. In the 1930s he was out of office, but returned in 1940 as prime minister. His inspirational wartime speeches and refusal to surrender did much to lift morale at home.

Although Hitler had defeated most of western Europe within three months and now had an empire that stretched from Oslo to the Mediterranean and from the Atlantic to the border with the USSR, some crucial mistakes had been made. His decision to delay an attack on the French coastal town of Dunkirk allowed the British to evacuate some 340,000 Allied troops. Moreover, Hitler underestimated the determination of the British not to surrender, personified in the new prime minister, **Winston Churchill**. Britain's unwillingness to negotiate with Germany led to Hitler ordering Operation Sea Lion, the invasion of Britain. However, in order to achieve this, Germany needed air superiority so that invasion barges could carry the troops across the Channel. The *Luftwaffe* (German air force) began by attacking radar installations and the bases of British fighter command in the south of England. The German air force suffered heavy losses and the invasion had to be abandoned. The *Luftwaffe* changed tactics and on 7 September began bombing British cities, particularly London, in the hope of destroying morale. This change in tactics provided fighter command with the time it needed to recover and replace lost aircraft, and it was also the first setback for Germany in the war so far.

Despite the end of military victories in the west, there were German successes in the east. In the period between August 1940 and February 1941, Hungary, Romania and Bulgaria were forced to become Nazi allies. Hitler then made the decision to attack the Soviet Union, despite the Nazi–Soviet Pact, which he had only ever seen as useful in preventing a war on two fronts.

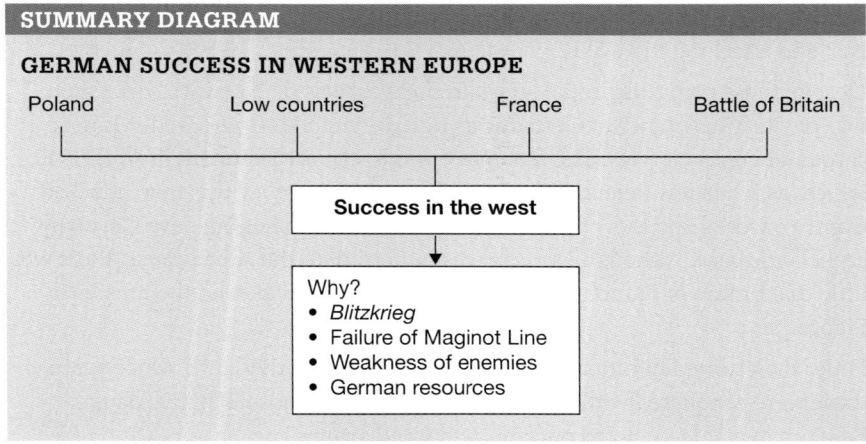

4 The turning point of the Second World War

- Why did Germany suffer defeats in 1942?

It had always been Hitler's intention to turn east. Hitler saw the south of the USSR as providing much needed raw materials, particularly corn and oil. He was convinced that Soviet forces would present little obstruction, which seemed to be reinforced by their poor performance in **Finland** in 1939–40. This, and the earlier success of *Blitzkrieg*, convinced Hitler that the USSR could be defeated in eight weeks. However, the attack was delayed as his ally, Mussolini, had launched assaults against the British in north Africa and also against Greece. These attacks faced setbacks and Hitler was forced to intervene. He was also forced into action in Yugoslavia when an anti-Nazi government, which could threaten his oil supplies from Romania, was established. The invasion of the USSR was delayed by only a month, but many historians have seen this as crucial.

The invasion of the USSR began on 22 June 1941. It was a huge operation involving 187 German divisions as well as forces from Romania and Finland. Initial advances were rapid as German forces appeared unstoppable and had been greeted as liberators by many in western Russia in their moves towards Leningrad, Moscow and Ukraine. By November, German troops were close to both Moscow and Leningrad. However, the Soviet leader, **Joseph Stalin**, rallied the people for what became known as the Great Patriotic War. He adopted a **scorched earth policy**, which meant that the Germans had to bring in their own supplies. This caused serious problems as they had to rebuild or convert the rail network to the German train gauge.

However, perhaps the most important issue in the ultimate failure of the campaign was the delay in launching the attack. As a result, the German troops suffered terribly in the Russian winter as they had not been equipped for the extreme weather and it led to their being halted at both Moscow and Leningrad.

Nonetheless, in 1942, German forces were able to push further south into the oil fields towards Stalingrad (see Figure 9.1, page 176). At the same time, it appeared as if Germany was succeeding in north Africa as the British were driven back to Egypt. Despite these apparent successes, it was on these two fronts that Germany suffered its greatest reverses. The British defeated the Germans in the desert of north Africa at El Alamein and drove them out of north Africa, while 300,000 German troops were surrounded and forced to surrender at Stalingrad. The German advance had been halted; the gamble on a quick victory had failed.

> **KEY TERMS**
>
> **Finland** The conflict from 1939 to 1940 is also known as the Winter War. The USSR invaded Finland in November 1939 and the war lasted three and a half months, ending with the Moscow Peace Treaty in March 1940.
>
> **Scorched earth policy** A military tactic of destroying everything that might be useful to the enemy when retreating.

> **KEY FIGURE**
>
> **Joseph Stalin (1879–1953)**
>
> A leading member of the Bolshevik Party in its early stages, he became commissar for nationalities and then general secretary of the party. Following Lenin's death, he took over the leadership and embarked on a massive modernisation programme with a series of Five Year Plans and a policy of collectivisation of Soviet agriculture. He signed the Nazi–Soviet Pact in 1939, which only delayed a German invasion of the USSR. During the war he provided strong leadership and it was Soviet forces that played a considerable role in the defeat of the Nazi regime.

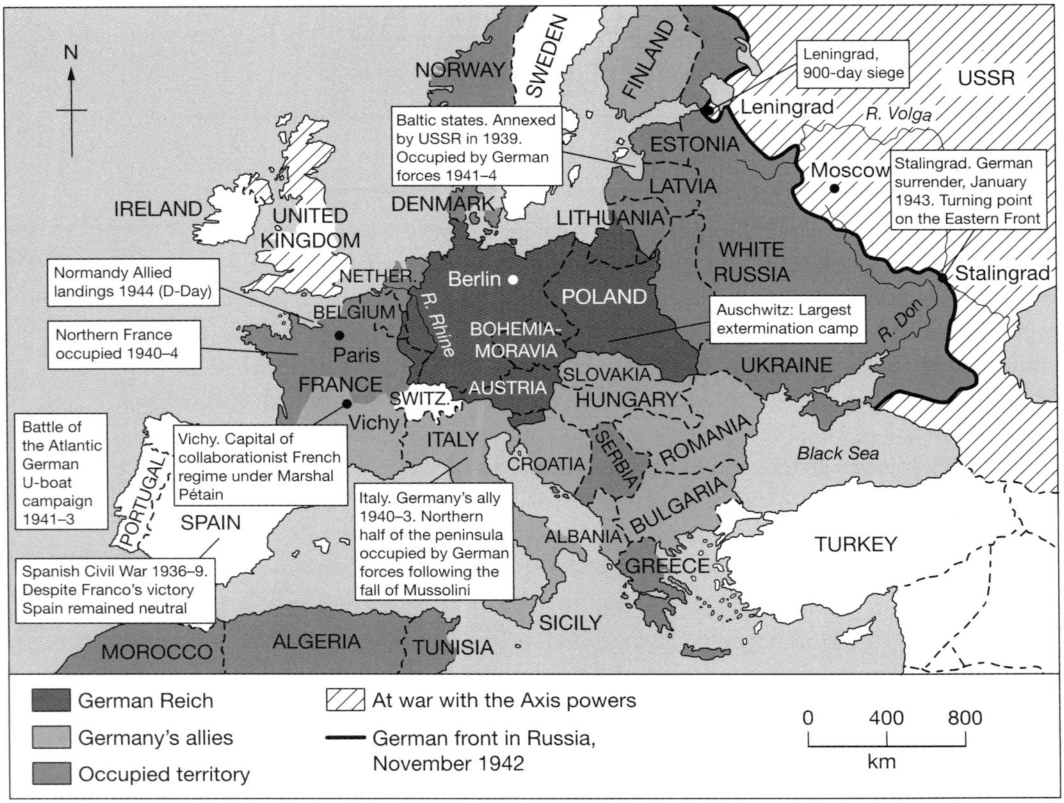

Germany: Democracy to Dictatorship c.1918–1945 for WJEC

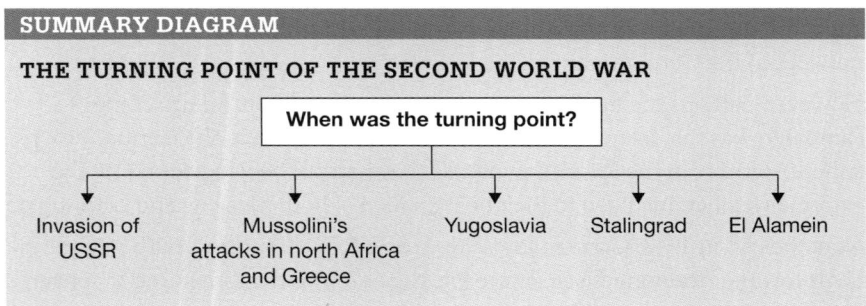

Figure 9.1 Europe, showing Nazi Germany at its height in 1942.

SUMMARY DIAGRAM

THE TURNING POINT OF THE SECOND WORLD WAR

When was the turning point?
- Invasion of USSR
- Mussolini's attacks in north Africa and Greece
- Yugoslavia
- Stalingrad
- El Alamein

5 The Wannsee Conference (1942) and the Final Solution

■ *Was the Final Solution a response to the war in the East?*

Hitler had already made dire threats against the Jewish population in his speech to the *Reichstag* on 30 January 1939 (see Source C, page 177).

Chapter 9 Nazi foreign policy and the Second World War 1933–45

> **SOURCE C**
>
> From a speech by Hitler to the *Reichstag*, 30 January 1939.
>
> *If the international Jewish financiers in and outside Europe should succeed in plunging the nations once more into a world war, then the result will not be the Bolshevising of the earth, and thus the victory of Jewry, but the annihilation of the Jewish race in Europe.*

> **SOURCE QUESTION**
>
> What was the purpose of Hitler's speech in Source C?

By the end of the war, an estimated 6 million Jewish people had been murdered. This event has probably generated more controversy and historical writing than any other, particularly over whether the Holocaust was the result of a long-term plan or was a response to the circumstances of the war. This has also led historians to discuss the question of where responsibility for the Holocaust lies. This section will consider how emigration turned into extermination and who was responsible for such events.

The impact of the occupation of lands in the east

The German occupation of Poland in 1939 brought some 3 million Jewish people under Nazi control. Before this, the regime had encountered only a few hundred thousand Jewish people in Germany, Austria and Bohemia. The outbreak of war also made resettlement to other countries more difficult and placed a considerable strain on food supplies and transport. This resulted in the creation of **ghettos** in cities such as Warsaw and Kraków. However, the conquest of France in 1940 appeared to open another possibility for resettlement. The French colony of Madagascar was considered as a site for Jewish resettlement, particularly as it was more than likely that the majority would have died from disease. However, such a plan was impossible because Britain was not only unwilling to make peace, but its Royal Navy controlled the Indian Ocean.

The use of ghettos and the building of a range of camps in Poland caused logistical problems for the Germans as they slowed the build-up for the invasion of the USSR. The invasion was the turning point in Nazi policy. Not only was it seen as a racial and ideological war aimed at destroying Jewish Bolshevism, but it also brought another 3 million Jewish people under German control. Moreover, by the spring of 1942, over half a million Jewish people had been killed by SS *Einsatzgruppen*, who followed the invading army. The murder of this large number of Jewish people was an obvious escalation of Nazi policy and, it could be argued, prepared the way for the more organised and systematic extermination, or 'Final Solution', as the Nazis now faced the practical problem of fighting a war and dealing with an ever-increasing number of Jewish people.

The end of resettlement

There has been much debate among historians as to when the regime abandoned the plans for resettlement and adopted the policy of extermination in the death camps. Structuralist historians argue that the extermination became

> **KEY TERMS**
>
> **Ghetto** An area of a city occupied by a minority group. During the Second World War, the Nazis created ghettos to where Jewish people were moved. Surrounded by high walls, barbed wire and guards, escape was very difficult, as was smuggling food or goods into the ghetto. Many inhabitants died of starvation or disease.
>
> ***Einsatzgruppen*** SS units who followed the regular German army in the USSR. Their task was to destroy potential opposition and the squads killed large numbers of suspected partisans, Communist officials and prisoners, as well as Jewish people. The killing was often done by enthusiastic local anti-Semites, and regular police battalions took part in rounding up and sometimes murdering people.

likely once it was clear that the war would not be won quickly. The resettlement, which would include housing and feeding, would create huge organisational problems for the regime. However, intentionalist historians challenge this view and argue that extermination was not just a response to the military situation. They contend that Hitler was committed to such a policy from early in his career and gradually increased pressures on the Jewish population, leading ultimately to extermination because that is what he had always wanted.

However, one thing does appear to be clear in this debate. Events suggest that the implementation of the killing was chaotic. Options were considered during the autumn of 1941 as the invasion of the Soviet Union had led to another 3 million Jewish people coming under Nazi control. Until this point there had been a variety of ideas, including resettling Jewish people in camps and ghettos in Poland or in Madagascar. It was only after this that a clear programme emerged, the detailed implementation of which was agreed at the Wannsee Conference in January 1942, although by late 1941 there were already many Nazi plans being issued for the eventual extermination of the Jewish population. Source D (see below) shows instructions issued to the German army on what to do with the large numbers of Jewish people that they captured as they advanced further east.

> **SOURCE QUESTION**
>
> What can we learn from Source D about the instructions given to the SS about Jewish people that they captured?

SOURCE D

From an order signed by Hermann Göring and dispatched to senior SS officers in July 1941.

To supplement the task that was assigned to you on 24 January 1939, which dealt with the solution of the Jewish problem by emigration and evacuation in the most suitable way: I hereby charge you with making all necessary preparations with regard to organisational, technical and material matters for bringing about a complete solution of the Jewish question within the German sphere of influence in Europe. Whatever other government agencies are involved, these are to co-operate with you. I request you further to send me, in the near future, an overall plan covering the organisational, technical and material measures necessary for the accomplishment of the final solution of the Jewish question, which we desire.

The meeting at Wannsee drew up plans to conscript Jewish people into labour gangs in eastern Europe, in which it was expected that a large number would die, while the others would be dealt with 'accordingly', with the euthanasia programme acting as the model. In November 1941, Heydrich had been given responsibility to draw up plans for the complete solution of the Jewish question in Europe.

> **SOURCE QUESTION**
>
> What can we learn from Source E about the nature of the Final Solution?

SOURCE E

From the minutes of the Wannsee Conference, drawn up by Adolf Eichmann, 20 January 1942.

In pursuance of the final solution, the Jews will be conscripted for labour in the east under appropriate supervision. Large labour gangs will be formed from those fit to work, with the sexes separated, which will be sent to those areas for road

> construction and undoubtedly a large number of them will drop out through natural wastage. The remainder who survive – and they will be certainly those who have the greatest powers of endurance – will have to be dealt with accordingly. For if released, they would, as a natural selection of the fittest form a germ cell from which the Jewish race could regenerate itself.

During 1942, a number of camps were converted into, or built as, extermination centres, such as **Auschwitz**, Sobibor and Treblinka, all of which were in Poland. On arrival in most camps, nearly all Jewish people were killed immediately in the camps' gas chambers. The whole process was turned into an industry. Not only were some inmates worked to death, but gold teeth were extracted from the bodies so the metal could be used elsewhere. Hair was shaved and used to fill mattresses. Camps were located near railway lines to speed up the transportation. As time went on, Jewish people were transported to these death camps from all over Nazi-occupied Europe. It is impossible to be certain of the numbers killed in the death camps, but it was several million. Millions more died in concentration camps and ghettos, and at the hands of *Einsatzgruppen*. An estimated 6 million Jewish people died in total. Of the 3 million Polish Jews, it is believed that only 4000 survived.

Such a horrific outcome has raised a number of questions and a range of answers. There is considerable disagreement among historians as to Hitler's role and influence. No written order from Hitler for the killing of Jewish people has been found, but in January 1944, Himmler claimed that he had been given an order by the Führer to prioritise the solution to the Jewish question. However, although no written evidence is available to show that Hitler himself gave the order, it does not mean that he did not approve the policy. Moreover, the nature of his authority meant that initiatives that followed his ideological vision were encouraged and it would be unreasonable to deny that Hitler had spoken of the destruction of the Jewish population from early in his political career. Even if the policy was the result of the chaos and complexity of the regime's administration (see page 111), institutions and decision-making, it does not mean that Hitler was any less responsible, even if it came about as a response to circumstances.

More controversial has been the debate among historians about the role of the German people. Ian Kershaw, in his book *Hitler's Role in the Final Solution* (2006), suggests that Hitler's followers carried out the policy because they believed that it was his intention and took responsibility to 'work towards the Führer'. This view was taken even further by Daniel Goldhagen in his controversial book, *Hitler's Willing Executioners* (1996), where he argues that the policy was carried out because German culture had developed a murderous form of anti-Semitism. He claims that 'The men and women who peopled the institutions of genocidal killing were overwhelmingly and most importantly German. This was above all a German enterprise. Comprehension and explanation of the perpetration of the Holocaust therefore requires and explanation of the Germans' drive to kill the Jews.' Such a view has been challenged by historians such as V.R. Berghahn in his book *Modern Germany* (1982), where he argues that 'The outbreak of war and

ONLINE EXTRAS **WWW**

Get to grips with analysing sources about the development of anti-Semitism in Germany in the years 1939–41 by completing Worksheet 34 at **www.hoddereducation.co.uk/accesstohistory/extras**

KEY TERM

Auschwitz Originally established as a concentration camp in 1940, on the grounds of a former Polish barracks. The Nazis then built Auschwitz II at the Birkenau camp in 1941. It was specifically chosen as a death and labour camp, in part because of the rail links which enabled Jewish and other prisoners to be brought there easily from many parts of occupied Europe. During its three years as a death camp, some 3 million murders may have been committed there.

its subsequent escalation into Total War seriously weakened the Jews' chances of survival. The military victories in the east and west suddenly added millions of Jews to the number who had been unable to leave the Reich before September 1939.' Other historians also contend that many of the individuals in the squads and camps were not violently anti-Semitic, but carried out the task because of peer pressure, alcohol, cowardice and for promotion, all exaggerated by the brutality of war on the Eastern Front, which was unlike any previous experience.

But while the extermination of Jewish people has dominated historians' writing, it should not be forgotten that other groups which were seen as enemies of the Nazi racial state were also killed. The Romani people, in particular, were an increasing focus of Nazi persecution, with large numbers sent to Auschwitz in 1943 and 1944. They were joined by political opponents, homosexuals, Jehovah's Witnesses, asocials and Soviet prisoners of war. Most died through starvation, disease or exhaustion, or were shot or beaten.

> **ONLINE EXTRAS**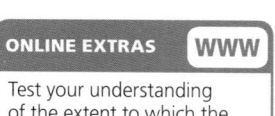
>
> Test your understanding of the extent to which the Holocaust was the result of the Second World War by completing Worksheet 35 at **www.hoddereducation.co.uk/accesstohistory/extras**

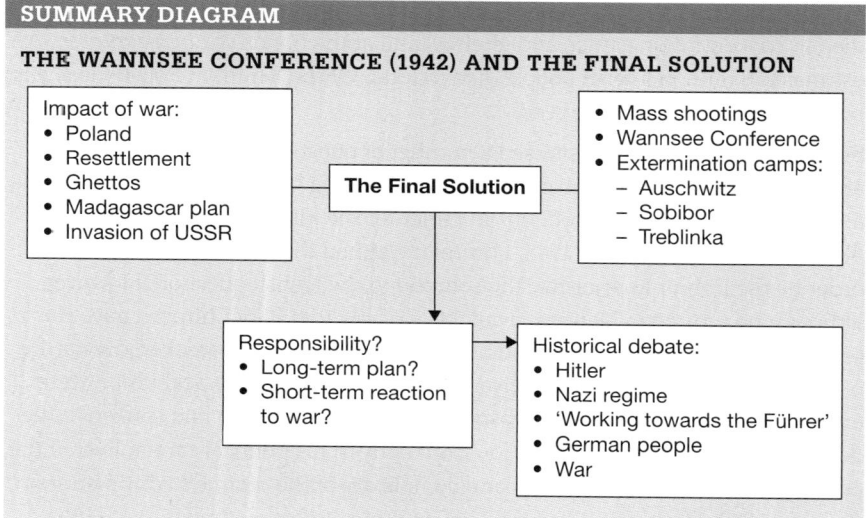

SUMMARY DIAGRAM — THE WANNSEE CONFERENCE (1942) AND THE FINAL SOLUTION

6 The defeat of Germany

■ *Why was Germany defeated?*

In many ways, 1942–3 represented a turning point for German forces after their initial military successes. The defeats in north Africa and the surrender at Stalingrad showed the Allies that the German military was not invincible. However, these defeats did not prevent Germany from continuing its determination to create a new racial order and, if anything, the Final Solution was pursued with even more vigour.

From 1943, German strategy was defensive. However, this strategy did not prevent the first major Allied aerial bombing of Germany in May 1943 and in the Atlantic, the tide also began to turn as Germany suffered serious U-boat losses as a result of Allied technology and US air power. In the east, Germany also suffered major setbacks, particularly in the largest ever tank battle at Kursk in May 1943, which led on to the Soviet advance into Poland, Bulgaria and Romania. Anglo-American forces also linked up in Africa and, in 1943, also established a hold on southern Italy.

By the start of 1944 it was apparent that, with the Allied advances and the heavy bombing raids of the British at night and the Americans during the day, Germany faced total destruction unless it agreed to an **unconditional surrender**. This became even clearer in June 1944 when the Allies opened the second front by landing troops in Normandy, France. Despite heavy German resistance, the Allies advanced and by August had retaken Paris. It was these developments that led to the attempted assassination of Hitler with the Stauffenberg Plot (see page 186). German forces did attempt a breakout and advance from the Ardennes in December 1944, but this failed and also resulted in heavy losses. On the Eastern Front in June to August 1944 there was also a major Soviet offensive, Operation Bagration, which destroyed the German Army Group Centre. It led to the loss of some 800,000 German troops and played a significant role in Germany's eventual defeat. The spring of 1945 witnessed further advances from both the west and east, but Hitler clung to the belief that a victory was possible and it was only when Soviet forces were within a mile of the Reich Chancellery that he killed himself, leading to a German surrender on 7–8 May 1945.

There were a number of reasons why Germany, after its initial successes, was defeated:

- The failure to defeat Britain or secure its neutrality meant that he had to fight a war on two fronts, something that he had been keen to avoid after the First World War.
- The German economy was not prepared for the war it had to fight, and it was put under further strain by Italian failures, which meant that German forces and resources had to be diverted.
- The delay in launching the invasion of the Soviet Union meant that many German troops were lost in the winter of 1941. The USSR, in contrast, had a vast amount of manpower available.
- The entry of the USA into the war provided the Allies with a vast supply of resources.
- Allied bombing meant that Germany could not fully benefit from the increase in production under Speer.
- Germany suffered from a shortage of labour and could not keep up industrial and agricultural production as well as sending men to fight.
- Hitler made several strategic errors.

ONLINE EXTRAS

Learn how to plan for essay questions by completing Worksheet 36 and get to grips with evaluating a range of factors as to why Germany lost the Second World War by completing Worksheet 37 at **www.hoddereducation.co.uk/accesstohistory/extras**

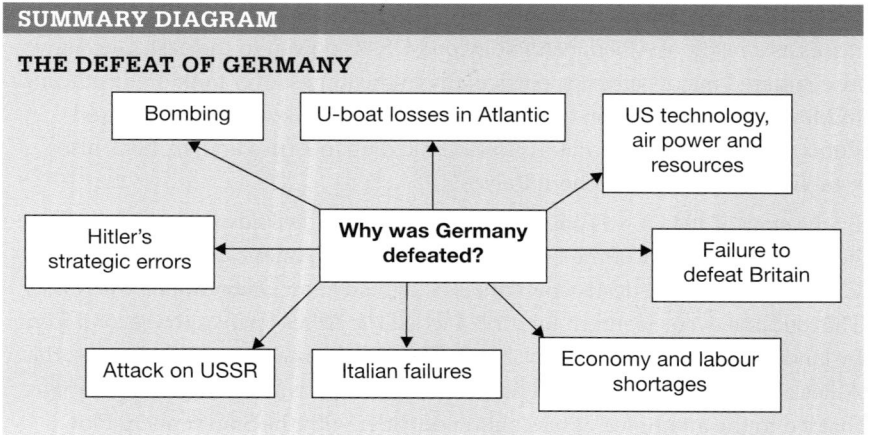

SUMMARY DIAGRAM
THE DEFEAT OF GERMANY

7 The impact of war on society

■ How seriously affected was German society by war?

When war was declared in September 1939 it was greeted in Germany with apprehension, unlike the euphoria that had met its declaration in 1914. However, early successes dispelled much doubt and it was only towards the end that the German people became resigned to defeat, although they still carried on fighting to defend the homeland.

The impact of bombing on morale on the home front

Propaganda had been a key element in bringing the Nazis to power and consolidating their position. It would play just as important a role in wartime. However, many Germans must have wondered why they were suffering so much damage from bombing if, as propaganda stated, they were winning the war. The regime, unlike that in the First World War, did acknowledge setbacks in the fighting, but these were used to rally the people and encourage them to put in even greater efforts to resist the enemy. Similarly, as with Britain and the 'blitz spirit', whereby civilians showed stoicism and determination to carry on, there is little evidence of a breakdown in morale. The predictions of such a collapse proved false despite the impact of bombing:

- it is believed that 400,000 German civilians were killed
- 500,000 were disabled and severely injured
- twenty per cent of the housing stock was destroyed.

Rather than reducing morale, the shared suffering often brought the Nazi Party and the people closer together and increased resentment against the enemy, instead of a wish to surrender. Goebbels gained popularity by visiting bombed areas, although Hitler himself stayed away.

Most people appeared willing to carry on fighting until the bitter end in May 1945, and there were a number of reasons for this outlook. Undoubtedly many, particularly those living in the east of the country, feared what would happen to them as Soviet troops advanced and whether they would be victims of revenge and the same brutality that their own soldiers had shown when invading the Soviet Union. Accounts of Soviet soldiers raping German women were circulating and there were suggestions that the number of rapes reached 2 million. Others feared the consequences of the racial policies towards Jewish people and saw the air raids as a sign of things to come in retribution for the genocide (see pages 178–80). The final phase of the war saw a horrific rise in violence by hardened Nazis against the civilian population as Allied forces advanced. Local Nazi officials killed many who showed signs of wanting to surrender and roving squads of SS men executed suspected deserters. Coupled with the death marches of concentration camp survivors, the final months living in Nazi Germany were often hellish.

> **SOURCE QUESTION**
>
> How does Source F show the impact of the Allied forces on Berlin?

SOURCE F

The ruins of Berlin in 1945.

It might also be argued, somewhat controversially, that there were many Germans who kept fighting because they shared Hitler's vision of the future, the establishment of the 1000-year Reich. Many Germans still clung to the idea that Hitler was an all-powerful leader who would come up with a superweapon to win the war. This view may not have been so far-fetched given the development of the **V-1 and V-2 rockets**, which inflicted considerable – but not sufficient – damage to the south of England in 1944–5.

However, there are also signs that towards the end of the war most Germans were more concerned about their own personal survival rather than fighting. With the breakdown in government support and little being done for refugees and evacuees, most were simply concerned with individual and family survival.

> **KEY TERM**
> **V-1 and V-2 rockets**
> Long-range aerial bombs. V-1s were flying bombs that were launched from France to England with indiscriminate targeting. V-2s were the first ballistic missiles and included a guidance system.

The impact on workers

The war added to the pressure on the workforce. In order to maintain productivity, bonuses and overtime payments, which the Nazis had ended, were reintroduced. However, these brought little benefit because of a rise in taxes on things such as beer and tobacco. The need to fight a Total War only added to the pressures:

- Working hours increased from 52 hours per week in 1940 to 60 in 1944.
- Foreign workers were used.
- There was a shortage of skilled workers.
- From 1944, the situation became desperate, holidays were stopped, bonuses ended and any rewards were limited to an increase in rations.

The impact on farmers

Conscription resulted in a shortage of agricultural labour. This led to an increasing reliance on bringing in peasants from eastern Europe, even though they were Slavs and seen by the regime as racially inferior. Although there were problems in obtaining farm machinery, those living in the countryside did not suffer the same shortages as those in the cities who suffered from the increasing air raids.

The impact on women

At the start of the war the use of women, even in essential industrial work, was limited and the number of female workers actually decreased. Speer, however, wanted to increase productivity and, therefore, with Total War, wanted the conscription of female labour. However, this went against Nazi ideology and it was also feared that the conscription would damage morale. Despite this conflict, the Nazi regime was forced to use women labour and the last two or three years of the war saw more women employed, with many playing an auxiliary role in the armed forces; by 1945 they made up 60 per cent of the workforce.

With many men away fighting, women also had to take on increased roles, not only working but also running the home. It was the same in the countryside, where, even before the war, a labour shortage had made life hard, but now women had to run both the farm and the home.

The impact on youth

The young suffered educationally as the number and the quality of teaching staff declined. There was also a far greater emphasis on military training rather than academic skills and this led to many being alienated by the regimentation and forming counter-groups.

Growing opposition?

In the years up to the outbreak of war, opposition to the Nazis had been limited and ineffectual (see pages 120–2). However, Hitler was concerned about the demoralising impact of the war and how it might lead to the development of opposition. Propaganda was used to try and counter this, but it became more difficult after the failure of the invasion of the USSR. Opposition did grow during the war, but it was really only towards the end of the war, with the July Bomb Plot (see page 186) in 1944, that it became a serious, and almost successful, threat to the regime.

Nazi youth policy

Nazi Youth policy lost support as a result of the war for a number of reasons. First, many of the leaders were called up to fight leaving the organisation to be run by youngsters who were little older than the members. Second, the almost complete emphasis on military affairs put many off and encouraged them to look for alternatives. Those disinterested in military ideology often attended gatherings of the Swing Youth and some joined the Edelweiss Pirates. The Swing movement was never going to topple the regime as its main aim was simply to listen to 'swing' music in the swing clubs that appeared in most cities, especially Hamburg. The Edelweiss Pirates were an umbrella movement and contained members from other groups, such as the 'Roving Dudes' and the 'Navajos'. Much like the Hitler Youth pre-war, they organised weekend hikes and camping trips, but they also hoped that they might meet and be able to attack Hitler Youth groups. Some did get directly involved in resistance to the regime, sheltering those who had escaped concentration camps or attacking military targets and Nazi officials. However, their impact was minimal and when the Edelweiss Pirates did successfully kill the head of the Cologne *Gestapo*, they were quickly caught and killed as punishment.

Perhaps, in retrospect, the most famous of the challenges to the regime came from the **White Rose** group in Munich, which printed leaflets encouraging people not to help the war effort and attacking Nazi policies towards Jewish citizens. But again, the members of the White Rose were soon caught and executed. Although it can be argued that their attacks on the regime were brave

> **KEY TERM**
>
> **White Rose** So-called because the white rose was a symbol of peace. A student group in Munich which distributed anti-Nazi leaflets, led by brother and sister Hans and Sophie Scholl. The leaflets condemned the moral and spiritual values of the Nazi regime. The weakness of the group's security meant that the six leaders were soon arrested by the *Gestapo*, tortured and executed.

and had gone beyond mere passive dissent, they achieved very little against the regime.

The Church

Although many within the Church supported, or at least failed to oppose Nazi policies, there were some individuals who did stand up to the regime, such as Dietrich Bonhoeffer. He did not believe that Christianity could accept Nazi racial policies. Bonhoeffer's attitude resulted in his being involved in the plot to assassinate Hitler and in October 1942, he was arrested and placed in solitary confinement in prison. As the war progressed, Hitler became more concerned by plots to assassinate him and as a result of this, Bonhoeffer was moved to a concentration camp. Finally, Bonhoeffer was put on trial and sentenced to death by hanging. Despite concerns about individuals such as Bonhoeffer, the Churches as institutions were not an active threat to the regime as they were more concerned with self-preservation and did not publicly condemn the policy towards Jewish people.

Upper classes

One of the most influential and active resistance movements came from Germany's conservative upper classes, mainly those in the civil service and the officer corps. Opposition within the army was a particular danger as they had access to arms and had never been fully co-ordinated into the Nazi regime.

It was the military failings of the winter of 1942–3 that encouraged opposition within the army to grow and led to the so-called **Kreisau Circle** being formed. This was clearly the most significant opposition to the regime as its members were potentially influential figures with the possibility of army support. These conservative opponents hoped to form a government which might have been acceptable to the western Allies and therefore bring an end to the war in the west. However, because of their anti-communist views, this group wanted to continue the war in the east. Their main concern was with ridding themselves of a populist dictatorship rather than in restoring democracy. However, they lacked any real popular support and it is not certain that the Allies would have abandoned their policy of unconditional surrender even if Hitler had been overthrown.

The opposition was not united and contained a range of opinions, with some opposed to the assassination of Hitler. Some in the army became convinced that only they had the power to remove Hitler and began to plot to assassinate him. The plot involved General Ludwig Beck and the conservative politician Carl Goerdeler, as well as Colonel **Claus von Stauffenberg**. Stauffenberg had turned against the regime following events in Russia and the brutality of the SS. However, the attempted assassination, known as 'Operation Valkyrie' or the July Bomb Plot, failed. The bomb, which had been placed in a briefcase and positioned under a table close to Hitler, was moved. As a result, when the bomb exploded Hitler was only injured; meanwhile, fellow plotters in Berlin failed to act quickly and seize the capital. The plotters were apprehended and soon

> **KEY TERM**
>
> **Kreisau Circle** A wide-ranging group of officers, academics, aristocrats and clergy, so-called because they met at the Kreisau estate of Helmuth von Moltke. They were drawn together by the massacres and destruction taking place in the east and by the defeats in 1942–3. Their discussions centred around plans for a new Germany after Hitler and they drew up 'Basic Principles for the New Order', which was a conservative and Christian vision for the future.

> **KEY FIGURE**
>
> **Claus von Stauffenberg (1907–44)**
>
> Stauffenberg was an able soldier, who initially admired Hitler but had come to believe that the only way the Nazi regime could be ended was by his assassination. He had been loosely connected to the Kreisau Circle but in 1944 drew up the plan – Operation Valkyrie – to kill Hitler. He took personal responsibility for placing the bomb in the briefing room at Hitler's headquarters in East Prussia. The briefcase containing the bomb was moved slightly and this resulted in Hitler sustaining just minor injuries. Stauffenberg was executed for his role in the plot.

executed, and Hitler used the plot as a reason to arrest some 7000 opponents, of whom nearly 5000 were killed. Although it failed, the plot had made clear that the only way to bring down the regime was to remove the head by assassinating Hitler. However, it had taken military disasters to persuade some within the army to act, showing how strong the regime was and how few were willing, at a time of national crisis, to act, with many army generals still loyal to Hitler.

Reasons for the lack of resistance

There has been wide debate by historians about the reasons for the absence of opposition to the regime. Some historians have put forward the view that there was a lack of resistance because the German people were being held down by force. Others have argued that there was resistance, but it failed because it was too divided. However, some have suggested that opposition was weak because many Germans acquiesced in the regime. It can also be argued that during the war the Nazis were linked to the whole survival of the nation and therefore resistance failed because it was seen as unpopular and treacherous.

There were acts of social defiance:

- the Catholic opposition to euthanasia
- the fraternisation with foreign workers against Nazi orders
- young people reacting against the disciplines of the regime
- desertions, especially towards the end of the war
- isolated acts of violence.

However, a concerted and effective resistance movement did not emerge, partly because of the repression by the regime – effective even with relatively low numbers of *Gestapo* agents – and partly because of the acceptance by so many Germans of the regime at different levels from active support to apathetic lack of open criticism.

Germany at the end of the war

The impact of the Second World War on Germany was far reaching. As a result of the aerial bombing campaign, many thousands were rendered homeless. Millions more became refugees who wanted to return to their homes having been prisoners of war, slave labourers or evacuees. There were some 12 million displaced German civilians from east of the River Oder who had fled west in the face of the advancing Red Army, fearful of what might happen to them if they were taken by the Soviets. In addition, places where refugees were housed were often unable to cope with feeding and caring for them. Many were still traumatised by their experiences of bombing and devastation, although that was nothing in comparison to the sufferings of the survivors of the concentration camps.

The problems facing the Allies when they entered Germany were immense. Some twenty per cent of housing had been destroyed and another 30 per cent had been badly damaged. Many of the larger cities, such as Berlin, Hamburg and Dresden, had been very badly bombed which, with the addition of the huge number of refugees, created a major housing crisis. This was accompanied by food shortages. The average calorie consumption had dropped from the recommended 2000 per day to about half of that. The lack of fuel added to the problem of transporting what food remained.

The economy had also been badly damaged. Much of the infrastructure had broken down at the end of the war. The state was in massive debt and inflation was rising. This led to a growth of the wartime black market. However, there were still many elements of continuity which would allow Germany to rebuild. Government authorities and the civil service still existed and there was a well-established banking system, even if it faced the problem of inflation. Most importantly, Germany did have an industrial base and, therefore, the potential for productivity.

There were vast social problems, as many men had been killed and injured fighting and, while prisoners of war from the west were soon released, some of those in the USSR remained captive until the 1950s. This put increasing pressure on women, and this was not helped by the behaviour of some Soviet troops in the east, with approximately one in three women in Berlin raped. However, there had not been a complete breakdown in the social order, and law and order was soon restored. Also, Christianity had survived, and religious faith continued to offer support to the many members of Germany's Protestant and Catholic communities. However, for some, the scale of death and destruction had undermined a belief in a merciful God and the support offered by some of the Church organisations to the regime had undermined many of their members' allegiance.

The German state itself had also ceased to exist. Following Hitler's suicide, a new government was briefly formed under Admiral Dönitz, but once it had signed an unconditional surrender on 8 May 1945, it was disbanded by the Allies, who now took over control of Germany.

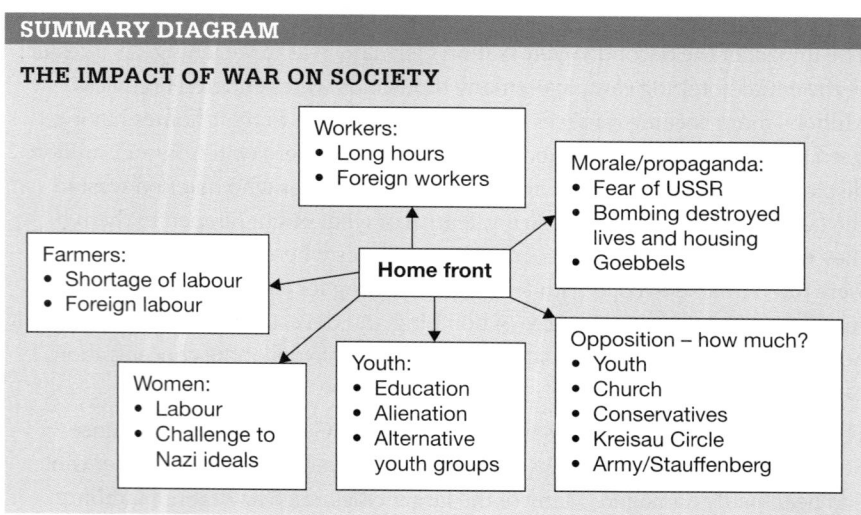

CHAPTER SUMMARY

Although the Nazis had not planned for a large-scale war in 1939, the initial *Blitzkrieg* tactics were a success and they came close to defeating the Soviet Union in 1941. However, delays in launching the invasion and the declaration of war on the USA were errors and from 1942 to 1943 the tide began to turn against Germany. The economy was not fully geared to war and there were labour shortages and poor economic co-ordination, which meant that production levels were never as high, even under Speer, as they could have been. The bombing of German cities helped to disrupt production. As the war continued, many on the home front suffered as the rationing system broke down and they had to rely on the black market. Although opposition to the regime did increase, it was largely ineffective, with few in the high command of the army willing to act. Most Germans carried on fighting until the end, fearing the advance of Soviet troops. The war also resulted in the abandonment of the plans to resettle Jewish people and played a crucial role in the development of genocide and the Final Solution.

Refresher questions

Use these questions to remind yourself of the key material covered in this chapter.

1 What were the main aims of German foreign policy?
2 Why was Germany successful in its military policy in the years 1939–41?
3 How well organised was the German economy in the early years of the war?
4 How successful was Speer in expanding the economy?
5 Was a Total War economy achieved?
6 When and why did military events start to turn against Germany?
7 Why was the policy of resettlement abandoned?
8 Why was the policy of genocide and the Final Solution adopted?
9 How did the war impact living and working conditions?
10 How did the war change people's attitudes towards the regime?
11 Why was resistance to the regime so limited?

Question practice: A level

Source analysis questions

1 Using your understanding of the historical context, assess the value of these three sources to an historian studying opposition to the Nazis between 1933 and 1944.

> **EXAM HINT** Responses should analyse and evaluate the three sources by considering the content, authorship and appropriate context of each in order to judge the value of each to an historian studying opposition to the Nazis in the period 1933–44.

SOURCE A

From an article in the *Völkischer Beobachter* (*The People's Observer*), the main official Nazi daily newspaper, January 1934.

The political opponents of National Socialism have not been removed by the prohibition of their organisations and newspapers, but have withdrawn to other forms of struggle against the State. Therefore, the National Socialist State has to trace out, to watch over and to render harmless the underground opponents fighting against it in illegal organisations, in camouflaged associations and in their foreign headquarters. The preventative activity of the Secret State Police consists primarily in the thorough observation of all enemies of the State in the Reich Territory. The Secret State police takes the necessary preventative measures against the enemies of the State on the basis of the results of the observation. The most effective preventive measure is without doubt the withdrawal of freedom, which is masked in the form of protective custody. The use of protective custody is organised by the directions of the Reich and the Minister of the Interior and by a special arrest procedure of the Secret State Police. The number of criminal proceedings continually being dealt with in the People's Court on account of high treasonable actions is the result of this tireless work.

SOURCE B

From a letter written by the Catholic Bavarian bishops and circulated to their clergy, expressing their disillusionment with aspects of the Nazi regime, December 1936.

The National Socialists seek to rid Germany of the influence of the Catholic Church and declare it to be a body foreign to our country and its people. In 1933, a Concordat was signed between the Holy Father and the German Reich. However, instead of the much wished for friendship, there has developed an ever-growing struggle against the Papacy, a struggle carried out in writings and speeches, in books and study courses, in organisations and school camps. A hate for Rome has been cultivated. Under the Concordat, Catholic organisations and societies were promised protection for their continued existence. But instead of this protection the exact reverse has taken place. The Führer can be certain that we Bishops are prepared to give all moral support to his struggles against Bolshevism. We will not criticise things which are purely political. What we ask is that our holy Catholic Church is permitted to enjoy her God given rights and her freedom to worship.

SOURCE C

From General Beck, writing in a pamphlet in which he set out a plan for a post-Nazi Germany. The pamphlet was never published but found in his private papers following his death in July 1944.

Germans! Monstrous things have taken place under our eyes in the years past. Against the advice of his experts, Hitler has unscrupulously sacrificed whole armies for his desire for glory, his presumption of power, his blasphemous delusion of being chosen as the inspired instrument of what he calls 'providence'. To maintain his power he has established an unbridled reign of terror, destroying justice, banishing decency, mocking the divine commands of pure humanity and destroying the happiness of millions. We must not continue on that course! Having examined our conscience before God, we have assumed executive power. Our brave forces will guarantee security and order. The police will do their duty. Without hatred we will attempt the act of domestic reconciliation. With dignity we will attempt foreign conciliation. Our first task will be to purge the war of its atrocities, and to put a stop to the disastrous destruction of human life.

2 Using your understanding of the historical context, assess the value of these three sources to an historian studying the development of Nazi social and religious policy and its changing impact on society between 1933 and 1945.

EXAM HINT Responses should analyse and evaluate the three sources by considering the content, authorship and appropriate context of each in order to judge the value of each to an historian studying the development of Nazi social and religious policy and its changing impact on society in the years 1933–45.

SOURCE A

From a report by the Social Democratic Party in exile (SOPADE), 1934.

Youth is still in favour of the system: the novelty, the drill, the uniform, the camp life, the fact that school and the parental home take a back seat compared to the community of young people – all that is marvelous. Many believe that they will find job opportunities through the persecution of Jews and Marxists. For the first time, peasant youth is associated with the State through the SA and the Hitler Youth. Young workers also join in: one day socialism may come; one is simply trying to achieve it in a new way. The new generation has never had much use for education and reading. Now nothing is demanded of them; on the contrary, knowledge is publicly condemned. The chaps are so fanaticized that they believe in nothing but their Hitler.

SOURCE B

From an American journalist writing in 1937 describing Nazi attitudes to women working.

How many women workers did the Fuhrer send home? According to the statistics of the German Department of Labour, there were, in June 1936, 5,470,000 employed women, or 1,200,000 more than in January 1933 … The vigorous campaign against the employment of women has not led to their increased domesticity and security; but has been effective in squeezing them out of better paid positions into sweated trades. Needless to say, this type of labour, with its miserable wages and long hours, is extremely dangerous to the health of women and degrades the family.

SOURCE C

From a sermon by Catholic Cardinal Clemens von Galen, Bishop of Münster, on 3 August 1941, protesting about the policy of euthanasia.

The Penal Code lays down in Article 139: 'He who receives credible information concerning the intention to commit a crime against life and neglects to alert the authorities or the person threatened in time ... will be punished.' When I learned of the intention to transport patients from Marienthal in order to kill them, I brought a formal charge at the State Court in Münster and with the Police President in Münster by means of a registered letter which read as follows: 'According to information I have received, in the course of this week a large number of patients from the Marienthal Provincial Asylum near Münster are to be transported to the Eichberg Asylum as so-called "unproductive national comrades" and will then soon be deliberately killed, as is generally believed has occurred with such transports from other asylums. Since such an action is not only contrary to the moral laws of God and Nature but also is punishable with death as murder under Article 211 of the Penal Code, I hereby bring a charge in accordance with my duty under Article 219 of the Penal Code, and request you to provide immediate protection for the national comrades threatened in this way by taking action against those agencies who are intending their removal and murder.'

3 Using your understanding of the historical context, assess the value of these three sources to an historian studying Nazi economic policy between 1933 and 1943.

EXAM HINT Responses should analyse and evaluate the three sources by considering the content, authorship and appropriate context of each in order to judge the value of each to an historian studying Nazi economic policy in the years 1933–43.

SOURCE A

From Gareth Jones, 'How Germany Tackles Unemployment', *Western Mail*, February 1933.

Wales and Germany have one grave problem in common – how to tackle unemployment. In Germany the fight has been carried on with energy. The German Government has encouraged a Voluntary Labour Service of public works, which has set up thousands of labour camps throughout Germany. The members of the camps are all volunteers. They work about six hours a day, some on roads, some in draining marshes, others in clearing the results of floods, some in building sports grounds. These young men do not work for profit, for they only receive pocket-money. They are given, however, plain but good food, work-clothes, exercise, health and comradeship, and work from four to nine months in the camp. All the work done is for the public good and not for the benefit of an individual. Indeed the Hitler Government wishes to make it compulsory and turn it into a kind of national conscription scheme. Perhaps by these labour camps Germany may be leading the way to a method of rescuing the youth of Europe from the effects of unemployment. The Trade Unions however, oppose the Voluntary Labour Service, which they see as a menace to the wage agreements they have struggled for.

SOURCE B

From a secret report for the leadership of the German Social Democratic Party in exile (SOPADE). The report assesses the economic situation in Germany in July 1938 and was circulated abroad.

Under the lash of dictatorship, the level of economic activity has been greatly increased. The exploitation of labour has been greatly increased by the abolition of the 8 hour day, which has been gained over generations, and by the extraordinary increase in work rate. A fascist system which makes marriage and the procreation of as many children as possible the highest duty of a subject, cannot afford in the long run continually to reduce housing capacity for the expanding and increasing number of households. 12–13 billions of Reich marks are squeezed from the national income for rearmament, but even then one cannot do everything at once with the extorted billions. One cannot simultaneously increase armaments for land and air, build up a massive fleet, build gigantic installations and construct grandiose buildings. On the basis of the living standards of the German people hitherto, one can either do one or the other or a bit of everything, but not everything at the same time and in unlimited dimensions.

SOURCE C

From Joseph Goebbels, minister of propaganda, speaking in a radio broadcast to the German people entitled 'Nation Rise Up, and Let the Storm Break Loose', Berlin, 1943.

We face a serious military challenge in Russia. Total war is the demand of the hour. The danger facing us is enormous. The efforts we take to meet it must be just as enormous. We can no longer make only partial and careless use of the war potential at home and in the significant parts of Europe that we control. We must use our full resources, as quickly and thoroughly as it is organisationally and practically possible. We are voluntarily giving up a significant part of our living standard to increase our war effort as quickly and completely as possible. This is not an end in itself, but rather a means to an end. The total war effort has become a matter of the entire German people. No one has any excuse for ignoring its demands. We must bear any burden, even the heaviest, to make any sacrifice, if it leads to the great goal of victory. Everyone must learn to pay heed to war morale, and pay attention to the just demands of working and fighting people. The problem is freeing soldiers for the front, and freeing workers for the armament industry. The reason for our current measures is to mobilise the necessary workers. The duty for women to work is vital. The more who join the war effort, the more soldiers we can free for the front. I am convinced that the German woman is determined to fill the spot left by the man leaving for the front, and to do so as soon as possible.

4 Using your understanding of the historical context, assess the value of these three sources to an historian studying the development of Nazi policy towards the Jewish people between 1933 and 1942.

EXAM HINT Responses should analyse and evaluate the three sources by considering the content, authorship and appropriate context in order to judge the value of each to an historian studying the development of Nazi policy towards the Jewish people between 1933 and 1942.

SOURCE A

From propaganda chief Joseph Goebbels' diary in April 1933 about the boycotts of Jewish businesses.

1 April 1933: The boycott against the international atrocity propaganda has burst forth in full force in Berlin and the whole Reich. I drive along the Tauentzien Street in order to observe the situation. All Jews' businesses are closed. SA men are posted outside their entrances. The public has everywhere proclaimed its solidarity. The discipline is exemplary. An imposing performance! It all takes place in complete quiet; in the Reich too …

In the afternoon 150,000 Berlin workers marched to the Lustgarten, to join us in the protest against the incitement abroad. There is indescribable excitement in the air. The press is already operating in total unanimity. The boycott is a great moral victory for Germany. We have shown the world abroad that we can call up the entire nation without thereby causing the least turbulence or excesses. The Führer has once more struck the right note. At midnight the boycott will be broken off by our own decision. We are now waiting for the resultant echo in the foreign press and propaganda.

2 April 1933: The effects of the boycott are already clearly noticeable. The world is gradually coming to its senses. It will learn to understand that it is not wise to let itself be informed on Germany by the Jewish émigrés. We will have to carry out a campaign of mental conquest in the world as effective as that which we have carried out in Germany itself. In the end the world will learn to understand us.

SOURCE B

From a secret report prepared by the Nazi Party Supreme Court after the events of *Kristallnacht*, 9–10 November 1938.

On the evening of 9 November 1938, Reich Propaganda Director and Party Member Dr Goebbels told the Party leaders assembled at a social evening in the old town hall in Munich that in the districts of Kurhessen and Magdeburg-Anhalt there had been anti-Jewish demonstrations, during which Jewish shops were demolished and synagogues were set on fire. The Führer at Goebbels' suggestion had decided that such demonstrations were not to be prepared or organised by the Party, but neither were they to be discouraged if they originated spontaneously.

The oral instructions of the Reich Propaganda Director were probably understood by all the Party leaders present to mean that the Party should not outwardly appear as the originator of the demonstrations but that in reality it should organise them and carry them out. Instructions in this sense were telephoned immediately (and therefore a considerable time before the transmission of the first teletype) to the bureaux of their districts by a large number of Party members present.

SOURCE C

From the minutes of the Wannsee Conference, drawn up by Adolf Eichmann, 20 January, 1942.

In pursuance of the final solution, the Jews will be conscripted for labour in the east under appropriate supervision. Large labour gangs will be formed from those fit for work, with the sexes separated, which will be sent to those areas for road construction and undoubtedly a large number of them will drop out through natural wastage. The remainder who survive – and they will certainly be those who have the greatest powers of endurance – will have to be dealt with accordingly. For if released, they would, as a natural selection of the fittest, form a germ cell from which the Jewish race could regenerate itself. (That is the lesson of History.)

In the process of carrying out the final solution, Europe will be combed through and through from west to east. The evacuated Jews will be brought initially to so-called transit ghettos in order to be transported from there further east.

Essay questions

1 'Opposition to the Third Reich in the period 1933–45 failed because the majority of Germans were enthusiastic supporters of the regime.' Discuss.

EXAM HINT Responses should discuss how far support for the regime brought about the failure of opposition before considering other issues, such as a divided opposition or the use of terror. Answers should reach a developed and balanced judgement about the role of support in the failure of opposition.

2 To what extent was the appeal of Nazi ideology responsible for maintaining the support of the German people between 1933 and 1945?

EXAM HINT Responses should analyse and evaluate the extent to which Nazi ideology was responsible for maintaining support for the regime, weighing its role up against other factors, such as terror, and reach a balanced and developed judgement about its relative importance.

3 How successfully did the Nazi regime deal with opposition groups between 1933 and 1945?

EXAM HINT Responses should analyse and evaluate the way in which the Nazi regime dealt with opposition groups in the period. Answers should focus upon the nature and extent of opposition ranging from youth movements to the army and reach a developed and balanced judgement on the role of the state in dealing with opposition groups.

4 How significant was the role of propaganda in the Nazi consolidation of power between 1933 and 1945?

> **EXAM HINT** Responses should analyse and evaluate the significance of the role of propaganda in the Nazi consolidation of power in the period. Responses should weigh up the role of propaganda against other developments such as the creation of jobs or terror, and reach a balanced judgement on its relative significance.

5 'Young people were the group most affected by Nazi social and racial policies in the period 1933–9.' Discuss.

> **EXAM HINT** Responses should discuss how far the young were affected by Nazi social and racial policies before considering their impact on other groups, such as women or workers. Answers should reach a developed and balanced judgement as to whether the young were affected the most.

6 How effective were social, religious and racial policies in maintaining support for the Nazi regime in the period 1933–1945?

> **EXAM HINT** Responses should analyse and evaluate the effectiveness of Nazi social, religious and racial policies in maintaining support for the Nazi regime, in order to reach a balanced and developed judgement about the effectiveness of the policies.

7 'The German people had more benefits than drawbacks from Nazi social, religious and racial policies.' Discuss.

> **EXAM HINT** Responses should discuss the benefits and drawbacks of the social, religious and racial policies of the Nazis. Answers should reach a developed and balanced judgement about the policies.

8 Discuss with reference to the period between 1933 and 1945 the impact of Nazi social policies on German society.

> **EXAM HINT** Responses should analyse and evaluate the impact of Nazi social policy on different groups within society such as women, Jews, working classes, the Church. Answers should reach a balanced judgement on the changing role and status of different groups within society.

9 To what extent was Nazi racial policy the most significant impact on German society in the period 1933–45?

> **EXAM HINT** Responses should analyse and evaluate the extent to which Nazi racial policy had the most significant impact on German society, weighing this against the impact of social and religious policies, in order to reach a balanced and developed judgement about the impact of the policies.

Question practice: A level

10 To what extent was Nazi economic policy responsible for Hitler's defeat in the Second World War?

EXAM HINT Responses should analyse and evaluate the extent to which Nazi economic policy was responsible, weighing this issues against other factors, such as US military might and the role of the USSR, in order to reach a balanced and developed judgement about its responsibility.

11 To what extent did Nazi economic policies prepare Germany for war?

EXAM HINT Responses should analyse and evaluate the extent to which Nazi economic policies prepared Germany for war, weighing success against failure, in order to reach a balanced and developed judgement about how well prepared they were.

12 Evaluate Nazi economic policy between 1933 and 1939.

EXAM HINT Responses should analyse and evaluate the nature and extent of Nazi economic policy in the period. A balanced judgement should be reached in relation to the relative success and failure of the Nazi economic recovery in the period.

13 'The Nazi economy failed to meet the needs of Germany in the years 1939–45.' Discuss.

EXAM HINT Responses should discuss how far the economy met the needs of Germany in the years 1939–45. There might be discussion of issues such as armaments production or Total War. Answers should reach a developed and balanced judgement as to how far the needs of Germany were met.

14 To what extent was Hitler's leadership responsible for Germany's defeat in the Second World War?

EXAM HINT Responses should analyse and evaluate the extent to which Hitler's leadership was responsible, including issues such as his command and strategies, against other factors such as US strength and the USSR's manpower, in order to reach a balanced and developed judgement about the reason for Germany's defeat.

15 How successfully did the Nazi regime deal with the economic challenges it faced between 1933 and 1945?

EXAM HINT Responses should analyse and evaluate how successfully the Nazi regime dealt with the economic challenges it faced in the period. Answers should reach a balanced judgement about the success of the regime in dealing with different priorities at different times.

16 To what extent were Britain and the USA responsible for Germany's defeat in the Second World War?

EXAM HINT Responses should analyse and evaluate the extent to which Britain and the USA were responsible for German defeat, weighing them against issues such as the contribution of the USSR or Germany's weakness, in order to reach a balanced and developed judgement about the responsibility of Britain and the USA in Germany's defeat.

17 How significant were the campaigns of the Western Allies to the defeat of Germany by 1945?

EXAM HINT Responses should analyse and evaluate the relative significance of the campaigns of the Western Allies. A balanced judgement should be reached on the significance of the campaigns in the West in comparison to other factors such as Hitler's leadership, economic policy and the Russian front.

18 'Germany's defeat in 1945 owed more to the strength of her opponents than to German weakness.' Discuss.

EXAM HINT Responses should discuss how far German defeat was due to the strength of its opponents before considering other issues such as the weaknesses of Germany, for example the economy or Hitler's leadership. Answers should reach a developed and balanced judgement as to whether Germany's defeat was due more to the strength of its opponents or its own weaknesses.

Exam focus: WJEC AS and A level

Exam guidance

The assessment of Units 2 and 4: Germany: Democracy and Dictatorship c1918–1945 for WJEC depends on whether you are studying it for AS or A level:

- AS level: you will answer one source question and one interpretation question
- A level: you will answer one source question and one essay question.

At AS level you will study unit 2, which covers the period from 1918 to 1933, and for the A level you will study Unit 4, which covers the period from 1933 to 1945. At AS and A level there is no choice for either the source question or the interpretation question.

AS question 1 and A level question 1: source analysis question

At both AS and A level you will have to answer one source question using three sources. At A level, the sources will have greater depth, range and complexity.

The skills needed to answer this question are made very clear by the mark scheme, which emphasises that the answer must:

- Focus on the question.
- Evaluate the sources using *both* the provenance and relevant/appropriate contextual knowledge.
- Use detailed and accurate date-specific contextual knowledge, and not just general contextual knowledge which is linked to the sources. The appropriate context is the key driver for this question. Context has two dimensions: the context of the origin of the sources and the context of the set enquiry.
- Reach a supported analysis of the sources in relation to the question.
- Reach a substantiated judgement about the issue.

There are a number of skills that you need to develop if you are to reach the higher levels in the marking bands for both the AS and A level questions:

- You have to *analyse and evaluate* the evidence. You need to link it to the issue or set enquiry in the question and decide what the evidence is saying about that issue.
- You need to consider *how valuable* the evidence is. This involves thinking carefully about a range of issues concerning the provenance of the source. You might think about who wrote it, why it was written, whether the person who wrote it would be in a position to know and how typical it might be.
- You need to apply relevant contextual knowledge to the source to judge the validity of the source and its view. You therefore need a good knowledge of the development of the topic or key issue in the question.
- You need to link your material to the issue in the question and not write a general essay about the topic.

WJEC-style questions

The focus of the question will be on a development over a set period of time.

Using your understanding of the historical context, assess the value of these three sources to an historian studying Nazi economic policy between 1933 and 1943.

The following example shows just one of the three sources. The other sources for this question can be found in the A level question practice section on pages 193–4.

SOURCE B

A secret report for the leadership of the German Social Democratic Party in exile (SOPADE). The report assesses the economic situation in Germany in July 1938 and was circulated abroad.

Under the lash of dictatorship, the level of economic activity has been greatly increased. The exploitation of labour has been greatly increased by the abolition of the 8 hour day, which has been gained over generations, and by the extraordinary increase in work rate. A fascist system which makes marriage and the procreation of as many children as possible the highest duty of a subject, cannot afford in the long run to continually reduce housing capacity for the expanding and increasing number of households. 12–13 billions of Reich marks are squeezed from the national income for rearmament, but even then one cannot do everything at once with extorted billions. One cannot simultaneously increase armaments for land and air, build up a massive fleet, build gigantic installations and construct grandiose buildings. On the basis of the living standards of the German people hitherto, one can either do one or the other or a bit of everything, but not everything at the same time and in unlimited dimensions.

Answering AS question 1 and A level question 1

- Keep a good focus on the question and do not drift off into describing everything the sources say. Avoid mechanistic source-based responses that focus only on the content and attribution of each of the three sources.

- Analyse and evaluate the sources within their appropriate historical context. Do not consider each source in isolation. Historical context goes beyond just general factual knowledge or the summary of the content of the sources. You must analyse and evaluate the sources within the distinct social, economic, religious, political or foreign policy contexts in which they appear, and also in relation to the development of the set enquiry. With these sources, on Nazi economic policy, economic policy goes through three distinct developments: recovery, rearmament and war. Each of these will have a distinct historical context. Furthermore, who produces the source and when it is produced will have a bearing on why it was produced and therefore how valuable it will be for a historian studying a set enquiry.

- You have to keep a balance. You should not write an essay on the topic in the question just by using knowledge, but you should not just explain what the sources say about the issue either. You need to apply some knowledge to all of the sources to answer the question, but additional information you bring should be linked to the appropriate historical context of each source.

In planning your answer to this question it might be helpful to construct a chart similar to the one below:

Source	View about the issue in the question	Evidence from the source	Provenance	Context	Judgement
A					
B					
C					

- In the second column you decide whether the source supports or challenges the view in the question.
- In third column you should enter evidence from the source which supports your view.
- The fourth column considers the provenance, which may affect the reliability of the source and therefore its value to a historian studying a specific line of enquiry.
- The fifth column is about placing each of the three sources within the appropriate historical context; in other words, what was going on in relation to the set enquiry/key issue at that time.
- The final column brings all this together to make a judgement as to whether the source is valuable to a historian studying the development of a specific issue.

If you complete this table it should provide you with the material you need to answer the question.

An opening paragraph to the question *using all the sources* could start as follows:

> These sources are valuable to a historian studying the development of Nazi economic policy in the period 1933-43[1] as they cover all three phases of Nazi economic development, namely the recovery in 1933, rearmament from 1936-8 and Total War in the period after 1943 under Albert Speer[2].

1 The response starts by offering a view about the value of the sources.
2 The response then explains why the sources are valuable and uses some contextual knowledge to show that each source considers a different phase of Nazi economic development.

Answers can deal with each source separately and, in considering Source B, an answer might take the following approach:

> Source B is from a report from the exiled Social Democratic Party[1]. It is commenting on the effects of the Four Year Plan, which was introduced by Göring in 1936. The plan set Germany on a course for vigorous rearmament at all costs[2]. The tone of the source is obviously anti-Nazi given that it is from the political opposition, and so a historian would have to treat the source with caution[3].
>
> The source is valuable to a historian studying economic policy because it gives a contemporary viewpoint of the developments in Nazi economic policy and shows how rearmament was the economic priority of the regime despite the social consequences. However, it is true to say that Hitler did not want to lose the support of the people by making the domestic situation impossible for them, even though Göring had coined the phrase 'guns or butter?'[4].
>
> The source is valuable to a historian because it shows that the Nazi regime was driven by its ideological goals for foreign policy and that it did not always make the right choices. Rearmament was the first step on the road to an aggressive foreign policy[5].

1 The opening sentence briefly outlines who has produced the source and this provenance will be used later.
2 There is some good contextual awareness.
3 The nature of the source is briefly considered but this would benefit from further explanation.
4 There is some explanation as to why the source has value and this reflects the general context of the source.
5 Although the focus is on the development of economic policy, it would have been helpful if there had been more focus on the date-specific historical context in order to produce a more reasoned judgement on the value of the source to a historian.

Having considered the provenance and used contextual knowledge, the response reaches a limited judgement about the source in relation to the question. This is vital for the higher levels and should be done for each source.

Answers should treat each source in a similar way and then use the judgements reached about each source individually to reach an overall judgement in a concluding paragraph. The conclusion should be based on the evaluation of the sources and not simply own knowledge, as is seen in the example below.

> Overall, the three sources are valuable to a historian because they show how Nazi economic policy had developed in the period 1933-43 and

how the economic priorities had changed[1]. *The sources show that in 1933 the issue was an all-out attack on unemployment, which would enable the Nazis to consolidate the regime. The second source shows how the Nazis were now on an ideological mission to rearm so that they could pursue the aggressive policies shown in Source C*[2].

1 The opening sentence relates to the issue in the question and is focused on the sources.
2 The remaining two sentences explain the ways in which all three sources are valuable and the focus continues to be on the sources and is not a general comment about Nazi economic policy.

Common mistakes

- Forgetting that this is the source element of the paper. Your answer needs to be driven by the sources in their appropriate historical context.
- Responses that consider *only* the provenance of each source or use *only* contextual knowledge to evaluate. You must use *both*.
- Avoid stock comments about provenance such as 'he was there and would therefore know' or 'it is written in a private diary so can be trusted'.
- Knowledge is simply deployed rather than used to evaluate the source. You need to make sure that you link your contextual knowledge to the sources to show the value of the sources to a historian for a specific enquiry within a set period.

AS question 2: interpretation question

Although this is an AS level paper it is not a historiography paper. The aim of this element of the unit is to develop an awareness that the past has been interpreted in different ways. The question will require you to analyse and evaluate the extracts within the wider historical debate and reach a reasoned judgement on the question set. The interpretations will always be extracts from historians and will not be primary sources.

You should be able to place the interpretations within the context of the wider historical debate on the key topic. However, you will not be required to know the names of individual historians associated with the debate or to have studied the specific books of any historians. You will be required to show a meaningful understanding of how and why historical interpretations are formed, with possible links to schools of thinking or schools of thought.

There are a number of skills you will need to develop if you are to reach the higher levels in the mark bands.

- Remain focused on the question throughout the answer.
- Assess and evaluate the two interpretations in the wider context of the historical debate about the issue. Consider how and why these interpretations have been formed – the evidence or facts surrounding the interpretations bring the context the historians might have considered in forming their judgements.
- Apply your knowledge of the topic to the interpretations in order to evaluate their strengths and weaknesses.
- Analyse the authorship of the interpretations.
- Ensure that you consider both interpretations.
- Evaluate the interpretations within the wider context of the historical debate.
- Consider another possible interpretation to the question from your wider historical contextual knowledge.

Answering AS question 2: interpretation question

Questions set will be similar to the one below:

How valid is the view that the years 1924–9 were mainly a period of domestic success for the Weimar Republic? [30]

The following example provides only one of the interpretations. The other interpretation can be found in the AS level question section on page 93.

Exam focus: WJEC AS and A level

INTERPRETATION 1

Golo Mann, in this extract from his book *The History of Germany Since 1789* (Praeger, 1968), provides a traditionalist interpretation.

Between 1924 and 1929 the Weimar political system functioned normally and the long-term future of the Republic looked rosy. The political violence that had characterized the period 1919–23 subsided. Germany's economic achievements after 1924 were considerable. The income of the nation returned to its pre-war levels. All the worn-out antiquated equipment was replaced. Germany had the most modern merchant fleet and the fastest railways. The workers worked well. The inventors, engineers and technicians were of high caliber. Industrial planning was magnificent and effective. If the Wall Street Crash of October 1929 had not led to a world economic depression, the Weimar republic would have been able to win the popularity of the German people permanently.

In answering the question, the opening paragraph could consider the view of Interpretation 1:

> Interpretation 1 supports the view that the years 1924-9 were mainly a period of domestic success for the Weimar Republic[1]. This is demonstrated through the fact that the extract says that 'the political violence which had characterized the period 1919-23 subsided' and 'Germany's economic achievements after 1924 were considerable'[2].

1 The opening sentence states the view of Interpretation 1 in relation to the question.
2 The next sentence then provides evidence from the interpretation to support the claim. The quotations are brief but relevant.

The answer for the question could then go on to evaluate the interpretation by considering the political or economic issues raised:

> In economic terms, the historian would recognise that these were 'golden years' of the Weimar Republic[1]. The Rentenmark had established financial stability, and the Dawes and Young Plans revised Germany's reparation payments. These were the years of economic growth and prosperity. The foreign investment from the USA allowed Germany to invest in new production techniques, and a welfare state was established. Stresemann was also able to get rid of some of the most unpopular terms of the Treaty of Versailles[2].

1 The opening sentence makes it clear that the response is going to deal with the economic argument of the interpretation.
2 A good range of contextual knowledge is used to show why the view of Mann could be considered to be correct.

The answer should also consider the other issue raised by the interpretation: the political situation. The answer should also consider how and why this interpretation has been formed by the historian, linking to the schools of thought and schools of thinking it relates to:

> Mann provides a traditionalist viewpoint of the years 1924-9 which are seen as a kind of 'golden age' for the Weimar Republic. According to this traditionalist school of thought, the years 1924-9 have been seen as years of domestic success with economic growth and political stability. There was a growth in prosperity, new production, management techniques and industrial planning. There was a decline in political violence and the constitution functioned normally[1].

> This a rather simplistic and optimistic view of the years 1924-9 which does not take into account the overall reliance on foreign investment or the high turnover of governments. This is the opinion of an historian who has been swayed by the veneer of 'stabilisation' under which there were many cracks both political and economic. Mann is too easily persuaded by the exaggerated extent of domestic success and has ignored the notion of the continuity of history so the accuracy of this interpretation should be questioned[2].

1 The answer considers the viewpoint of the interpretation and places this in the context of the debate about Weimar 1924–9.
2 The response develops a judgement about the interpretation and provides some evidence to support the claim, and again places the interpretation in the wider context of the debate about Weimar's achievements.

A level question 2: essay questions

The skills are made very clear by both mark schemes, which emphasise that the answer must:

- focus on the demands of the question
- be supported by accurate and relevant factual knowledge
- be analytical and logical
- reach a supported judgement about the issue in the question.

There are a number of skills that you will need to develop to reach the higher levels in the marking bands. Essentially, you should scan, plan and write:

- understand the wording of the question
- focus on the exact key concept in the question
- plan an answer to the question set
- write a focused opening paragraph
- avoid irrelevance and description
- write analytically about the main developments and cover the set period within the question
- write a conclusion which reaches a supported judgement based on the argument in the main body of the essay.

These skills will be developed in the section below.

Understanding the wording of the question

To stay focused on the question set, it is important to read the question carefully and focus on the key words and phrases. Unless you directly address the demands of the question you will not score highly. Remember that in questions where there is a named factor you must write a good analytical paragraph about the given factor, even if you argue that it was not the most important.

These are the command words you may find on your exam paper:

'Statement'. Discuss; Discuss … ; Evaluate … ; How effective/effectively … ?; How significant … ?; How successful/successfully … ?;

'Statement'. To what extent … ?; To what extent … ?

Some types of A level questions you might find in the exams	The factors and issues you would need to consider in answering them
1 How effective were social, religious and racial policies in maintaining support for the Nazi regime in the period 1933–1945?	Answers should focus on the three issues named in the question and consider how they did and did not help to maintain support for the regime in the period. Having considered how they were both effective and ineffective, a balanced judgement as to their overall effectiveness should be reached
2 To what extent was Hitler's leadership responsible for Germany's defeat in the Second World War?	Answers should consider the importance of Hitler's leadership in Germany's defeat and then discuss a range of other factors that played a role, such as the German economy, Soviet forces and the contribution of the western Allies, before reaching a balanced judgement as to what extent Hitler's leadership was responsible
3 'Fear of the Nazi police state was mainly responsible for the lack of effective opposition to the Nazis between 1933 and 1945.' Discuss.	Answers should analyse the role of the police state in preventing effective opposition, considering both its strengths and weaknesses in preventing opposition. Responses should weigh this factor up against other issues, such as divided aims or weak leadership, in causing opposition to be ineffective

Planning an answer

Many plans simply list dates and events – this should be avoided as it encourages a descriptive or narrative answer, rather than an analytical answer. The plan should be an outline of your argument; this means you need to think carefully about the issues you intend to discuss and their relative importance before you start writing your answer. It should therefore be a list of the factors, developments or issues you are going to discuss and a comment on their relative importance.

For question 1 in the table, your plan might look something like this:

- Indoctrination of the young at school and through youth movements, disillusionment and alternative youth groups.
- Women given honours but policy inconsistent, role in labour market.
- Christian support for Nazism and why, attitude of Confessional Church, Catholic Church and euthanasia.
- Hostility to alien elements in society allows discrimination and persecution, support for racial policy and extermination camps?
- Control of institutions, army? Civil service?
- Effectiveness of *Volksgemeinschaft*.

The opening paragraph

Many students spend time 'setting the scene'; the opening paragraph becomes little more than an introduction to the topic – this should be avoided. Instead, make it clear what your argument is going to be. Offer your view about the issue in the question – how effective were the policies – and then introduce the issues you intend to discuss. In the plan it is suggested that there were limitations to all policies. This should be made clear in the opening paragraph, with a brief comment as to why – perhaps that it was impossible to win over all people and that some simply conformed. This will give the examiner a clear overview of your essay, rather than it being a mystery tour where the argument becomes clear only at the end. You should also refer to any important issues that the question raises. For example:

> It could be argued that the social, religious and racial policies were effective in maintaining support for the Nazi regime, although they led to changing levels of support for the Nazi regime at different times and to different degrees[1]. For example, the Concordat of 1933 ensured the immediate compliance of the Catholic Church, but it did not stop the Church criticising the euthanasia programme in 1937[2]. While the banning of trade unions in 1933 may have effectively silenced the voice of the working classes, it did not prevent unofficial strikes and go-slows over poor pay and long hours[3].

1. The student is aware that the three issues have to be considered and starts to enter into a debate on the key concept, offering a view about the issue in the question.
2. The opening sentence of the answer has offered a view about the issue in the question and goes on to provide some support for this.
3. The justification for the view is further developed.

Avoid irrelevance and description

Hopefully the plan will stop you from simply writing all you know about Nazi social, religious and racial policies and force you to weigh up their effectiveness. You will not lose marks if you do that, but neither will you gain any credit, and you will waste valuable time.

Look at the paragraph below written in answer to the question: How effective were social, religious and racial policies in maintaining support for the Nazi regime in the period 1933–1945?

> The Nazi social, religious and racial policies were mostly effective in maintaining support for the regime[1]. The Nazis introduced a range of policies in these areas designed to win support for the regime[2]. The Nazis took control of education, changing the curriculum and also encouraged the young to join the Hitler Youth, later making it compulsory[3]. The policies were effective as children were easily influenced and indoctrinated[4].

1. The answer offers a view about the issue in the question.
2. The answer describes the aims of the policies.
3. The descriptive approach continues with, at best, a hint that it was effective as all children were subject to the education programme and later forced to join the Hitler Youth.
4. The response asserts that it was effective, but this has not been shown.

There is no real explanation as to the effectiveness of the policy, which would be essential for the response to reach the higher levels.

Write analytically

This is perhaps the hardest, but most important skill you need to develop. An analytical approach can be helped by ensuring that the opening sentence of each paragraph introduces an idea, which directly answers the question and is not just a piece of factual information. In a very strong answer it should be possible to simply read the opening sentences of all the paragraphs and know what argument is being put forward.

If we look at the question on the effectiveness of social, religious and racial policies (see page 204), the following are possible sentences with which to start paragraphs:

- Educational policies were effective as the young were indoctrinated.
- Policies towards the young were not always effective as alternative youth groups were established.
- Many reacted in a positive manner to Nazi ideas and policies towards them.
- The Churches were keen to protect their institutions and compromised with the regime.
- The Nazis were able to control most institutions.
- Nazi policies appealed to people's sense of community.

You would then go on to discuss both sides of the argument raised by the opening sentence, using relevant knowledge about the issue to support each side of the argument. The final sentence of the paragraph would reach a judgement on the effectiveness of the issue you are discussing. This approach would ensure that the final sentence of each paragraph links back to the actual question you are answering. If you can do this for each paragraph you will have a series of mini essays, which discuss a factor and reach a conclusion or judgement about the importance of that factor or issue. For example:

> The social policies of the Nazis resulted in changing levels of support but were mainly effective in maintaining support for the regime[1]. The youth policy, for example, was initially very successful in attracting the support of the young and German people in general. The young were indoctrinated into becoming loyal Nazis although SOPADE reports challenge this general support by suggesting that the young were more supportive of the organisation itself rather than the Nazi Party which had implemented it. The young people were thirsting for action and were rebellious by nature. However, despite the widespread initial support there developed a separate Swing Youth culture as the Hitler Youth became more military based and many young people also turned to Church organisations[2].

1 The sentence puts forward a clear view that social policies were mainly effective.
2 The claim that the effectiveness of the policies declined is developed and a limited judgement is reached, suggesting that the policy was less effective over time; this is explained and support provided.

The paragraph above explains the effectiveness of the Nazi policy towards young people. There is a limited judgement, but this will not take you to the highest level even if this approach was repeated in all the paragraphs.

In order to reach the higher levels there needs to be clear evidence of the evaluation of factors – how effective the policies were. The paragraph above does start to move towards that as it suggests that the policies were less effective over time. The paragraph also provides some support for that claim and it is this that turns an assertion that they were important into a judgement and takes the response to the higher levels.

In some responses the judgement is likely to be present only in the conclusion. However, at the very top it is likely that there will be a judgement about the effectiveness of each factor as they discuss it, so that there will be a series of interim judgements which are then pulled together in an overall conclusion.

Questions for practice

Write six opening sentences for the following questions:

- 'The main reason for Germany's defeat in the Second World War was its economy.' Discuss.
- To what extent was propaganda responsible for maintaining support for the Nazi regime between 1933 and 1945?

- 'The Enabling Act was the most important event in Hitler's consolidation of power in the period 1933 to 1934.' Discuss.

The conclusion

The conclusion provides the opportunity to bring together all the interim judgements to reach an overall judgement about the question. Using the interim judgements will ensure that your conclusion is based on the argument in the main body of the essay and does not offer a different view. For the essay answering question 1 (see page 204), you can decide how effective the policies were, but for questions 2 and 3 (page 204) you will need to comment on the importance of the named factor – Hitler's leadership or the police state – as well as explain why you think a different factor is more important, if that has been your line of argument. Or, if you think the named factor is the most important, you would need to explain why that was more important than the other factors or issues you have discussed.

Consider the following conclusion to question 1: How effective were Nazi social, religious and racial policies in maintaining support for the Nazi regime in the period 1933–1945?

> To conclude, social, religious and racial policies were at times both effective and ineffective in maintaining support for the regime[1]. Initially, it is probably true that the policies were effective because the Church was content with the fact their institutions were protected, and the Nazis destroyed communism. The early racial policies were accepted although there was some opposition as they developed during the war. Social policies were met with little or no opposition[2]. It is probably true that most Germans lived in fear of Nazi terror and so that would have made the policies appear more effective than they actually were[3].

1 The conclusion does reach a judgement, although it would be stronger if it was more decisive.

2 The judgement is developed and this view could have been used to improve the opening sentence by stating that the policies were effective at the start but became less so over time.

3 The judgement is developed further and this is a useful point, which could have been further elaborated on.

Timeline

Year	Domestic events	Foreign policy
1918	Naval mutiny at Kiel Kaiser Wilhelm II abdicated	Armistice to end First World War signed
1919	Spartacist rising in Berlin Weimar constitution adopted	Treaty of Versailles signed
1920	Ruhr rising Kapp *Putsch*	
1923	Hyperinflation Beer Hall *Putsch*, Munich Stresemann became chancellor	French and Belgian troops occupied the Ruhr
1924	Hitler released from jail after Munich *Putsch*	Dawes Plan
1925	Ebert died Hindenburg elected president	Locarno Conference
1926	Bamberg meeting	Treaty of Berlin Germany joined the League of Nations
1928	Müller's Grand Coalition	
1929	Stresemann died	Young Plan Wall Street Crash
1930	Nazis made major gains in elections Brüning appointed chancellor	
1931	Goebbels put in charge of propaganda Failure of banks in Germany	
1932	Hitler won 37 per cent of vote in presidential election Nazis won 37 per cent of vote in June elections Von Papen appointed chancellor Nazis lost votes in November elections Von Schleicher replaced Papen as chancellor	
1933	Hitler appointed chancellor *Reichstag* fire Boycott of Jewish businesses Enabling Act Creation of DAF Confessional Church established One-party state established Creation of Strength Through Joy	Concordat signed with papacy
1934	Night of the Long Knives Death of Hindenburg Office of chancellor and president combined Army oath New Plan	
1935	Mass arrests of socialists and communists by *Gestapo* Nuremberg race laws *Lebensborn* introduced Reich Labour Service	

Year	Domestic events	Foreign policy
1936	Four Year Plan	Germany occupied demilitarised Rhineland
1937	Hossbach Memorandum	
1938	*Kristallnacht* Decree for the Struggle Against the Gypsy Plague Euthanasia campaign started	*Anschluss* with Austria Sudetenland given to Germany
1939	War economy decrees	German takeover of Bohemia and Moravia Nazi–Soviet Pact Germany invaded Poland Outbreak of Second World War
1940		Germany occupied Denmark, conquered Norway Invasion of Netherlands, Belgium and France Battle of Britain German plan to invade Britain failed
1941	Bishop Galen attacked euthanasia Rationalisation Decree	Germany invaded Yugoslavia and Greece Germany invaded USSR German advance in USSR halted at Moscow and Leningrad
1942	Wannsee Conference Speer appointed minister of armaments Extermination facilities established at Auschwitz, Sobibor and Treblinka	German offensive at Stalingrad
1943	Romani people sent to Auschwitz Goebbels' Total War speech	
1944	Execution of Edelweiss Pirates in Cologne Stauffenberg Plot	Allies launched D-Day
1945	Hitler killed himself Germany surrendered	Yalta Conference Potsdam Conference

Glossary of terms

Abdication The act of a monarch giving up his or her throne.

Alsace-Lorraine Largely French-speaking provinces that had been taken by Germany in the Franco-Prussian War of 1870–1.

Anschluss The union of Germany and Austria. Although the population of Austria was German, the Treaty of Versailles outlawed the union of the two countries.

Anti-capitalism Opposition to a system which operates on the principle of private ownership and profit.

Anti-democratic Opposed to democracy.

Aryans The non-Jewish peoples of northern Europe who, Hitler believed, were supreme or the 'master race'.

Asocial people Those who showed behaviour that was deemed unacceptable.

Auschwitz Originally established as a concentration camp in 1940, on the grounds of a former Polish barracks. The Nazis then built Auschwitz II at the Birkenau camp in 1941. It was specifically chosen as a death and labour camp, in part because of the rail links which enabled Jewish and other prisoners to be brought there easily from many parts of occupied Europe. During its three years as a death camp, some 3 million murders may have been committed there.

Austro-Hungarian Empire Austria-Hungary had been Germany's closest ally since 1879. The multinational empire ended when Austria was forced to accept defeat. The 8-million-strong state of Austria, despite being German in language and culture, was forbidden to join with Germany. The new states created from the empire had German-speaking minorities.

Autarky Self-sufficiency in both food and raw materials.

Autocrat Rule by one person, usually a monarch, who will have absolute power.

Balance of trade The difference between the value of goods exported and imported. Where a country imports more than it exports then it has a deficit and is considered to be in the 'red'.

Barter An exchange where goods are swapped rather than sold for money.

Bavarian monarchy Bavaria was one of the oldest states in Europe, but was part of Imperial Germany, and kept its monarchy until November 1918.

Bilateral trade treaties A trade agreement between two countries.

Black Death A disease that struck Europe during the fourteenth century and killed about a third of the population. It was carried by fleas on rats, but this was not understood at the time and a variety of prejudiced theories were offered, including blaming the Jewish community.

Black market The underground economy where goods are sold at unregulated prices.

Blitzkrieg 'Lightning war'. The strategy used by Hitler in 1939–40 to avoid the static war of 1914–18. It used dive-bombers, paratroopers and motorised infantry to ensure that there was a rapid advance.

Block warden A Nazi official who provided information on people in his or her neighbourhood.

Blood and soil (*Blut und Boden.*) A romantic nationalist ideal which glorified the rural role of peasants.

Bolshevik Revolution of 1917 The Bolsheviks were the majority within the Russian Social Democratic Party, which, under its leader Lenin, seized power in October 1917 and established the world's first communist state.

Boycott Refusal to deal commercially with someone; in this case, refusing to use Jewish owned shops.

Cartel A group of companies which control the market and prices through a joint monopoly.

Confessional Church Established in 1934 in opposition to the Reich Church, the Confessional Church upheld traditional Protestant beliefs and rejected Nazi distortions.

Constitution The rules and principles that govern a state.

Constitutional monarchy A system where the monarch's powers are limited by a constitution.

Day of Potsdam Ceremony for the opening of the new *Reichstag* on 21 March 1933 following the *Reichstag* fire.

Deficit financing The policy whereby the government spends more than its income in order to stimulate economic growth.

Degenerate A term used by the Nazis to describe something of which they did not approve.

Demobilisation The removal of troops from active service at the end of a war.

Diktat A dictated peace, where a treaty is imposed without negotiation.

Ebert–Groener Pact Agreed in November 1918; by this, Groener, the supreme army commander, agreed to support the new government under Ebert and use troops to maintain the stability of the republic.

Einsatzgruppen SS units who followed the regular German army in the USSR. Their task was to destroy potential opposition and the squads killed large numbers of suspected partisans, communist officials and prisoners, as well as Jewish people. The killing was often done by enthusiastic local anti-Semites, and regular police battalions took part in rounding up and sometimes murdering people.

Elites Conservative groups within German society who dominated the army, judiciary and civil service. Most were opposed to the republic and wanted a return to traditional, authoritarian government.

Ersatz Substitute.

Eugenics A programme to genetically improve the race.

Euthanasia Nazi programme of killing those too ill, old or handicapped to work, known to the party as 'useless mouths'.

Federal state A state in which powers are shared between central and regional governments.

Feudal structure This term has been used to describe the dominance of Nazi leaders who were at the head of agencies. These leaders owed ultimate loyalty to Hitler, but that did not stop them building up their own power. It also led to quarrels between them, which Hitler viewed as a good thing as it diluted any threat to him.

Finland The conflict from 1939 to 1940 is also known as the Winter War. The USSR invaded Finland in November 1939 and the war lasted three and a half months, ending with the Moscow Peace Treaty in March 1940.

Fixed income Where people rely on a guaranteed set income, be it from a salary or bonds. It does not change in response to economic changes.

Freikorps The Free Corps, a right-wing group of former soldiers. Nationalist in their outlook, they acted as a paramilitary group who were willing to take action against communist activity.

Führerprinzip The 'leadership principle', whereby a one-party state is led by an all-powerful leader.

Gauleiters Leaders of a regional area. The Nazi Party was organised into 35 regions.

Genocide The extermination of a whole race.

German Empire This is also known as the Second Reich, 1871–1918, or Kaiserreich.

German National People's Party (DNVP) A coalition of nationalists that included the Fatherland Party and the Pan-German League. Many of its members were racists and extremists. Its support came from landowners and industrialists, but it also had backing among the middle classes and was the largest of the more radical right-wing parties.

Gestapo The secret state police, which played an important role in surveillance and repression.

Ghetto An area of a city occupied by a minority group. During the Second World War, the Nazis created ghettos to where Jewish people were moved. Surrounded by high walls, barbed wire and guards, escape was very difficult, as was smuggling food or goods into the ghetto. Many inhabitants died of starvation or disease.

Great Depression The severe economic depression from 1929 to 1993. It started in the USA with the Wall Street Crash and resulted in mass unemployment.

Gross national product (GNP) The total value of products and services produced by a country.

Grossdeutschland and *Kleindeutschland* A debate within the states of Germany in the nineteenth century as to whether a unified Germany should include Austria, *Grossdeutschland*, or exclude Austria, *Kleindeutschland*. It was the latter which prevailed.

Guns or butter? A phrase used to describe the debate as to whether Germany should focus on rearmament (guns) or consumer goods (butter).

Hard currency A currency that financial markets consider to be reliable because its value does not fluctuate.

Harzburg Front A right-wing nationalist alliance, formed in 1931, against Brüning's government.

Heavy industry The manufacture of large products, often through several processes and in large factories, usually associated with the production of coal, iron and steel.

Hitler myth Historian Ian Kershaw (1987) has described the 'Hitler myth'. While there were complaints about the party, local officials and policies, there was a widespread belief that Hitler was not to blame and that, as the embodiment of Germany, he stood above such matters. If only he knew what was going on, then he would step in to help his beloved people. The devotion to the leader only waned in the latter stages of the war and to that extent showed the power of the leader-orientated propaganda that portrayed him as a super-man who could solve all of Germany's problems.

Horst Wessel anthem This was a song written by a Nazi stormtrooper who was later killed in a street battle with communists. It became a Nazi marching song.

Hyperinflation A very rapid rise in prices. In Germany, this was caused by the government printing large amounts of money so that the value of the currency fell dramatically.

Indoctrinate To impose a set of beliefs.

July Bomb Plot An attempt to assassinate Hitler on 20 July 1944. It involved both civilian resistance figures and army officers, including Colonel von

Stauffenberg. He placed a bomb in a meeting room, but it was moved before the meeting and that probably saved Hitler's life. In the confusion afterwards, supporters of Hitler were able to arrest the conspirators.

Junkers The landowning aristocracy, they were particularly dominant in Prussia and other parts of eastern Germany.

Kredit Anstalt An Austrian bank that went bankrupt in July 1931. The collapse encouraged other investors to withdraw money from other banks and helped to initiate the Great Depression.

Kreisau Circle A wide-ranging group of officers, academics, aristocrats and clergy, so-called because they met at the Kreisau estate of Helmuth von Moltke. They were drawn together by the massacres and destruction taking place in the east and by the defeats in 1942–3. Their discussions centred around plans for a new Germany after Hitler and they drew up 'Basic Principles for the New Order', which was a conservative and Christian vision for the future.

League of Nations An organisation set up at the end of the war to help maintain peace, and to improve living and working conditions; it is often seen as the forerunner of the United Nations. The League was the brainchild of US President Woodrow Wilson. However, the US senate refused to approve it and the USA never joined the League. The defeated powers were initially not allowed to join.

Lebensraum 'Living space', Hitler's aim for land in the east to settle the surplus German population.

Ludendorff Offensive A German offensive launched in the spring of 1918 on the Western Front, designed to win the war before large numbers of US troops arrived to aid the French and British.

Maginot Line French defence fortifications built along the Franco-German border by the French during the 1930s. They were supposed to be impenetrable, but the Germans simply bypassed them.

Mandates The supervision of former German and Turkish colonies that were administered by the Allies after the First World War.

Martial law Government by the military.

Mass suggestion A psychological term suggesting that people can be unified by the atmosphere of an occasion.

Messianic Having the character of a messiah or saviour.

Military dictatorship Rule by the armed forces.

Mittelstand Literal translation means middle class, but in Germany it refers specifically to the lower middle classes, which includes shopkeepers, craft workers and clerks. They were self-reliant but had come under increasing pressure from big business and industrial labour.

Müller's coalition government This was one of the longer-lasting governments during the Weimar period, surviving from May 1928 until March 1930. It was the last Weimar government that had a majority in the *Reichstag* and its collapse led to the start of rule by emergency decree and presidential government. It was often called the Grand Coalition and was made up of the German Social Democratic Party (SPD), Centre Party (ZP), German Democratic Party (DDP) and German People's Party (DVP), with the SPD returning to government for the first time since the start of the period.

Mutiny The refusal of the armed forces to obey orders.

National Opposition Used to describe the political groups that came together in 1929 in opposition to the Young Plan and which opposed all reparation payments.

Nationalised When an industry is owned and run by the government.

New Order Used by the Nazis to describe the economic, political and racial integration of Europe under the Reich.

November criminals Those who agreed to the armistice; was later used as a term of abuse for those who supported the republic.

NSV National Socialist Welfare Organisation: this oversaw the expansion of welfare facilities, such as rural health clinics and improved childcare, leading to a reduction in infant mortality.

Pan-German League A nationalist organisation, founded in 1891, it gradually became more racist in its views.

Passive resistance The refusal to work or cooperate with occupying forces.

Pastors Ministers in charge of a church or congregation.

Plebiscite A people's vote on an issue, similar to a referendum.

Political intrigue Scheming and the attempt to create deals between leading politicians to ensure that their goals are achieved.

Polycratic Used to describe the many different bodies in the state. Often, Nazi institutions overlapped with existing ministries and Hitler even set up more to deal with problems that arose.

Proportional representation An electoral system by which the number of seats given to a party depends on the number of votes it gains.

Prussia The wealthiest, most powerful and largest German state in the 1800s, making up 62 per cent of the population of the German Empire.

Glossary of terms

Public works schemes Employment schemes that are financed by the state in order to create jobs and reduce unemployment.

Putsch An uprising, usually by a small group in an attempt to overthrow the government.

Rapallo A pact signed with Soviet Russia in 1922. It included trade and secret military links.

Rapprochement The re-establishment of good relations.

Rationalisation Decree A decree issued by Hitler to eliminate waste and ensure that resources were used in a more efficient way. Committees were established with responsibility for producing a particular class of weapon or equipment.

Reich Food Estate Government body responsible for everything involved in agricultural production. It fixed prices, regulated supplies and even decided what fertilisers and seeds were to be used. It also secured protection from the selling of foreign food supplies in Germany.

Reich governors The representatives of the Nazi government in the states following the abolition of the federalist structure of Germany.

Reich Labour Service (RAD) Introduced in 1935, it required young men to do six months' unpaid work, usually in military construction projects, before joining up for military service.

Reichskonkordat An agreement between the Nazi state and the Catholic Church signed in July 1933.

Reichstag The German parliament. It had limited powers.

Reparations Money and goods paid by a defeated power to cover the cost of damages caused by war.

Revolution from below The more radical elements within the Nazi Party wanted local Nazi groups to direct the revolution. This would take control away from the leadership.

RSHA Reich Security Office, which brought together all police and security organisations.

Schlieffen Plan Drawn up by General Schlieffen to avoid Germany fighting a war on two fronts by defeating France on the Western Front before dealing with the threat from Russia. The plan was to defeat France in six weeks, but this failed because of Belgian, British and French resistance. Russia also mobilised more quickly than the Germans expected and so more men had to be sent to the Eastern Front, weakening the German attack in the west. Its failure led to trench warfare and a war of attrition.

Schutzstaffel **(SS)** Commonly referred to as Blackshirts, so-called because of the colour of the uniforms. Set up in 1925 as an elite bodyguard for Hitler and then grew further to become a major paramilitary organisation under the control of Himmler. It developed a reputation for obedience and loyalty.

Scorched earth policy A military tactic of destroying everything that might be useful to the enemy when retreating.

SD The intelligence branch of the SS.

Self-determination The right of people of the same race to decide their own government.

Škoda Works An armaments factory in the Sudetenland region.

Social Darwinism A belief that the world comprised a struggle between the different races.

Social Democratic Party (SPD) In Germany, a moderate socialist party, which should not be confused with Russia where the Social Democrats were more radical, with one part forming the Bolshevik or Communist Party.

Socialism A political and economic theory that argues the means of production should be owned by the community for its collective benefit.

Sovereignty Where ultimate power to make decisions resides.

Soviet A Russian word for an elected council, often comprised of workers.

Stab-in-the-back myth The belief that the army had not lost the war but had been let down by groups at home, such as Jewish people and socialists. This made it much harder for the new Weimar government to gain popular support.

Stahlhelm A German First World War ex-servicemen's organisation. It was the paramilitary wing of the DNVP.

Stalingrad The initial invasion of Russia in 1941 failed to take Moscow and Leningrad. The strategy for 1942 was to thrust into the south of Russia but the attack was held up at Stalingrad by very determined Soviet opposition. A long siege developed in the winter of 1942–3. Facing bitter winter conditions and shortage of supplies, the Germans surrendered in February 1943. This was the beginning of the end of German advances and one of the great turning points of the war.

State within a state Where another power can threaten the authority of the government.

Sturmabteilung **(SA)** Members were known as the Stormtroopers or Brownshirts, after the colour of their uniform. Many were supporters of the more radical or socialist aspects of Nazism.

Successor states Term used to describe the states created from the break-up of the Austro-Hungarian Empire, such as Poland and Czechoslovakia. These were often weak and this would make it easy for Germany to take them over in the 1930s.

Sudetenland A largely German-speaking region of Czechoslovakia, which was annexed by Germany in 1938.

Tenant farmer A farmer who rents land from a landlord.

Total War A war that involves the whole population, both economically and militarily.

Treaty of Brest-Litovsk The treaty signed between Germany and Russia in March 1918 that ended the war in the east. It was much harsher than Versailles, with Russia losing 62 million people, 27 per cent of farmland, 26 per cent of railway lines and 74 per cent of iron and coal resources.

Treaty of Versailles The Allied powers met in Paris during 1919–20 and drew up five treaties with the defeated powers and created the League of Nations. The Treaty of Versailles was signed with Germany on 28 June 1919 and was much harsher than the Germans had expected, leading to national outrage.

Universal suffrage An electoral system in which every adult has the right to vote.

Untermenschen Sub-human or racially inferior people.

V-1 and V-2 rockets Long-range aerial bombs. V-1s were flying bombs that were launched from France to England with indiscriminate targeting. V-2s were the first ballistic missiles and included a guidance system.

Veto The right to block laws or decisions.

Volksgemeinschaft A people's community that was socially unified and racially pure.

Voluntary Labour Service Established by Brüning in 1931. It was a state-sponsored employment organisation that provided services to civic and land improvement projects. By 1932, it had enrolled some 300,000 men.

Waffen-SS Racially 'pure' and fanatical units of the SS which were involved in the advances into eastern Europe.

Wall Street Crash The collapse of share prices on the New York Stock Exchange, based on Wall Street, in October 1929.

War bonds In order to finance the First World War, the German government encouraged people to invest in government funds in the belief that their money was secure and they were helping the war effort.

Weltpolitik The policy of the German government in the 1890s and 1900s by which it sought to advance German interests throughout the world.

White Rose So-called because the white rose was a symbol of peace. A student group in Munich which distributed anti-Nazi leaflets, led by brother and sister Hans and Sophie Scholl. The leaflets condemned the moral and spiritual values of the Nazi regime. The weakness of the group's security meant that the six leaders were soon arrested by the *Gestapo*, tortured and executed.

White Terror First used to describe the suppression of the soviet or 'Red' republic in Bavaria in 1919, it became used to describe the murders and violence that took place in 1919–22.

Wilson's Fourteen Points When the USA entered the First World War its president had drawn up the Fourteen Points to explain what the USA was fighting for. The aim was to create a more just world. One of the Fourteen Points called for disarmament as many believed the First World War had been the result of an 'arms race'.

Winterhilfe Winter relief: a scheme to provide extra help for the unemployed during winter months. Money for it was raised by donations resulting from the savings made by eating a 'one-pot' meal on a Sunday once a month.

Working towards the Führer A situation in which Hitler's followers carried out what they presumed to be his intentions. In this way, others took responsibility for trying to determine what the Führer wanted.

Further reading

Books relevant to the whole period

V.R. Berghahn, *Modern Germany* (Cambridge University Press, 1987)
The focus is on social and economic history

William Carr, *A History of Germany 1815–1990* (Hodder Arnold, 1991)
A narrative history of the period which puts political developments in context

A.J.P. Taylor, *The Course of German History* (Routledge Classics, 2001)
A controversial, yet thought-provoking book written in a wonderful style. First published in 1945 but reprinted many times

Chapter 2

Richard Bessell and Edgar J. Feuchtwanger, editors, *Social Change and Political Developments in Weimar Germany* (Croom Helm, 1991)
A series of essays on Weimar Germany; the first, on the revolution of 1918, is particularly relevant to this chapter

Ruth Henig, *Versailles and After, 1919–1933* (Methuen, 1984)
A short but useful analysis of the impact of the Treaty of Versailles

Chapter 3

Gordon A. Craig, *Germany 1886–1945* (Oxford University Press, 1978)
A collection of essays, of which 'Inflation, stabilisation and political realignment in Germany, 1924–8' is the most helpful

Jonathan Wright, *Gustav Stresemann: Weimar's Greatest Statesman* (Oxford University Press, 2002)
A biography of Stresemann which portrays him in a positive light

Chapter 4

Richard J. Evans, *The Coming of the Third Reich* (Allen Lane, 2003)
A very readable book which goes beyond the period to 1933

Conan Fischer, *The Rise of the Nazis* (Manchester University Press, 2002)
A valuable introduction to the rise and appeal of the Nazi Party

Jeremy Noakes and Geoffrey Pridham, *Nazism 1919–45, Volume 1: The Rise to Power 1919–34* (University of Exeter Press, 1994)
A collection of primary sources with a valuable commentary about the formative years of the Nazi Party

Chapter 5

Martin Broszat, *Hitler and the Collapse of Weimar Germany* (Berg, 1987)
Provides a clear analysis of the factors leading to Hitler's appointment as chancellor

Ian Kershaw, editor, *Weimar: Why Did German Democracy Fail?* (Weidenfeld & Nicolson, 1990)
A collection of essays on the collapse of the Weimar Republic

Hans Mommsen, *The Rise and Fall of Weimar Democracy* (University of North Carolina Press, 1996)
This provides a very thorough analysis of the collapse of Weimar looking at both domestic and international events

Chapter 6

Martin Broszat, *The Hitler State* (Routledge, 2013)
A structuralist examination of the nature of government in the Third Reich

David Crew, editor, *Nazism and German Society, 1933–45* (Routledge, 1994)
A series of essays which question the extent of control the Nazis had over the German people

Robert Gellately, *Backing Hitler: Coercion and Consent in the Third Reich* (Oxford University Press, 2001)
A helpful study that considers the role of coercion in maintaining Hitler in power

Chapter 7

Michael Burleigh and Wolfgang Wippermann, *The Racial State: Germany 1933–45* (Cambridge University Press, 1991)
A study which looks at a range of groups within Nazi Germany, including Romani people, asocials and the mentally ill

Henry Metelmann, *A Hitler Youth: Growing up in Germany in the 1930s* (Spellmount, 2004)
A fascinating and readable account of a working-class child growing up in 1930s' Germany

David Schoenbaum, *Hitler's Social Revolution: Class and Status in Nazi Germany, 1933–9* (Weidenfeld & Nicolson, 1997)
Probably the classic text on the topic

Jill Stephenson, *Women in Nazi Germany* (Pearson, 2001)
Provides a lively guide to a controversial topic

Chapter 8

Tim Mason, *Social Policy and the Third Reich: The Working Class and the 'National Community'* (Berg, 1993)
The work argues that the Nazis did not do enough to win over the working class to make the economic sacrifices needed for rearmament

Richard J. Overy, *The Nazi Economic Recovery 1932–1938* (Macmillan, 1982)
This book looks at the main areas of debate and argues that war preparations that took place at this time were incompatible with long-term economic recovery

Richard J. Overy, *War and Economy in the Third Reich* (Clarendon Press, 1995)
A series of essays which examine the tensions between Hitler's vision of an armed economy and social and economic life

Chapter 9

P.M.H. Bell, *The Origins of the Second World War in Europe* (Longman, 1997)
A clear guide through the major developments in light of historical debates

Richard J. Evans, *The Third Reich at War* (Penguin, 2009)
A modern interpretation of the impact of war on Germany

Richard J. Overy, *The Origins of the Second World War* (Pearson, 1998)
An accessible introduction

A.J.P. Taylor, *The Origins of the Second World War* (Hamish Hamilton, 1961)
An interesting, if somewhat controversial, but classic book

Index

25-Points programme 21, 22

Agriculture and farming 37, 39, 56, 63, 71, 149, 156, 181, 184
Anschluss 8, 47, 129, 131, 154, 156, 166–7
Anti-capitalism 21, 53
Anti-democratic 22, 72, 92, 97
Anti-Semitism 18, 21, 22, 64, 119, 127–31, 179, 180, see also Holocaust
Article 48: 13, 14, 74, 78, 98
Asocial people 110, 132–3, 180

Beer Hall *Putsch* 24
Berlin Olympics 107, 129
Bismarck, Otto von 1, 2, 3
Bombing campaigns 144, 155, 161, 169, 172, 174, 180–1, 182–4, 187
Bonhoeffer, Dietrich 143, 186
Bormann, Martin 115
Brüning, Heinrich 59, 62, 73–5, 76, 82, 85, 95

Catholicism 18, 23, 53, 66, 99, 121, 143, 159, 187, 188, 190, 192
Catholic Youth Movement 135, 143
Censorship 104, 105, 106, 123
Chamberlain, Neville 167, 168
Christians and Nazism 142, 144, 188
Churchill, Winston 174
Communists 6, 16, 18, 23, 31, 59, 66, 76, 97, 98, 101, 121, 141, see also German Revolution; Spartacist rising
Concentration camps 100, 109, 110, 120, 123, 129, 133, 143, 159, 172, 179, 183, 185, 186, 187
Concordat (*Reichskonkordat*) 143, 190
Confessional Church 142, 143
Conservative elites 14, 81, 85, 99, 103, 122, 186
Cuno, Wilhelm 27, 34
Czechoslovakia 167–8

DAF, see German Labour Front
DAP (German Workers' Party) 18, 21, see also Nazi Party
Dawes Plan 34, 37, 38–40, 43, 44, 47
Diktat 10
DNVP (German National People's Party) 12, 18, 28, 40, 41, 59, 76, 77

Ebert, Friedrich 5, 6, 11, 20, 30, 31, 54
Ebert–Groener Pact 20
Einsatzgruppen 177, 179

Eisner, Kurt 17
Emigration 131
Enabling Act 99–100, 114
Euthanasia campaign 120, 121, 133, 143, 145, 178, 187

Federal states 1, 12, 100
Final Solution 176–80, 195
Foreign labour 171
Freikorps 16, 17, 19, 87
Führer cult 63, 113, 144, see also Hitler, Adolf
Führerprinzip 54, 113, 115

Galen, Clemens von 121, 192
Gauleiters 55, 100, 115, 158, 172
German Faith Movement 144
German Labour Front (DAF) 100, 121, 141, 159–60
German National People's Party, see DNVP
German Revolution 5–6, 15, 17, 19, 29, 30–2
German society 2, 61, 62, 66, 71, 100, 126
  impact of First World War 6
  impact of Second World War 182–5, 187–8
  policies 134–40
Gestapo 108, 109, 110, 120, 121, 122, 133, 145, 185, 187
Ghettos 177, 178, 179, 195
Gleichschaltung (co-ordination) 100–1, 146, 159
Goebbels, Joseph 55, 63, 79, 90, 105, 107, 117, 129, 130, 146, 158, 172, 183, 194–5
Göring, Hermann 23, 24, 117, 129, 131, 152, 154, 156–7, 178
Grand Coalition 73
Great Depression 35, 37, 58, 60, 70–2, 150, 155
Grossdeutschland 1
Gypsies 110, 132

Hess, Rudolf 115
Heydrich, Reinhard 109, 178
Himmler, Heinrich 56, 109, 110, 179
Hindenburg, Paul von 4–5, 40, 41, 59, 73–4, 76–80, 82–4, 85, 91, 94, 96, 97, 99, 102, 103, 104, 111
Hitler, Adolf
  anti-Semitism 22, 64, 127, 129, 130, 131
  appointment as chancellor 3, 76, 79, 80, 82–4, 96–104
  as Führer 23, 104, 111, 112, 116–17

  character 111, 113
  cult of personality 63, 113, 144
  early years 18, 21–4, 28, 29, 41, 52–9
  leadership 60–1, 63, 78, 105, 111–13, 114, 117–18, 119, 143, 145, 150–2
  Mein Kampf 24, 53, 62, 131, 164
  myth 108, 113, 119
  political ability 65–6, 84–6, 167
  opposition to 120–3
  racism 22, 127
  responsibility for Holocaust 131, 176–80
  war aims 152–3, 154–5, 173–6
  Zweites Buch 164
  see also Nazi Party
Hitler Youth 55, 114, 122, 135–7, 185
Holocaust 119, 127, 131, 177, 179, see also Anti-Semitism; Final Solution
Hugenberg, Alfred 41, 58, 59, 83
Hyperinflation 11, 14, 25, 26, 27, 28, 29, 33, 37, 74, 81

July Bomb Plot 122, 185, 186
Junkers 2

Kahr, Gustav von 23, 24
Kapp *Putsch* 19, 20, 87, 91
Kapp, Wolfgang 19, 29
Kellogg–Briand Pact 45, 47
Kerrl, Hanns 143
Kleindeutschland 1
Kreisau Circle 122, 186
Kristallnacht 120, 129–30, 131, 195

League of Nations 7, 8, 9, 46, 71, 89, 166
Lebensborn 138
Lebensraum 22, 164
Liebknecht, Karl 16, 17
Locarno Pact 45, 46
Lubbe, Marinus van der 97
Ludendorff, General 4, 5, 23, 24, 87
Ludendorff Offensive 3
Luxemburg, Rosa 16, 17

Marxism 53, 63, 64, 135
Mass culture 105, 106, 134, 179
Mass suggestion 62
Mittelstand 28, 56, 63, 65, 66
Morale 3, 78, 82, 104, 144, 160, 171, 174, 182–4
Müller, Hermann 14, 72, 73
Mussolini, Benito 166, 167, 175, 176

National Assembly 5, 11, 12, 15

217

National Opposition 41, 166
National Socialism, see Nazi Party
Nationalism 18, 21, 22, 63, 107, 126, 127, 134
Nazi Party (NSDAP)
  anti-Semitism 22, 64, 127–31
  calendar 107–8
  culture 107–8
  defeat 175, 180–1, 187
  divisions within 54–5
  economy 64, 141–2, 149–61, 169–71
  election results 57, 59, 64, 76, 79
  emergence 21–4
  establishment of dictatorship 84–6, 96–104, 116–17
  foreign policy 164–8
  growth 23, 53–7, 60–4
  ideology 21–3
  opposition 101, 120–3, 185–7
  policy towards 'asocials' 132–3
  political system 111–15, 117
  propaganda 62–3, 104–8
  racism 22, 126
  reorganisation 55–6
  socialism 22–3, 54
  support 53–7, 65–7, 118–19
  views on religion 142–4, 186
  views on women 137–40
  views on young people 134–7, 185–6
  violence and terror 61–2, 108–10
  wartime victories 173–4
  see also Hitler, Adolf; Night of the Long Knives; Volksgemeinschaft
Nazi–Soviet Pact 168, 174
New Plan 134, 152, 155–6
Niemöller, Martin 143
Night of the Long Knives 101–3, 116, 121, 128
North Africa 175, 180
Noske, Gustav 16
November criminals 22, 63
NSDAP (National Socialist German Workers' Party), see Nazi Party
Nuremberg laws 128–9

Opposition to Nazi regime 120–3, 143

Papen, Franz von 62, 73, 76, 78, 79–80, 82–3, 84, 85, 96, 103
Poland 168, 177–9, 181
Propaganda 55–6, 63, 79, 104–8, 117, 145, 182, 185
Proportional representation 12, 13, 14, 55, 65, 73
Protestantism 18, 66, 67, 121, 142–3, 188
Prussia 1, 8, 74, 78

Rapallo Pact, see Treaty of Rapallo
Reich Food Estate 151
Reich Labour Service (RAD) 142, 151
Reichskonkordat 143, 190
Reichsrat 12, 99
Reichstag 1, 2, 12, 114
  elections 1, 11, 17, 20, 29, 53, 76–80, 98
  fire 97–8, 101, 121
  relationship with president 12, 13, 14
Religion 66, 85, 134
Reparations 7, 9–10, 20, 25, 26, 34, 38, 39, 40, 41, 46, 47, 71, 74, 81, 150
Ruhr occupation 11, 14, 17, 27–9, 33, 34, 38, 39, 44, 45, 46, 48
Röhm, Ernst 23, 61, 102, 103
Romani people 110, 126, 132, 133, 180

SA (*Sturmabteilung*) 23, 61–2, 67, 76, 78, 98, 100, 101–3, 109, 117, 128, see also Night of the Long Knives
Schacht, Hjalmar 34, 129, 152, 155–6, 164
Schleicher, Kurt von 73, 74, 76, 77, 78, 79, 80, 82, 103, 150
Scholl, Hans and Sophie 185
Schlieffen Plan 3
Social Darwinism 22, 126
Spartacist rising 15–16
SPD (Social Democratic Party) 2, 5, 6, 11
Speer, Albert 154, 155, 157–8, 161, 172, 181, 184
SS (*Schutzstaffel*) 56, 76, 78, 102, 103, 108, 109, 110, 111, 114, 117, 120, 138, 158, 170, 172, 183, 186
Stab-in-the-back myth 6, 92
Stalin, Joseph 116, 175
Stauffenberg Plot 122, 181, 186
Stauffenberg, Claus von 122, 186
Strasser, Gregor 54, 55, 57, 79, 80, 103
Strasser, Otto 54, 61
Streicher, Julius 23
Stresemann, Gustav 18, 28, 33, 34–7, 38, 40, 41, 42–8, 50, 89
Students, resistance to Nazis 122, 185

Todt, Fritz 154, 157
Totalitarianism 116–18, 147
Total War 154, 156, 157, 158, 161, 171, 172, 180, 184, 194
Trade unions 2, 18, 19, 49, 66, 78, 80, 100–1, 110, 121, 141, 142, 150, 159–60
Treaty of Berlin 46, 47

Treaty of Brest-Litovsk 9
Treaty of Rapallo 43, 46, 47
Treaty of Versailles 9, 10, 11, 15, 18, 19, 34, 45, 46, 48
  German reaction 10, 25, 81
  impact on Germany 7–8, 37, 42, 43, 81, 87, 92, 93, 168
  Nazis' views 21–2, 63, 127, 164, 167

Untermenschen 126
USSR 46, 116, 155, 158, 164, 168, 169, 170, 172, 173, 174, 175, 177, 181, 185, 188

Volksgemeinschaft 23, 63, 104, 126, 131, 134, 145–7

Wall Street Crash 14, 48, 58, 70, 81, 84
Wannsee Conference 176–80, 195
War guilt 7, 10, 41, 47, 92
Weimar Republic
  challenges from left and right 15–20
  collapse 80–2
  constitution 11–14
  economy 25–7, 35–7, 38–41, 49–50, 70–1, 72, 81
  foreign policy 42–7
  governments 73–5
  Hitler's appointment as chancellor 82–4
  impact of First World War 6
  impact of Great Depression 70–2
  impact of occupation of the Ruhr 27–9
  impact of the Treaty of Versailles 7–11
  phases 81–2
  political parties 18
  presidential power 73–5
  social conditions 36, 37, 71
  see also Brüning, Heinrich; Nazi Party; Reichstag, elections
White Rose group 122, 185
Wilhelm II, Kaiser 2, 3, 5
Wilson, Woodrow 7, 9, 87
Women in Nazi Germany 55, 137–40
Workers 141–2, 184, see also DAP (German Workers' Party); Foreign labour; German Labour Front (DAF)

Young people in Nazi Germany 122, 134–7, 185–6
Young Plan 40–1, 46, 47, 58, 85